UNIVERSITY OF WASHINGTON PUBLICATIONS ON ASIA

Sponsored by

THE FAR EASTERN AND RUSSIAN INSTITUTE

This book is a product of the Russia in Asia Project carried on by the Far Eastern and Russian Institute of the University of Washington. Members of the group represent various disciplines in the social sciences and humanities. The work of the project is of a cooperative nature with each member assisting the others through critical discussion and contribution of ideas and material. The responsibility for each study rests with the author.

SIBERIA AND THE REFORMS OF 1822

By Marc Raeff

Seattle
UNIVERSITY OF WASHINGTON PRESS
1956

957
R12

© 1956 by the University of Washington Press

Library of Congress Catalog Card Number: 56-11036

Lithographed in the United States of America

To the memory of my father

Acknowledgments

This study would have been impossible without the interest and support of many persons. My thanks go first to
the officers and staff of the Far Eastern and Russian Institute
of the University of Washington and, more particularly, to
its director, Professor George E. Taylor, who gave me the
opportunity to devote a full year to the research and writing
of this study. I am grateful to my friend, Professor Donald
W. Treadgold, acting director of the Russia in Asia Project
during most of the time I was with it, for his encouragement
and support. In spite of our differences--rather, because of
them--I benefited greatly from his research orientation, his
comments, and his criticisms. Professor N. N. Poppe
generously shared his vast first-hand knowledge of Siberia's
ethnic and cultural development. The spirited discussions
provoked by my friends and colleagues in the Russia in Asia
Project called my attention to new points of view and subjected my conclusions to unsparing but highly rewarding
criticism. I wish to thank them all, in particular Professors
Franz Michael, Victor Erlich, Franklyn Holzman, Paul
Kirchhoff, William Ballis, and Hellmut Wilhelm. The late
Professor George Lantzeff and Professor Michael Karpovich
read the manuscript and helped with many valuable suggestions. Whatever defects and errors the book still contains
are, of course, entirely my own responsibility.

The staffs of the Hoover Library, the Library of the
University of California at Berkeley, the New York Public
Library, the Library of Congress, and the Widener Library
of Harvard University were most generous with their time in
helping me to trace rare publications and obscure references.

I wish to thank them here for their assistance. I also wish to thank Mr. Martin Kilcoyne and the Geography Department of the University of Washington for preparing the Siberian map. I was relieved from the essential but laborious task of preparing an index thanks to the industry of Miss Jane F. Perry and the generosity of the Bland Fund of the History Department of Clark University. Mrs. Betty Charouhas and Mrs. Beverly Plank cannot be thanked enough for the cheerful patience with which they prepared a clear typescript.

My wife's understanding encouragement and support meant more to me than I can express here.

Marc Raeff

Worcester, Mass.
June, 1955

Contents

Note on Dates and Transliteration

All the dates are given according to the Julian calendar, which was in effect in Russia until 1917. The dates given are therefore eleven days late on the Gregorian calendar in the eighteenth century and twelve days late in the nineteenth century.

The transliteration system used is a somewhat simplified version of the system adopted by the Widener Library of Harvard University and the Library of Congress; the simplification was possible because no Slavic language other than Russian was involved. Furthermore, for the sake of consistency and simplicity, all Russian titles have been transliterated according to the modern rules of spelling.

Introduction

FOR CLOSE TO thirteen centuries from the time of the maximum expansion of the Roman Empire, Europe was on the defensive against invaders and conquerors from east, south, and north. A small peninsula at the tip of the Eurasian continent, Europe seemed sure to be engulfed by the masses pressing on it from three sides. Yet it withstood the menace; and even while the last of the Eastern invaders, the Ottoman Turks, were at the walls of Vienna, Europe broke out of its narrow confines and launched on an adventure which was to conquer the world for Western civilization. This reversal in the fortunes of the European nations took place at the turn of the fifteenth century and was dramatically brought to their consciousness by the exploits of Vasco da Gama, Columbus, and Magellan. A new continent was opened for exploration and conquest, and an old one became directly accessible to the cupidity and exploitation of European enterprise. Coming to a highly sophisticated and creative generation, the dazzling results of these discoveries received immediate recognition and stimulated the love of adventure, the imagination and energies of Western Europe, whose sons set forth across the oceans, "ivres d'un rêve heroique et brutal." Throughout the next centuries Europe lived and fought on the proceeds of these conquests and built empires. European isolation, maintained against its will for centuries, had come to a close, and awareness of the world beyond the seas never ceased to haunt the peoples of Western Europe.

The eastern borderlands of Europe participated but little in the excitement over this widening of horizons. Not that they failed to take part in the process of expansion into new

lands and continents; on the contrary, since the early sixteenth century Moscow, following the lead of its new subject,
Novgorod, had been pushing beyond the traditional boundaries
of Europe into the uncharted wastes of northeast Asia and
Siberia. But this expansion did not have the dramatic features
of the maritime discoveries of Spain and Portugal, revealing
at a stroke exciting civilizations and riches hitherto unknown.
To the peoples of the northern forest and plain, the advance
into Asia was but a continuation of the age-old slow and patient
whittling away of the possessions of their nomadic neighbors.
In this gradual process the end of the Mongol domination,
symbolically dated in 1480, made a greater impression on the
Russians than did Novgorod's attainment of the northwestern
slopes of the Urals: the Russian people had become again
masters in their own house. As they had plenty of territory,
the acquisitions in the East were not needed and went largely
unnoticed. Even a century after the fall of the Tatar yoke, when
profiting by the new-won freedom of movement and spurred
on by the traders of Novgorod and Pomor'e, Ermak opened
up Siberia for the Russian people and state, the significance
of the event was not grasped immediately. A new continent
was added to the Tsardom of Muscovy and Moscow too became
the capital of a colonial empire; but neither the people nor
the rulers quite realized this. True, it was now possible to
penetrate further eastward into Asia and more furs could be
brought to the tsar's treasury for sale to Western European
merchants, but this was the extent of the impact that the
opening of Siberia had on Russia in the sixteenth and seventeenth centuries.

We need not go into the many reasons for the difference
between the reactions to the discoveries in Siberia and to those
in Africa, America, and Asia. Climate and geography, easy
access to coveted resources, the presence of rich civilizations
capable of striking the imagination of the discoverers are some
of the factors which come easily to mind. But whatever the
causes, the fact remains that the Russian people did not become
aware of their new possessions. And although Siberia did
attract a few hardy adventurers, served as a refuge for the
criminal and persecuted, and provided ways to quick wealth
for an unscrupulous bureaucracy, it was not truly part of the
experience of the Russian peasant or even of the educated
nobleman. Under these conditions it was natural enough that
the government would not concern itself too much with this new

possession. In the very apt characterization of F. F. Vigel',
Siberia was like the remote estate of a very wealthy landowner:
its possession was appreciated as the source of an additional
income and of a few interesting and pleasant items, but it
played only a small role in the general economy of the domain
and little attention was paid to it. As long as there was no
serious trouble there, as long as the items of revenue came
in regularly, there was no need to be concerned and the remote
estate could be left to its own devices.[1]

Over two centuries later Siberia had been transformed
into an organic part of Russia. By the end of the nineteenth
century, the Russian people had come to regard Siberia as a
new Eldorado, a place of escape from the depressing poverty
and lack of opportunities at home. The government too no longer
looked on Siberia as a remote source for minor items in its
general economy but viewed it as a most valuable possession
of the Crown, whose connections with the central areas had
to be developed and whose safety had to be insured. Even for
the lowly prisoner condemned to hard labor and exile, Siberia
was no more the fearful "house of the dead," but "after all
Russian land" (ved' tozhe russkaia zemlia).

This shift of attitude toward Siberia was long in the making.
In a sense, the process was part of a growing realization of
the fact that Russia was an empire. This development was one
of the by-products of Russia's Europeanization in the eighteenth
and early nineteenth centuries; for not until the Russian state
had abandoned the Muscovite conceptions of political, social,
and economic relations under the influence of Western ideas
and models, could this imperial outlook be developed. Once
it had been realized that Russia was an empire and Siberia an
important and organic part of it, the way was paved for the
Russification of this vast region. It now became possible to
view Siberia's problems and features in their proper light and
to adapt the administrative and social organization of the region
to the new relationship. As an organic part of Russia, Siberia
could help to provide a solution for the economic, social, and
political problems which beset the country; it could offer new
areas for settlement and exploitation--it could be the "frontier"
for the Russian peasantry.

The close connection of this transformation with Russia's
Europeanization permits us to place the process in a fairly
precise chronological frame. It is contemporaneous with the
absorption of the cultural and ideological influences of the

West by Russia's ruling circles which occurred during the second half of the eighteenth century and the first quarter of the nineteenth. For reasons which will become apparent in the following pages, the process reached its most active stage in the early nineteenth century and culminated in a series of legislative acts, the statutes on Siberian administration of 1822.

In the pages to follow, it will be our intention to trace this process which transformed Siberia from a neglected and exploited colonial backyard into a full-fledged--although particular and "Asiatic"--province of the empire. Our purpose will not be to give a complete account of all the events which preceded and accompanied this transformation; we shall rather attempt to analyze the character of the circumstances--both Siberian and Russian--which made this transformation possible and shaped its course. This process might be called a "second discovery" in the sense both of opening up the great economic and social potentialities of the region and of giving it meaning and value for all segments of the country's population. The emphasis will therefore be on the change in the political attitude towards Siberia on the part of Russian statesmen in the crucial period of the reign of Alexander I, and also on the effort to give institutional and legislative expression to this newly gained awareness of the particular problems presented by Siberia's belonging to Russia.

The limitations imposed by the character of our sources leave us a twofold task: first, to seek out the circumstances and conditions in Siberia which made a new administrative approach imperative; second, to characterize and analyze the resulting change in the attitude of the imperial government in St. Petersburg as it expressed itself in legislative action. It would have been equally desirable to investigate this transformation from the vantage point of Siberia and its population, but this approach is unfortunately barred by the nature of the sources accessible to us. Russian local archival material is very scant indeed, and very little of it has ever been published. To this situation Siberia is no exception; on the contrary, as long as direct search in Russia is impossible, we can study Russian local and regional history only through the materials of the central government.[2] The obvious limitations this imposes on our understanding and knowledge should always be kept in mind by the reader.

Two very distinct groups composed Siberia's population in the first quarter of the nineteenth century and the decades immediately preceding. These two groups were not unrelated, yet each lived in its own separate way. The inhabitants of Russian ethnic origin --officials, settlers, exiles, or convicts-- formed one group, and the numerous native peoples of varied racial and linguistic background--the original occupants and owners of the territory--the other. Obviously there existed important and frequent social intercourse between the two, intercourse which was not always friendly or equally beneficial to both but social contact nonetheless. The recognized institutional and political organization of Siberia, however, maintained a rather sharp separation between the Russian and native elements of the population. While there was a significant area where interplay and fluidity existed, i. e., the Russification of the natives and the adoption of native languages and customs by Russian settlers, it was an informal process, not yet fully institutionalized and certainly inadequately recognized by the authorities. It is therefore almost impossible to describe this process fully within the framework of the task we have set ourselves. All we can do is to indicate the general character of this interaction, for its exhaustive analysis is still a task for the cultural anthropologist. This writer would be happy indeed if the cultural anthropologist and student of the Siberian peoples could be prodded by the following pages into an investigation of the dynamics of this process.

The present book, then, consists of two parts--independent but by no means unrelated. The first deals with the administrative and political problems of the Russian population of Siberia; the second takes up the situation of the natives and their treatment and government by the authorities. Together, the two studies are intended to give a rounded picture of the administrative transformation of Siberia in the reign of Alexander I. Both a result and a cause of the changed attitude towards Siberia, this transformation in its turn prepared the ground for the role Siberia played in the social and economic evolution of Russia in the last period of the imperial regime.

PART ONE
The Second Discovery of Siberia

"Like a second Ermak, I have
discovered Siberia politically."
--Speransky

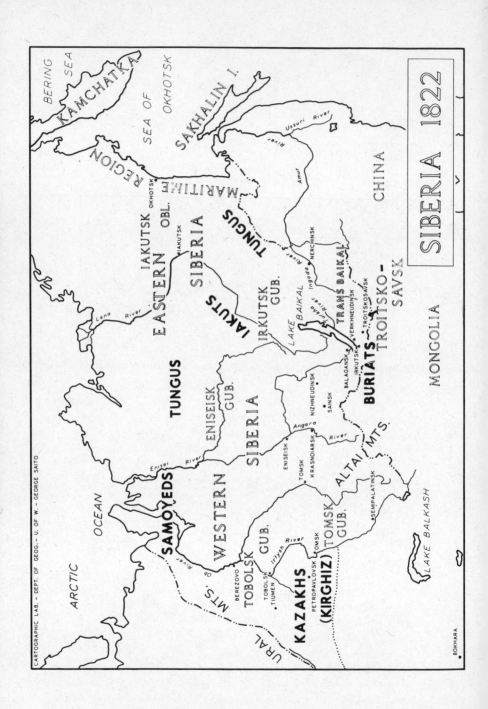

SIBERIA 1822

CARTOGRAPHIC LAB. - DEPT. OF GEOG.- U. OF W. - GEORGE SAITO

CHAPTER I
Changing Attitudes in the Eighteenth Century

1. Administration

HISTORY OR tradition had not prepared sixteenth-century Muscovy, or for that matter the other European states in the Age of Discovery, for the role of a colonial power. The conquest of Siberia, not unlike that of America by Spain, presented Moscow with a new problem in administration for which its old methods of absorption of Russian principalities could not easily serve. A long time passed before the Russians achieved a clear understanding of what was necessary for the governing of an immense area populated by many people of different cultures. The groping solutions hit upon by the Russians were not essentially different from those devised by the Spaniards in South America, except for the latter's forced Christianization of the natives. The social pattern of the native societies was not changed but made to serve the conquerors' purposes, and the Russians recreated for themselves those conditions to which they were accustomed at home. This was not so much the result of clearly recognized policy decisions made in Moscow as it was the natural outcome of a situation in which conquest or establishment of Russian control took place haphazardly. Russian penetration was carried out by individuals similar to the conquistadores of Latin America, who only later secured the recognition of their acts by the home government.

The officials who were sent to watch over the interests of the state were provided with very vague instructions, whose usual formula was "to look out for the interests of the state

3

in everything and to act in accordance with the situation as
God will inspire."[1] This lack of precise instructions, together
with the fact that the Russian system of administration left
its local agents to collect their subsistence on the spot, offered
great temptations to the officials to exploit the weak natives and
make their personal fortunes. Whatever the good intentions of
the tsars' governments concerning the well-being of Siberia,
their representatives brought them to naught and even provoked
the violent opposition of the new subjects. The impossibility
of keeping a close check over these representatives in Siberia,
as well as the inability of the natives and Siberian settlers to
obtain satisfactory action on their complaints to the throne,
resulted in the development of satrapic habits on the part of
the Russian voevodas and governors. As a saying of the
peasantry indicated, "God was high above, and the Tsar was
far away," and nothing remained but to bow to the will and
whims of the Siberian governors.[2]

The earlier decades of the eighteenth century, which
witnessed a radical transformation of the administrative
machinery of the Russian state, brought much less change in
Siberia. Peter the Great did not tackle many of the numerous
problems involved in administering a remote, far-flung, and
variegated region, but he did concern himself with bringing
Siberia under more centralized control. He put the several
voevodas under the control of a single official, the governor-
general. In 1708 he established the governorship of Siberia,
which in 1719 was subdivided into five regions (provintsiia).
In characteristic fashion Peter neglected to provide the
governor-general with clear-cut instructions and failed to
specify to whom he should be responsible. Thus the governor-
general found himself ruler over an enormous territory with
unchecked power over both the officials and the inhabitants of
Siberia. The temptations inherent in such a situation were too
great to resist. The governor-general abused his powers and
used his authority for his personal advantage. The example of
the first governor-general, Prince Gagarin, appointed by
Peter the Great himself, is instructive: his misrule and
defrauding of the treasury led him to the gallows. The successors of Gagarin, however, proved to be no better. If they
remained unpunished, it was not owing to their better behavior
but to weakness or lack of interest on the part of the emperors
and empresses in St. Petersburg. The only change brought
about by Peter was that the area was now under the despotic

rule of one individual rather than of many. It is doubtful that this change was of great benefit to the Siberian population.

In line with its traditional hands-off policy in local affairs (cf. the pattern of the "gathering" of Russian lands by the grand dukes of Moscow) Muscovy had not interfered in the ways of life of the native peoples it had encountered in Siberia. True enough, as all Siberian historians have pointed out on the repeated evidence of the chronicles and sources, this benevolent policy of Moscow was not always followed by its representatives in Siberia. But their intervention in native affairs aimed only at obtaining personal benefits, and they cared little about transforming the natives' way of life or social organization. In 1728, this traditional policy of allowing internal autonomy to the native tribes was clearly restated by the Russian Ambassador to China, Savva Vladislavich, Count Raguzinskii, in his instructions to the Siberian Border Commissioner, Firsov.[3] As a result, the administrative history of the native population of Siberia took a somewhat different course from that of the Russians, and it will be discussed separately in the second of these studies.

In the middle of the eighteenth century, and especially after Catherine II's ascent to the throne, a change became apparent in the imperial government's attitude towards Siberian administration. The government was becoming increasingly aware of Siberia as a political and administrative problem per se and beginning to realize that Siberian conditions were different from those of European Russia and should therefore be dealt with separately. Even before Russian political leaders had become fully aware of Siberia's special character and problems, the need for putting an end to the maladministration of the region had been felt by even the most obtuse advisers of the empress. Not only did the prevailing pattern in Siberia lead to abuses and an inefficient exploitation of the natural resources, but it also caused disorders and discontent which imperiled the state's revenues. In a sense Catherine's attempts to improve Siberian administration were but part of her more energetic, and perhaps more fruitful, efforts to introduce better administrative practices in Russia itself: to reaffirm the prestige of the government by making the rule of law prevail in Siberia and to subject the local officials to more effective supervision.

The solutions attempted involved two alternative views. On the one hand, there was a tendency to regard Siberia as a true colony of Russia. Drawing on a superficial and erroneous analogy with the colonial possessions of England and Spain, Catherine II and her councilors referred to Siberia as "our India, Mexico, or Peru." On the other hand, there was the view proceeding from the philosophical assumption of the eighteenth century that "everything which pertains intimately to human nature is much the same from one end of the world to the other."[4] According to this view there was no need to develop a special approach for Siberian problems; it sufficed to extend to Siberia the same laws and regulations, allegedly based on reason, which were deemed suitable for European Russia. In line with the former view, Siberia was called a "realm," implying that it was an independent territory joined to Russia not organically but by virtue of having a common sovereign.[5] This new nomenclature also served to stress the government's intention to preserve the natives' inner autonomy in full under the paternalistic protection of the Russian monarch. (This intention was clearly expressed in the instructions given in 1763 by Catherine to Major Shcherbachev for his census and general survey of Siberian economic conditions, but as these instructions affected the history of the natives more particularly, they are discussed in Part Two.) The view that Siberia was subject to the same laws as Russia found its legislative expression in the abolition, in 1763, of the Siberian Prikaz, the special government office which heretofore had been concerned with Siberian matters. The general political and administrative tasks performed by the Prikaz were now distributed among the central departments of the empire along functional lines.[6]

In 1775 Catherine II reorganized the system of local administration in European Russia by introducing provinces (guberniia) and lieutenancies (namestnichestvo); and she proceeded, though with some delay, to introduce the same organization into Siberia.[7] Some slight changes were unavoidable: thus, in the organization of the Lieutenancy of Irkutsk in 1783, its regional subdivisions received a greater number of judiciary and fiscal officials than their counterparts in European Russia because of the greater distances in Siberia.[8] The statute of 1775 avowedly aimed at fostering the self-rule of the Russian nobility in the countryside, but Siberia had no nobility and the government was too distrustful of the other classes to allow them initiative and autonomy. The only social group that could conceivably play a political role in Siberia was the merchants. But ever since Peter the Great, the Russian government had had no great love or respect for the traditional merchant class of Russia.[9] Furthermore, the merchants' constant complaints and denunciations of Siberian administrators--complaints which more often than not went unanswered and unheeded--had given the Siberian traders a reputation of being ever dissatisfied slanderers. This reaction is well illustrated by Catherine's comments on the file of complaints against Governor-general Jacobi. She wrote: "From all these thousands of sheets I have derived nothing but the impression that these are slanders and lies of irresponsible and malignant people who wish to discredit the government."[10] It is not surprising, therefore, that Catherine II ruled out the possibility of developing local self-government in Siberia. And to compensate for the absence of the nobility, some of their functions in local affairs were entrusted to bureaucrats.[11]

It was natural that the defects of the statute of 1775 would come out more sharply in Siberia than in European Russia. The most important of these defects was a lack of clarity concerning the authority of the head of the province (guberniia)--the governor (gubernator) or lieutenant (namestnik)--and in particular his responsibility to the central government.[12] As the personal representative and direct appointee of the sovereign, he was responsible to the monarch alone. This position gave the governor extremely wide powers, for he could easily nullify or neutralize the decisions and policies of the other officials or departments by dealing with the monarch directly. Under the circumstances, the tendency of the governor to become a viceroy was a natural one, especially in such a faraway region as Siberia.[13]

Some of the defects of the application of the statute of 1775 to Siberia were clearly brought out by the well-known adviser and State Secretary of Alexander I, M. M. Speransky, in the survey of the Siberian administration which he made in 1821 when he was governor-general of Siberia. Speransky listed five major defects: (1) excessive distances from the local points to the various headquarters of the administration; (2) the lack of a local nobility, which forced the government to appoint officials to positions in courts and to other "elective" offices; as a result, the very spirit of the idea of division of functions and independence of action by the officials was nullified; (3) the fact of a sparse and small population was ignored, and there was a great number of bureaus, courts,

etc. for a small number of people; (4) the nature of the population was not taken into consideration--the fact that natives
could not be "on the same plane as Russians"; (5) there was a
general lack of clear and fast rules on which the various
authorities could base their actions. [14]

The failure of the attempt to apply to Siberia rules which
had been developed for European Russia led the government to
see more clearly that Siberian problems should be treated
separately. It was becoming apparent that the need was for an
over-all fundamental reorganization of the pattern of Siberian
administration. To the task of finding the basic principles for
such a reorganization the leaders of Russia applied themselves
in the last decade of the eighteenth century and in the first
quarter of the nineteenth.

During a discussion of Siberian affairs in its session of
May 27, 1801, the Council of State reasoned:

> Because of its great area, the circumstances of its geo-
> graphic location, the condition of the peoples that inhabit
> it and the great variety which prevails in their mores,
> customs, industries, and ways of life, this country needs
> special regulations for its administration as well as for
> its subdivisions. [15]

Soon it was realized that a sound basis for such regulations
would be possible only if the government possessed more
complete and accurate information on Siberian conditions than
had been available before. The Council therefore proposed
that a special official be sent to survey the situation and to

> ...present his comments on all particulars, so that on
> their basis one could determine precisely whether the
> present division of the area into the Perm', Tobolsk,
> Irkutsk, and former Kolyvansk provinces was consonant
> with the situation and the size of the country, or whether
> it would be more convenient to find some other basis for
> administrative division; [he should also] find out and
> determine which method of administration would be more
> fitting to the great variety of peoples settled there. [16]

Privy Councilor Selifontov, at the time governor of
Tobolsk, was selected for this task, which carried with it the
title of inspector general, and was given instructions which

read in part:

> Occupied at the present with the examination of the internal organization of the provinces, We [Alexander I] find that Siberia, because of its large area, the variety of its geographic conditions, the situation of the peoples inhabiting it... requires in its administrative division as well as in the actual system of government a special statute; but the statute should be based on accurate and detailed knowledge of local conditions which are to be brought into necessary unity. This is impossible to accomplish from such a distance [i.e., from St. Petersburg].

Selifontov, already quite familiar with the problems of the region, was then enjoined to do the following: (1) survey the whole of Siberia; (2) find out what the most convenient administrative divisions for the region would be and on what principles the system should be reorganized; (3) ascertain whether the present division into three parts was the most appropriate in view of the distances, population, etc.; (4) determine the defects of the present system, establish what should be done to secure the maximum of well-being, education, increase of population, etc. in the area, and recommend any changes in the system that might appear desirable; (5) collect all useful data, statistics, etc.; (6) present a report to the emperor. [17]

To what extent a general reorganization had become necessary can be seen from the following incident which is drawn from the archives of the Council of State. In 1800 the prominent merchant and mayor[18] of Irkutsk, M. Sibiriakov, had submitted a lengthy complaint against Governor-general Lezzano. There were eleven major points in his complaint: (1) Grain prices had been artificially raised. (2) The population was being distracted from useful work by forcible impressment for road building. (3) The administration had neglected to apportion the required amount of land to each village. (4) The peasants were compelled to transport grain to remote places. (5) The governor-general had forbidden the planting of tobacco in Irkutsk. (6) The mansion of the governor had been repaired with the help of conscripted labor. (7) Military barracks had been built in the square in front of the cathedral. (8) A distribution point for forced labor had been established at the very gates of the city, thus making the outskirts of the town unsafe. (9) The barracks of the police had been transferred to another

spot in the city at the expense of the people. (10) The transportation of merchandise over Lake Baikal had been prohibited
and the merchants had been compelled to use a longer route
around the lake. (11) Sibiriakov himself had been deprived of
his office of mayor without any reason.

This jumbled list of grievances shows the extent to which
Siberian administrators were felt to interfere in the lives of
the people through their highhanded method of governing.
The complaint reached the full assembly of the Senate only
after heavy pressure had been brought to bear by the Minister
of Justice and long after Governor Lezzano had been replaced
by Selifontov. Disagreement within the Senate as to the validity
of the complaints and the means by which the situation could be
remedied resulted in the matter's being brought to the Council
of State in 1809, nine years after the filing of the original
complaint. Without going into the details of the discussion
that took place in the Council of State, discussion which is
reported in full in the archives of that body, two points should
be noted. On the one hand, the validity of the complaint was
determined almost exclusively on the basis of the counter-
statements and evidence presented by Lezzano himself. Small
wonder then that the petition was rejected and that Sibiriakov
was branded as a slanderer whose actions should be watched
carefully. On the other hand, the discussion in the Council
clearly brought to light the absence of any criteria and rules
for deciding whether the governor-general had exceeded his
powers and acted beyond the limits set by his instructions. [19]
Instances such as this came up periodically on the agenda of the
Council of State, the Senate, and the Committee of Ministers.
All this served only to confirm the emperor in his conviction
that a fundamental reorganization alone would prove adequate.

Selifontov had been appointed inspector general with the
specific task of initiating temporary measures in preparation
for the general reorganization of Siberian administration. But
in this instance, as in so many others, the government of
Alexander I expressed pious wishes but took little action. For
almost twenty years the intention of drafting a general statute
for Siberia remained unfulfilled. In the meantime, the former
Inspector General Selifontov was appointed governor-general
of Siberia and was given wider powers than any of his predecessors in the eighteenth century, under the pretext of enabling
him to prepare the new general statute. In addition to the
regular powers vested in him as a personal representative

of the emperor, Selifontov was authorized to take immediate
measures to supply the region with foodstuffs, fight epidemics,
and cope with highway robberies and gangster activities.
Although these measures were supposed to be only temporary
ones, the governor-general often took steps which were far
from temporary in their effect. And also, though he was
supposed to consult with other local officials and bodies on
any measure of permanent policy, Selifontov's voice was
decisive and his powers went almost unchallenged. The area
of his authority was widened to include the state mining enterprises of Siberia, giving him absolute control over very
important and extensive areas. To reinforce his position all
military forces in the region were placed under his control.
Finally, and most important of all, he was given the widest
powers to hire and fire subordinate officials. His duties, on
the other hand, were left rather vague. He was to improve
the quality of the bureaucracy (without being given any criteria
or standards); he was to eradicate the "chain of quarrels and
slanders," which again could only mean an extension of his
wide discretionary powers. Finally, he was to establish the
causes of Siberia's decline and recommend a new system of
administration consonant with its conditions.[20]

The only change in administrative structure undertaken
by Selifontov in accordance with his very broad instructions
was to establish "commissariats" (1804).[21] These commissariats had as their laudable purpose to make more effective
and adequate the supervision of far-flung districts. However,
as Speransky was to point out later, this positive gain was
nullified by the multiplication of officials and government
bodies in an area which was already overburdened with bureaucrats. Moreover, considering the widespread corruption among
Siberian officials, the creation of these commissariats could
only lead to more abuses and confusion.[22]

Until the second decade of the reign of Alexander I,
the government had found no better means of coping with
the situation than to continue the old tradition of widening
the power of its representatives without providing effective
means of controlling and supervising them. The full effect
of this situation, in both its positive and negative aspects,
came clearly to light during the long administration of Ivan
Borisovich Pestel, 1805-1819.

2. Social and Economic Life

While the government was searching for a solution of the administrative problems of Siberia, it was also beginning to change its attitude towards the economic possibilities of the region. This change can fairly safely be ascribed to the influence of ideologies received from Western Europe. Catherine II and her advisers adopted the physiocratic belief in the paramount importance of agriculture to the prosperity and wealth of a nation. [23] This doctrine found easy reception in Russia not only because Russia was an agrarian country and based its wealth on the products of its peasants' labor but also because the physiocratic doctrine did not preclude political absolutism, in particular in the form of "enlightened despotism." Insisting on increased agricultural production, the physiocrats also emphasized the need for the free circulation of agricultural products within the boundaries of the country. In line with this view, Empress Elizabeth had abolished a great many of the internal customs boundaries and Catherine II in 1767 made trade free throughout her empire. [24]

The ground for the application of these economic ideas to Siberia had been prepared by the investigations of Siberia made by various scholars and scientists throughout the eighteenth century. The potentialities of the region were first brought to the attention of the government by Swedish officers who came to Siberia as prisoners of war during the Great Northern War. They had seen, as their Russian predecessors and contemporaries had not been able to, the manifold possibilities of the natural resources of Siberia. [25] Following up these reports, scientists were sent by the Imperial Academy of Sciences to make further studies of the geography, population, and economic potential of the area. As a result the Russian government had become aware of the agricultural possibilities of southern Siberia, in particular the region beyond Lake Baikal, while its attention was also directed to the opportunities for trade from points on the Pacific Coast. It is not surprising then that by the 1770's, when a great deal of this information had been accumulated and the ideas of the physiocrats digested, the government tried to apply the latter to Siberian circumstances.

Trade and commercial opportunities were the first to receive the attention and encouragement of the government.

This was quite natural, for trade had always been a traditional occupation of the Russian settlers in Siberia. Siberia had been discovered and conquered by merchants and their agents, coming from the area of the Pomor'e of northeast European Russia, while the Russian nobility with its predominant agricultural interest had tended to keep away from Siberia.[26] The officials sent by Moscow had as their primary task the collection of tribute in furs from the natives, and this led them to engage in commercial enterprises for their own benefit. The connection between trade and officials was a very close one indeed throughout the seventeenth century. The example set by these officials was often followed by other Russian settlers and even by the clergy.[27] As a result, there had developed very active trade, both external and internal, which was carried on by practically every class of the population. The soldiers and Cossacks traded with the natives and across the steppe "line";[28] big merchants engaged in the transit trade between Russia and China; officials used their position to trade with the natives in furs;[29] and the peasants sold supplies to the military, the cities, and the bureaucracy.[30]

The easy rewards of this trade turned quite a number of people away from agriculture, mining, and hunting. If we are to believe a serious, though somewhat dogmatic, student of Siberian history, A. Shchapov, the eighteenth century witnessed a large influx of population into Siberian cities but little settlement in the villages.[31]

Besides trading in the articles derived from hunting, trapping, agriculture, and foreign imports, the Siberian population also indulged in the slave trade, which was promoted by the establishment of serfdom in Russia. While the holding of serfs was restricted to the nobility, a class almost nonexistent in Siberia, the government permitted (1767) the purchase of slaves from the natives. One of the mainstays of slavery was the traffic in Kalmyk and Kazakh (Kirghiz) children on the basis of the ukaz of November 16, 1737. Paragraph 7 of the ukaz reads: "Kalmyks and peoples of other origin, who, as is known, are baptized and come to their masters as children, can be bought by everyone, be baptized and kept without the payment of any capitation, merely by registering in the chanceries of the province or of the voevoda."[32] Although by repeated and energetic measures the government prevented the slave trade from growing very much, it remained, until the first decades of the nineteenth century, a

lucrative and important business along the southwestern "line"
of Siberia. [33]

Not all of this trade was equally profitable nor could it be
carried on by anyone. For some of it, in particular the most
important Chinese trade, big capital was necessary. Also,
government rules allowed only merchants belonging to the first
guild to engage in foreign trade. It was natural that trading
associations be formed and that they attempt to monopolize
commerce. The state, no doubt, fostered the creation of
monopolies by its economic policies. In the seventeenth century
the fur trade had been largely a state monopoly, all the most
valuable furs being reserved for the government; in the early
eighteenth century, Peter the Great replaced the monopoly by
granting special privileges to selected individuals and companies. The China trade, which was the most profitable,
remained a closed government preserve until 1762 when it was
opened to merchants in the first guild. [34]

Following this example set by the state, the traders
in Siberia, especially those dealing with export articles,
clamored for special privileges and monopolies. Their claims
can be illustrated by the petition their delegate presented to
the Commission on Codification of 1767. Iadrintsev reports that
the deputy Samoilov, on behalf of the merchants of Eniseisk,

> ...asks that all trade in the Eniseisk and Turukhansk
> regions be given to them in exclusive monopoly; that
> they be given the monopoly of water transportation between
> Irkutsk and Eniseisk, and that the merchants of Irkutsk
> be prohibited from carrying their merchandise on the
> Angara River in their own ships. He asks that they be
> granted the monopoly of wine-making and wine-selling.
> He asks that serfdom be introduced into the Eniseisk
> province. He asks that children of paupers be legally
> recognized as indentured and that in return for being
> taken care of by their employers, they be confirmed as
> slaves [kholopy]. Finally, the town of Eniseisk asks for
> subsidies from the treasury. [35]

By the middle of the eighteenth century these merchants
as well as the government were becoming more and more
aware of the possibilities existing for the export of local
Siberian products. Besides the constant demand for furs by
China there were now greater opportunities for trade with

the nomads along the southern border. Also Russian discoveries and attempts at settlement on the North American
continent and the consequent contact with the southern Pacific
area gave rise to the belief that there were great opportunities in maritime exchanges between eastern Siberia and
the Pacific.[36]

The drive to expand these trade opportunities found its
expression in a series of developments in the second half of
the eighteenth century. First of all, as we mentioned, the
state surrendered its monopoly on the Chinese trade in 1762;
trade with China increased, a greater number of goods and
people became involved, and as a result there was a development of agricultural activity in Eastern Siberia in the form of
horse and cattle breeding (horses for transportation, cattle
for leather goods which were readily taken by the Chinese).[37]

Before the Russian conquest of Siberia there had been
very active and close relations with the southern steppes and
Central Asia.[38] This contact, weakened even before the
appearance of the Russians, had almost completely broken
down after the conquest in the seventeenth century. In the
eighteenth century, however, this old trade was revived,
apparently on the initiative of the Central Asian peoples.
Merchants from Central Asia, called Bukhartsy because most
of them were believed to come from Bokhara, traded in Siberia
in large numbers and formed small settlements in the larger
centers of western Siberia. These merchants were interested
in the purchase of Siberian products as well as in the sale of
their home manufactures. As one alert traveler, Radishchev,
noted, most of the inhabitants of western Siberia were clad in
textiles of Central Asiatic origin.[39] In return, Central Asia
imported from Siberia leather goods and the products of
Siberia's mineral wealth. For example, the Council of State
decided (1808) to permit the export of iron to the Central
Asiatic countries. It reasoned that if Russia would not export
the iron these countries would have to turn to other sources
of supply and this would be harmful to the iron industry.[40]
The importance and the desirability of this trade across the
southern border can be gauged from another decision (1812),
this time of the Committee of Ministers, by which passport
rules were relaxed to enable merchants from Central Asia to
travel more easily through Siberia to inland cities.[41]

Increasing interest in maritime trade in the Pacific led
to the organization of the Russian-American Trading Company

in 1798. This company, a stock company, was set up on the
model of the British and Dutch East India Companies. It was
given complete monopoly of commerce as well as a large
degree of political power. It was hoped that the activities of
this company would lead to an intensification of the use of
natural resources in this remote corner of the empire.

In the past, Siberian agriculture had been fostered by
the Muscovite state as a means of supporting the officials and
soldiers in that area. [42] In the second half of the eighteenth
century the combined demands of trade and of physiocratic
doctrine resulted in a renewed stress on the advantages of
agriculture and the desirability of its expansion into Siberia.
As in European Russia in former times, the major problem
in developing an active agriculture was that of obtaining enough
labor. In the eighteenth century Siberia was still largely empty
country, and the development of agriculture was therefore
intimately linked with colonization and a policy of settlement.
However, a true solution of the problem remained impossible
while the government continued to protect serfdom in European
Russia. As long as serfdom remained, the government was
restricted to a compulsory colonization policy. While the
government realized the advantages of an energetic colonization policy, Catherine II, as well as her son Paul I, was very
careful not to give any support to the opponents of serfdom. [43]

Greater production of grain was also needed to make
possible further development of the mining and manufacturing
possibilities of Siberia. Villages and agricultural areas were
needed to feed the workers of the mines and mills. [44] This had
been the reason for settling exiles and state peasants near
the major factory towns (Kolyvansk, Nerchinsk), a policy
inaugurated by Peter the Great. But colonists were unwilling
to settle of their own choice as factory-ascribed peasants. [45]
Furthermore, the demands of trade had transformed many
peasants into cart drivers who had no time to till the soil,
and yet they too had to be fed. More agricultural labor was a
crying need.

Attempts to meet this problem were made throughout the
eighteenth century. For example, a decree of December 3,
1760, permitted serf owners to meet their obligation to furnish army recruits by sending peasants to settle in Siberia. [46]
These peasants were to be sent to areas near factories to help
provide workers with food. Other measures were taken to help
the peasants meet their obligations towards the state. Thus

already in the first half of the eighteenth century their obligation to work a parcel of state land (desiatinnaia pashnia) was
replaced by the obligation to deliver a fixed quantity of grain,
a change which gave the peasants more freedom in their
activities. [47]

The government's hesitancy and difficulty in finding a
correct solution are illustrated by the policies of Governor
Soimonov in the 1750's and 1760's. He still was not convinced
of the agricultural potential of the area he administered, and
he advocated the return to the old system of compelling the
peasant to work a plot of state land or to surrender a specified
part of his total crop to the state. Upon leaving Siberia and
becoming a senator, he continued to defend this approach
and managed to convince quite a number of his colleagues.
Needless to say, in so doing he helped hold back the progress
of agriculture in Siberia. [48]

Fortunately, however, Catherine II did not share this
skepticism, and she pursued a policy of active and energetic
colonization of the outlying districts of the Russian Empire.
Because she did not want to undermine serfdom by freeing or
resettling state serfs on more liberal terms, she tried to find
suitable colonists abroad. As is well known, her colonization
activities were mainly directed towards settling South Russia,
the fertile steppe area which had just been made secure as a
consequence of the wars with Turkey. But she tried to foster
colonization in Siberia as well. There is no doubt that in
Catherine's mind this colonization policy was closely connected
with an imperial outlook. As in the South Russian provinces,
colonization of Siberia meant to her the consolidation of
Russia's political and economic control of the area. She used
the Old Believers who had lived in the area wrested from
Poland; in the 1760's she sponsored the settlement of "Family
Old Believers" near Lake Baikal. These settlers came voluntarily but with government support and were granted extensive
benefits such as land allotments and some exemptions from
taxes and services. These colonists, an energetic, hardy
group of people, were quite successful and managed to transform a poor and backward area into a flourishing granary. [49]
Furthermore, Catherine II continued to encourage serf owners
to send their serfs to Siberia, although her efforts in this
direction, as might have been expected, found little response.

The example set by Catherine II was not forgotten. Her
son, Paul I (r. 1796-1801), who as a rule gleefully reversed

the policies of his mother, in this part cular respect followed willingly in her footsteps. In 1799 Prince Gagarin proposed to settle the area beyond Lake Baikal. This region, the Prince claimed, was rich but still unused; it was particularly suited for growing grain and for raising cattle. (He probably got this information from the explorers who had surveyed this region.) The cultivation of grain and the raising of cattle not only would provide food for the Siberian population but would also form the basis for a textile and leather industry whose products should find a ready market in China, just across the border.

Prince Gagarin therefore suggested that the government settle 10,000 "souls" (males of working age) within an unspecified period of time. These settlers should be drawn from among the ranks of retired soldiers, petty criminals (to be rehabilitated within ten years), and serfs not more than forty-five years of age whom their masters were willing to send to Siberia. The government would provide thirty desiatin per soul as land allotment. (1 desiatina = 2.703 acres.) The colonists were to settle in villages of no more than one hundred households; preferably, separate villages were to be established for regular settlers and for petty criminals. The state was also to build houses for them and provide the minimum of tools and cattle. The money for this operation, Prince Gagarin thought, could be obtained by the state's receiving a contribution from the landowners in return for a cancellation of recruit obligations. The first group of settlers would help build houses and villages for later colonists. Besides the initial help given by the state, the settlers were to receive various benefits and exemptions (for example, no tax payments for ten years). Finally, Prince Gagarin suggested that the administrators appointed to these villages be agricultural experts who would teach and guide the new colonists in the use of modern techniques. This proposal was approved by the emperor and put into effect by the decree of October 17, 1799.[50]

The subsequent story of this settlement plan is instructive, for it sheds light on the actual conditions in Siberia which hampered the realization of the government's intentions. We find the details of this story in the lengthy debates which took place in the Council of State over a decade later. In typically bureaucratic fashion the government thought it had done everything that was needed, once it had proclaimed the emperor's will. But the implementation of the policy hit upon many difficulties. First of all, the serf owners were not very willing to send their serfs to Siberia--a reaction that could have been predicted on the basis of Catherine's earlier experience along these lines. Furthermore, the exiles and criminals who were sent to the Transbaikal area found nothing provided for them and suffered such hardships that many of them fled, spreading rumors on their return which did not make this enterprise attractive to others and undoubtedly did much to discourage prospective settlers. Last, but not least, Siberian bureaucrats looked upon this plan not as a way to improve conditions in Siberia but as an easy means of obtaining personal benefits. Instead of helping the settlers get started, the local officials misappropriated the money allotted to the project, pilfered and sold implements, and used the settlers' labor for personal profit or to further public works. The disorder and confusion became appalling. An official, Councilor Laba, was sent to investigate these conditions, and after several years of long and weary work he managed to bring some order into the situation (1806). Unfortunately, the attempts at improvement were hampered again by a series of mishaps and crop failures in the years between 1809 and 1817. By 1807 only 1,312 persons had been settled in the area--a far cry from the 10,000 planned. In 1807, 1,267 settlers came; 2,375 in 1808 and 2,000 in 1809. This experiment made clear the need for definite and comprehensive rules for settlement and colonization. An attempt at this was made in 1806, but a complete solution was not achieved until 1822.[51]

Besides these attempts at colonization and settlement, the government undertook several measures to foster existing agriculture. Along with exemptions from taxation for Russians, efforts were made to encourage agriculture among the natives. In 1806, the Buriats were given a large land allotment to be used for agriculture. And since no permanent and stable peasant settlement--either native or Russian--could take place until the land had been surveyed, the first consistent efforts at surveying the vast territory were begun toward the end of the eighteenth century.[52]

Thus we see that the government was coming to a clearer realization of the economic problems in Siberia and had begun, however gropingly and ineffectively, to take some steps toward solving them. Yet its efforts were bound to remain inconclusive as long as the basic structure of Siberian government and society remained the same. A thorough reorganization,

demanded by purely administrative considerations, was also
essential to foster the growth of Siberia as a productive region. It was to this task that both Siberian and St. Petersburg
officials applied themselves in the course of the reign of
Alexander I.

CHAPTER II

Governors Pestel and Treskin and Siberian Society

GOVERNOR-GENERAL Selifontov started his administration in 1802 with the avowed intention of putting into practice these changes in attitude towards Siberia. But as had happened so often before, the good intentions were never realized. Following the tradition of former governors-general, Selifontov rapidly slipped into the rut of neglect and abuse of power and was incapable of carrying out his mission of reorganization and reform. He cared only to secure his personal finances and let his mistress and her friends run the country. His rule came to an end as a result of the inspection that Ambassador Count Golovkin conducted on his way to China. Although it appears that Golovkin's report was largely dictated by his dislike for Selifontov and was even gloomier than the situation warranted, [1] Selifontov was dismissed and in 1805 Alexander I appointed in his stead Ivan Borisovich Pestel, who remained the nominal head of Siberia for the next fourteen years.

The task Pestel set himself, on orders from the emperor, was to put into practice the changed outlook on Siberia we have just attempted to describe. Pestel was not brilliant, but he was a man of ruthless determination. A typical product of the Russian bureaucracy of the late eighteenth century, thoroughly imbued with the methods of Peter the Great and Paul I, he intended to carry out the plans and reach the objective, whatever the obstacles. Like other administrators of this school Pestel showed a complete disregard for popular sentiment and for traditions and customs. In the task of establishing a new order of things against the will of the population, Pestel, like his imperial masters, relied on the help of the regular bureaucracy exclusively and patterned his administration on

the army.[2] Very detailed regulations, unquestioned obedience,
and a disregard of the cost to the people--these were the
principles on which the army operated at that time and which
officials of Pestel's kind applied to the civilian administration as well. On a minor scale and with much less talent,
Pestel followed the practice of the more famous assistant
to Alexander I, Count Arakcheev.[3]

Pestel was lucky enough to find an extremely able assistant, N.I. Treskin, whom he appointed as civilian governor of
Irkutsk, and who became for well over a decade the actual
ruler of Siberia. Pestel had come to know Treskin as a clerk
in the Postal Department, had recognized his abilities, and
made use of him for the furtherance of his own career. We
know relatively little of Treskin's background and early life--
he came from Siberia, was the son of a village priest, and
like some of the more famous political figures of his time,
had received a good education in a theological seminary. As
was not uncommon for people of his class, he exchanged the
poverty of priesthood for the more promising future that
government service offered to an energetic, ambitious, and
intelligent individual. Both friends and enemies of Treskin
agreed that he was a man of remarkable energy, industry, and
devotion to duty. People in Irkutsk often wondered when their
governor slept, for he seemed to be working almost twenty-
four hours a day. He kept close watch over everything and
was able to find practical solutions for all the problems that
he had to face.

A very useful gift was his ability to choose efficient
advisers and assistants. The chief of his private chancellery,
Beliavskii, was, in the opinion of such an expert in the matter
as Speransky, one of the best "pens" for official correspondence that could be found in Russia. Treskin also selected and
appointed various subordinate officials who, like himself,
were energetic and capable executives, and even, as in the
case of Gedenshtrom, persons of vast erudition.

These good qualities, however, were offset by the harsh
methods Treskin used in imposing his will and his utter disregard for the principles of humanity and kindness. He was
ruthless in punishing disobedience or breaking any opposition
to his will. It was this trait which, in the long run, undermined
his administration and brought his efforts at improvement to
naught. One naturally wonders if Treskin was more than the
bureaucrat we have just described. Did he sincerely desire

the good of Siberia? Did he have any over-all plan for the
reorganization of the area? These are questions which cannot
be answered on the basis of available data but would require
a careful analysis of evidence which is preserved, if at all,
only in local archives.[4] We can merely give a summary of his
activities and perhaps attempt to indicate some very general
principles on which these actions seem to have been based.

Pestel and Treskin set to work to apply the insight into
Siberian problems that the government had gained at the end
of the eighteenth century.[5] In the first place stood the need to
improve and put into workable condition the physical facilities
of the region. A very energetic program of road building,
bridge repair, etc. was initiated. Treskin established the
ground work for better transportation between Irkutsk and
the vital border point of Kiakhta; he also improved the roads
between Irkutsk and the rich agricultural region of Lake
Baikal. Up to this time the few existing highways had not
been safe, for gangs of highway robbers and escaped convicts
were attacking travelers even in the suburbs of towns. Treskin
put an end to this situation by energetic police action which in
a relatively short time eliminated almost all of the bandits
and made travel much safer.[6]

Treskin also turned his attention to the improvement of
towns in Siberia. Until then even the largest cities in Siberia
had been but overgrown villages built without any plan and
open to devastation by fire and flood. Treskin had whole
sections of the major towns torn down and rebuilt according
to more progressive principles of city planning. He replaced
many wooden public buildings with stone structures and took
steps, though not with complete success, to control the flow
of rivers in and near these towns.

Unfortunately, these good measures were carried out
without regard for the feelings of the population. To build the
roads peasants were impressed against their will, sometimes
even at the height of the harvest. It has been claimed, perhaps
accurately, though our sources are inconclusive, that these
abuses were not due to Treskin's directions but to the mismanagement of his subordinates. Whatever the truth of this
claim, Treskin's building program and his rezoning of towns
were resented because of the ruthless fashion in which old
houses were razed to the ground and their inhabitants forced
to move. And all of it had to be paid for by the city people
themselves through municipal taxation. While many Siberians

realized the benefits of some of these measures, the hardships
that accompanied them produced a general wave of dissatisfaction. [7] Treskin also paid some attention to the cultural life
of the region. It seems, however, that the initiative was not
his, and he did not show any consistent interest in the matter.
He established a series of local schools, both in villages
and in towns, but did nothing to provide them with adequate
financial support and let them disappear eventually through
neglect. [8]

Along with these improvements of the physical plant of
the region, Treskin made efforts to facilitate the economic
activities of the local population. He introduced various
measures which aimed at simplifying the administrative aspects of economic life. For example, he obtained for Siberians
the right to conclude contracts locally up to the sum of 5,000 r.
without being required to certify this transaction in the provincial capital. [9] At another time Treskin, through Pestel,
obtained permission for Siberians to put up for auction houses
and real estate of a value not to exceed 500 r. without referring
to St. Petersburg. [10] Finally, he attempted, though without
success this time, to liberalize the rules for loans backed by
movable property so that it would not be necessary to put up
estates as security; for estates, in the technical definition of
the term, were rare in Siberia. [11]

But these measures were only preparatory. Treskin's
and Pestel's main interest was focused on the development
of agriculture in Siberia and the increase of the general
economic wealth of the area. To this end they took steps which
were far more systematic and effective than those of their
predecessors, though the method used often provoked more
resistance than was desirable. As Pestel himself stated to the
Council of State, the economic activity of the local administrator should consist of: (a) "the improvement of the well-being
of the population by encouraging it to engage in agriculture,
cattle raising, and industry" and (b) the devising of means to
increase the revenue of the government. Government revenue,
Pestel and Treskin believed (as the physiocrats and other
economists had held), depended upon the economic prosperity
of the population itself. [12]

To promote agriculture and the settlement of peasants
became one of Treskin's major concerns. In a circular of
1808 he stressed the desirability of agriculture and he set as

an example the success of the Old Believers who had settled
in the Baikal region:

> An example of rare diligence and industry in agricul-
> ture is given by the Old Believers settled in the Verkhne-
> udinsk district. About forty years ago they were settled on
> sandy and stony land where the possibilities for agricul-
> ture could not even be foreseen [an interesting retrospective
> comment on the government's ignorance of local conditions
> in the eighteenth century]. But unceasing labor and soli-
> darity made, so to speak, even the stones fertile. Today
> they have the best fields, and their agriculture gives them
> not only abundant subsistence but is the mainstay of the
> Verkhneudinsk and Nerchinsk districts. The authorities
> consider it their duty to cite to the entire province the
> rare diligence, industry, and usefulness to the community
> of the Old Believer peasants of the Verkhneudinsk district
> ...and express to them their sincere gratitude. [13]

Both Pestel and Treskin supported various applications
and petitions by individuals who wanted to set up households,
even if they wanted to establish noble estates, which were
almost unknown in Siberia. In 1812 the request of the medical
inspector of the province of Tobolsk that he be granted an
estate on which to settle his personal serfs was supported by
the Siberian administration and eventually approved by the
Committee of Ministers. [14] At another time the Committee of
Ministers acted favorably on the application of an official in
Iakutsk for a grant of 1,000 desiatin of land in that area. [15]
   But it was in connection with peasant settlement that
Treskin was most active. He petitioned the Committee of
Ministers and was granted the right to issue passports to
convicted criminals and exiles incapable of heavy forced
labor, thus enabling them to move around Siberia more freely
and settle down wherever they found it convenient to establish
a household. [16]
   Treskin also tried to bring to a satisfactory conclusion
the matter of the settlements on Lake Baikal in accordance
with the decree of 1799 which we have discussed earlier.
We recall that the early years were very difficult because of
maladministration and the exploitation of settlers by officials.
These disorders led to a special investigation by Councilor
Laba in 1806, as a result of which new regulations were

worked out. These rules of 1806 aimed at the establishment
of settlements whose population would be more or less uniform
in religion, nationality, and social background--which made
for more harmonious relations within the villages and for
less burdensome police and administrative problems. The
results of these new regulations we know only from the discussions and records presented by Speransky during his
administration of Siberia. They show that by 1819, in spite
of difficulties and bad harvests, the settlements had more
than adequately covered the government's outlay for tools,
surveying, etc. [17]

Attempts to induce the nomadic natives of Siberia to
lead a settled life and to engage in agriculture had already
been made by the Russian administration in the seventeenth
century. The results had generally been negative and most
of the natives still followed their traditional occupations of
trapping, hunting, and cattle raising. But as we shall see in
greater detail in the second part of this study, towards the
end of the eighteenth century the Russian administration had
become aware of the fact that the native and Russian ways
of life were becoming more similar; that closer and more
frequent economic, social, and institutional contacts had
developed; and that both the natives and the Russian settlers
were objects of the government's concern. It was but natural
that energetic officials like Pestel and Treskin, who were
promoting agricultural colonization and development for the
Russian population of Siberia, would attempt to push the natives
into the same path. And though the history of the natives is
the subject of another part of the present study, Treskin's
promotion of Buriat settlement and agriculture can be taken
up here.

At the beginning of the nineteenth century the Buriats
were already engaged in agriculture on a minor scale, perhaps
stimulated by the example of the Old Believers who had settled
in their vicinity. Pestel's administration tried to develop this
activity further. [18] On the proposal of the Siberian administration the Council of State decided to allot thirty desiatin to
any Buriat who expressed a willingness to settle and till the
soil. He would have full possession of this land, including
even the right to exploit the mineral resources that might be
found beneath the surface (in other words, his legal rights
were equal to those of European Russian landowners). Treskin
further implemented these measures by establishing better

roads, by having the local administrators teach the Buriats agricultural techniques, and by providing a ready market for their produce. [19]

Another effort, less successful, was made to entice the Kazakhs[20] into Russia and have them settle down to agriculture. In 1812 some Kazakh princelings were promised government subsidies, various exemptions, and a permanent house free if they would move into Russia and persuade their tribesmen to do the same. For one reason or another, the princes did not succeed in getting their fellow tribesmen to follow them and the whole scheme collapsed. [21]

But it was by his direct intervention in the grain trade that Treskin most energetically fostered the development of agriculture. His own personal predilections and a bureaucratic tradition which stemmed from Peter the Great led Treskin to believe that only the state could guide the people into this new way of life, and that therefore the government had to make agriculture worth while by manipulating the market. For this reason Treskin pursued a consistent policy of extensive grain purchases by the Treasury to fill the state-owned granaries. The price offered was usually a very good one, and the peasants, finding it to their advantage to have such a ready market, extended their agricultural activities. As a result of these purchases, Pestel claimed, the crop yield had increased between 1806 and 1815 from 200,000 to 300,000 chetverts. [22] Furthermore, 66,700 desiatin were under cultivation in 1816, 72,100 in 1817, and 91,200 in 1818. [23]

Treskin recognized that Siberian climatic and geographic conditions made for irregular harvests, especially in the more remote areas among the native people who were not yet accustomed to regular agricultural work. These irregularities in the harvest resulted in devastating famines. The unreliability of the crop yield and the incapacity of the population to make provisions for the future meant that the government had to expand the system of state granaries. [24] Thus Treskin, with Pestel supporting him energetically in St. Petersburg, directed his efforts toward keeping the state granaries always filled. Treskin greatly distrusted the merchants of Siberia and believed that their monopolistic practices resulted in the exploitation and impoverishment of the peasantry and the country. He wanted the state to buy up all available grain and, in order to prevent speculation and abuses by the merchants, to concentrate all the exchanges and dealings in grain in the

hands of the bureaucracy. In line with this policy, Pestel
worked on the Committee of Ministers to obtain for Treskin
complete freedom to make decisions affecting the export of
grain and the grain trade within Siberia according to local
needs. If he obtained the right to control--even stop--the
export of Russian grain to Kiakhta and the steppe areas,
Treskin would be able to make more grain available for the
state stores. This too, Pestel claimed, was to the advantage
of individual peasants, for previously this export trade had
been controlled by the big merchants who pulled prices down
almost below the level of adequate profit. [25] In essence, the
Committee of Ministers approved Treskin's request for control
over grain export, and this gave him wide powers to dictate
prices and to move the crops. The local administration also
received the right to make purchases whenever it deemed
necessary, and was instructed to pay for them in cash and in
advance. This latter rule, incidentally, increased the circulation of money in Siberia and also seems to have benefited the
peasantry. All these measures were to be carried out either
directly by, or under the supervision of, the officials, that is,
the representatives of Treskin. [26] Private merchants could
not easily compete with them.

By extending the purchases for the state granaries,
Treskin came into conflict with another government office,
the Ministry of Finance--a conflict which was to play an
important role in the downfall of his administration. The
distilling of alcoholic beverages (generically called "wine" in
those days), which had been in European Russia the exclusive
privilege of the nobility since 1765, was in Siberia a state
monopoly administered by the Ministry of Finance. Through its
local agents, the Ministry had been in the habit of purchasing
large quantities of grain at low prices for the distilleries in
Siberia, thereby playing an important role in the economic
life of the region.

Pestel, in his drive for complete control of all facets
of the government's activities by the Siberian provincial
administration, strove to have the distilleries put under the
supervision of the civil governor of Irkutsk, i.e., Treskin.
The discussion of this proposal in the Committee of Ministers
and the Council of State lasted for many years. In the meantime, Treskin acted as if permission to control and direct
the grain purchases for the distilleries had already been
granted to him. As the Minister of Finance pointed out in

his complaint to the Committee of Ministers in 1812, Treskin
and the provincial administration were interfering in the work
of the Treasury agents by prescribing the maximum purchase
price and the districts where the distilleries could buy their
grain. But not only did the local administration thus interfere
directly in the affairs of the Treasury, it also was encouraging
practices which were financially detrimental to the state
distilleries. Thus, while setting the maximum price for the
agents of the distilleries, the provincial administration was
paying higher prices to the individual peasants in its own grain
purchases for the state granaries. Naturally the peasants
preferred to sell to the higher bidder, the officials of the
provincial administration (whose police powers may have been
important in fixing the peasants' choice of a purchaser). As
a result, the distilleries were compelled to buy their grain
from the state granaries at still higher prices. Thus, for
example, the Minister of Finance noted that a pood (36.113
lbs.) of grain was costing the distilleries 2.29 rubles instead
of the 1.20 previously paid. Although Treskin's practices
were to the disadvantage of the Ministry of Finance (and the
Treasury), they profited the larger individual grain producers
of Siberia, who now could sell a larger crop to the state
granaries at better prices than to the distilleries. This,
Pestel and Treskin claimed, had stimulated the development
of agriculture and a more active economy in Siberia.[27]

To carry out their program Pestel and Treskin relied
on the bureaucracy. In the tradition of eighteenth-century
enlightened despotism they felt that the development of Siberia
could not be left to the people but depended on the work of an
efficient officialdom. The difficulty which they and their
colleagues in St. Petersburg encountered was the lack of
qualified personnel. It is illustrative of the situation and
attitude that in 1804 a decree had to be issued that "officials
should be appointed to Siberia not on the basis of their rank
but on the basis of their abilities."[28]

Not only was the staff mediocre, but there was also a
lack of clarity and coordination in the relation between various
bureaus and organizations. For example, the Committee of
Ministers had to point out to the civil authorities that in case
of trouble on the border they should get in touch with the
military commandant directly rather than by way of St.
Petersburg. This reminder had become necessary when,
as a consequence of the enmity between civilian and military

authorities, the former failed to warn the military of im-
pending danger on the border. [29] One way to obviate these
difficulties was to select officials who would do their chief's
bidding and to subordinate all military and civilian agencies
under one head. Pestel and Treskin endeavored to do both.
In the effort to bring all administrative matters under his
control, Treskin requested through Pestel in St. Petersburg
that the civil functions of the local military commanders
should be transferred to his subordinates. For example, he
secured this authority over the Okhotsk region by divesting
the military commander of his administrative duties and
transferring them to the local chancellery which was directly
subordinated to Treskin himself. [30] By the end of the fourteen
years of Treskin's regime, the military authorities had been
pushed into the background and relegated to the performance
of strictly army and navy matters. [31]

With the help of an obedient and personally devoted bureaucracy, Treskin put his program of economic development
into execution. He scorned the assistance and participation
of all other groups of society. It was natural that his program
would not find support among the merchants since the eventual
aim of the policy was to decrease their hold on the Siberian
economy. The prevailing sentiment in Siberia at the time
was that the merchants were keeping a stranglehold over
the economy of the region through their buying monopolies.
The administration of Pestel-Treskin became a fourteen-year-
long history of clashes and conflicts between the bureaucracy
and the merchants. Treskin and the officials accused the
merchants of monopolizing not only the trade but all the
economic life of Siberia, thereby preventing its full development. Unfortunately, we are not in possession of statistical
evidence which would prove or disprove this assertion. The
only materials we have are personal reminiscences and
correspondence, and even these are not completely reliable
because of the manner in which they have been collected and
published. Yet the general tenor of this evidence strongly
points to a monopolistic and reactionary (in the sense of
defending out-of-date economic practices) attitude of the
merchant class. We remember the privileges demanded by
Siberian merchant deputies in Catherine's commission, and
if we believe the contemporaries of Pestel and Treskin, these
efforts to secure complete control over almost all sections
of economic life had not been abandoned by the merchant

group. Thus around 1804 or 1805 two merchants tried to
secure a monopoly over the sale of meat in the city of Irkutsk.
Another contemporary writes that only a few individual merchants went to the fairs and brought various manufactured
goods to Siberian towns. Needless to say, they profited from
this advantageous circumstance to dictate their own prices. [32]

But in the countryside too, it seems, the monopolist
was calling the tune. For example, the peasant Novikov from
the village of Berezov in the Upper Tomsk township (volost')
had secured complete mastery over a whole village area by
moneylending and other operations. Once he had obtained
control, he monopolized all economic exchanges between
this village and the outside world; by means of bribery, he
had acquired the benevolence of local officials and made his
position impregnable. In the words of the historian who reports
this case, the rich trading peasant was but the first and lowest
unit of the army of exploiters of Siberia. [33]

Treskin tried to counteract this great influence of the
merchants by letting other groups share in their privileges
and rights. For example, in 1812 he was of the opinion,
eventually given legislative sanction by the Committee of
Ministers, that the agent of a merchant or any "burgher"
(meshchanin) should be given the right to act as interpreter
and intermediary with Chinese merchants. On Treskin's
behalf, Pestel supported this proposal before the Committee
of Ministers by pointing out that, first, these agents and city
dwellers were often best acquainted with the languages and
customs of the Asiatic natives and foreigners, and, second,
that there were too few merchants of the first guild in Siberia
to carry on this foreign trade. It is obvious that he hoped to
stimulate competition and break the monopoly of the few merchants by increasing the number of persons eligible to carry on
foreign trade. [34] Also, as the Minister of Finance complained
to the Committee of Ministers in 1812, the governor-general
of Siberia insisted that state factories make their purchases
of supplies (in particular of grain) through officials and not
through the regular private merchants. [35]

Unfortunately for Treskin and Pestel, this policy met
with resistance from the Ministry of Finance and its local
agents, the Chambers of the Treasury (Kazennaia Palata).
Ever since Catherine II, and especially since the beginning
of the reign of Alexander I, the Russian government had been
converted to the idea of unrestricted free trade as a basis

for healthy economic life. In this respect the state was well
ahead of "society." The Russian merchants in particular had
remained extremely conservative, still living in the world
of seventeenth-century Muscovy, thinking only in terms of
privileges, monopolies, and special rights. [36] The efforts
of Peter the Great to drag them out of their narrow confines
had been successful only in individual instances; the majority
of the merchants had remained untouched. This perhaps explains not only their insignificant social and political role in
Russia in the eighteenth and nineteenth centuries but also the
government's dislike and distrust of the class--a distrust
which probably made its acceptance of free trade principles
much easier.

The Ministry of Finance believed that in order to stimulate
freedom of trade, the officials should be given as little power
in economic matters as possible and individual merchants
should freely compete for whatever benefits were to be derived
from dealings with the state. In principle, this position was
unassailable. It seems, however, from the material available
to us, that the Ministry of Finance was not very well informed
on the actual conditions which prevailed in Siberia. The
Minister did not know that in fact freedom of trade was nonexistent, not because of government interference but because
of the control exercised by a small group of merchants. The
Ministry took the complaints of the merchants at their face
value, not realizing that these complaints against interference
and arbitrary decisions by the authorities were in the interest
of monopoly rather than of freedom of trade.

There may, however, be another side to the story. The
Russian government of the time was in a dilemma not unlike
that faced by the United States in the second half of the nineteenth century, though in a different area of economic
activity. As in the period of the first antitrust legislation
in the United States, the federal government did not quite
realize the positive functions fulfilled by the big trusts, so
the officials of Alexander I did not realize that perhaps, under
the conditions prevailing in Siberia, monopolies were the
only available means of fostering the economic development
of the region. At any rate, monopolies by merchants did not
disappear, in part surely because they were the most convenient institutional framework for the full exploitation of
Siberian resources and economic potentialities.

Nor should we exclude altogether the possibility that

the struggle between Pestel and the Ministry of Finance in the name of economic freedom might have also been a contest for power between rival government agencies or a conflict between the personal interests of high dignitaries. We do know that Pestel was the butt of many attacks in St. Petersburg for reasons both personal and political. But the evidence is not adequate or conclusive on this point, and the hypothesis of a struggle for power, however suggestive, must remain unproven and, in this writer's opinion, not very convincing. Yet here was certainly a conflict between different philosophies of government: bureaucratic absolutism (however enlightened it may seem in historical perspective) and freedom of individual initiative in the domain of economic action.

In any case, the Ministry of Finance and its agents waged a long war with Treskin and Pestel. This conflict lasted for almost a decade and rose to particular intensity in the last years of Pestel's regime. Treskin had requested that the major functions of the Ministry of Finance in Siberia, control of salt and wine monopolies, supplying of state factories, etc., be put under his direct control. [37] Without even waiting for confirmation and permission, he proceeded to exercise this control. For example, on his own initiative he replaced military service in remote districts by a general tax--not an uncommon practice but one which needed special authorization by the central government. This he did several years in succession. When the matter eventually reached the Council of State he was censured for it, but Alexander I refused to take any disciplinary action against him, thus assenting to the accomplished fact. [38] The conflict with the Ministry of Finance led to some very harsh and arbitrary measures against its representatives. Thus for several years Treskin persecuted the chief of the Chamber of the Treasury in Tobolsk, Levitskii, and another official, Gornovskii, in Irkutsk. He had them put under house arrest, prevented them from communicating with St. Petersburg, and denounced them to the central government as troublemakers and slanderers. The conflicting reports of Treskin and the representative of the Ministry of Finance were the subject of lengthy discussion in the Committee of Ministers, the Senate, and the Council of State. The fact that some of the instructions had to be repeated many times over the years indicates how little attention was paid to them by Pestel. [39]

The extreme claim for freedom of trade by the Ministry

of Finance was to some extent qualified by the feeling of many
outstanding government officials that Russia was not yet ready
for complete freedom of economic activities. The Minister
of the Interior (probably through the pen of Speransky, who
for a time was chief writer of reports for the Minister) stated
the belief that Russia would have to be brought to complete
freedom of trade by a long process of government leadership. [40] This conception, Treskin claimed, was implemented
by him in Siberia. He gave two reasons for his interference:
(1) the harm that could be done by private monopoly, (2) the
conditions of Siberian agriculture, in particular the recurring
crop failures which made government help essential if the
population were to survive. His reports stressed the fact
that private merchants were pulling down prices and that
only the government could promote agriculture by paying more
for the peasants' products. The agents of the Ministry chal-
lenged this contention; they claimed that in fact the peasant
received little benefit from these higher prices when he was
compelled by government officials to sell his grain and had
to buy it back later from the state stores. Of course, we
must not forget that the Ministry was defending not only the
interest of the peasantry but also the interest of the Treasury
in the profits derived from distilling alcohol from cheap
grain. [41]

To support his contention that crop failures were very
frequent in Siberia, Treskin kept on sending reports which
described the plight of the local population. The agents of the
Ministry of Finance questioned the accuracy of these reports
and insisted that Treskin was presenting false data. If the local
population was suffering hardships, the Treasury officials
claimed, it was not owing to natural causes but to the intensive
and arbitrary grain purchases by the office of the governor-
general. The central government seems to have been inclined
to believe Treskin, for it did not act on the request of the
Ministry of Finance except for repeating its advice that
freedom of trade and of economic activity should be fostered
and not stifled. [42]

So far we have been giving the impression that right was
on Treskin's side, that he acted for the benefit of Siberia, as
he saw it. This picture, however, must be qualified. Treskin,
as we have intimated, was a very harsh and demanding task-
master. He gave free rein to his subordinates, who often
abused this confidence or acted with much greater ruthlessness

than was perhaps necessary. They clung to the principles
of paternalistic despotism; they believed in prescribing the
actions of their subjects down to the last detail, and they also
felt that obedience and fulfillment of duties should be exacted
not by kind words lost on an illiterate and crude people but
by harsh, repressive punishments. Qui aime bien, châtie bien
could have been their motto.

Of anecdotal interest but a good illustration of this
attitude is a story told about Loskutov, the district chief of
Nizhneudinsk, and the peasant Emelian. This peasant, a
chronic vagrant whom no one had ever been able to compel to
work, had been exiled to Siberia for some minor misdemeanor.
He was assigned compulsory settlement in Loskutov's district.
Loskutov came to the village during an inspection tour and,
upon hearing of Emelian's aversion to work, sent for him.
In his usual sarcastic manner Loskutov said that either he,
Emelian, would till the land like everyone else, or his skin
would not remain on his body for long. Emelian was allotted
a piece of land and provided the necessary implements.
Loskutov even gave him some money and set him the task of
delivering a certain quantity of grain by the following year.
Emelian did not think much of this order and decided to disregard it. A year passed and Loskutov came around once
more. He asked whether Emelian had been a good farmer
and, upon hearing that the latter had been idling away his
time, had him seized and savagely beaten, promising to let
him perish under the knout next time if he did not settle down
and do as he was told. This time Emelian decided to heed the
warning, and he worked the plot assigned to him in such an
effective manner that by the following year he was well on
his way to prosperity. Encouraged by another loan from
Loskutov, within a few years he became a well-to-do peasant,
a leader of his community. [43] This anecdote shows the results
achieved by the methods used by Treskin and his assistants
but also the price that was often paid for the achievement.
Petty regulations and constant interference in the daily lives
of the population were a source of recurring annoyance and
friction. Treskin himself set an example by his constant
investigations of markets and of public and even private
kitchens and stores. Rules governing the quantity and quality
of foods were set forth in all details, reminiscent of Peter the
Great's regulations and with the same questionable effect. [44]

Under Siberian circumstances such methods were bound to

lead to a great deal of arbitrariness and abuse. The officials, given wide powers to interfere in the daily life of the people, took advantage of their position to fill their own pockets and to allow free play to their whims. Peasants avoided the annoyance of numerous petty regulations and interferences only by bribing the local authorities. As the Old Believer peasants testified, they were left alone and were free to pursue their work in the way they saw best, with very good results, only because they paid a yearly bribe to the local officials. [45] The governor-general had to intervene to stop an official of a grain store from exacting bribes from the peasants, cheating them on weight, and hampering their normal routine by keeping them waiting for days before taking their grain. [46] Even the chancellery of the governor-general in Irkutsk was not free from the taint of bribe-taking and abuse of power. The governor's office had such wide powers and so many functions that all important affairs had to be brought to it. This was, of course, a great opportunity for the officials to make some extra money. It is not proven that Treskin and Pestel indulged themselves in these unethical practices, but there is strong suspicion that they did. At any rate, it seems that Treskin's wife took advantage of the situation (though this is confirmed by many witnesses, one still cannot be entirely sure of its accuracy). Contemporaries assert that in order to succeed in one's business the best way was to go to the secretary Beliavskii, a favorite of Mrs. Treskin, with appropriate gifts. Treskin's wife and the secretary had established a regular store for selling these gifts. No doubt many other smaller functionaries and their families followed this example. For instance, when Loskutov, whom we mentioned earlier, was dismissed by Speransky, he was found in possession of furs and other articles to the value of over 150,000 r. These examples could be multiplied but would not in any way add to the picture. [47]

The conflict between Treskin and the Siberian merchants resulted in some very dramatic episodes. It is not our purpose here to relate all of these events, but a brief account of this conflict may help set the stage for some of the measures taken later by Speransky. Already in the first years of his administration Pestel got into difficulties with prominent members of the merchant group. In the last decades of the eighteenth century these merchants had secured for themselves a rather influential position, and had been able, by intrigues and petitions, to force the recall of unpopular governors. The dismissals of Lezzano and Selifontov, for example, took place after some pressure had been exerted by prominent merchants. [48] Most prominent among these merchants was Sibiriakov, mayor of Irkutsk, author of the previously discussed complaint against Lezzano. As could be expected in view of Treskin's policies, Sibiriakov became involved in a bitter conflict with the administration. He had attempted to obtain various economic privileges, such as the right to transport and supply grain to state factories, and had run into opposition from Treskin who felt that these functions lay within the province of the bureaucracy. [49] The struggle of Sibiriakov, assisted by another prominent merchant, Myl'nikov, against the powerful governor ended in the victory of the latter. Treskin accused Sibiriakov and his associates of fomenting discontent and of slandering the administration, and had them exiled to remote places. In spite of all the efforts of the families of these prominent men and in spite of appeals to St. Petersburg, supported by the Minister of Justice (the poet G. Derzhavin), Sibiriakov and Myl'nikov remained in exile until their deaths. This harsh treatment of influential and respected leaders incensed the merchant community, but it also instilled fear. If Treskin dared to treat prominent leaders so harshly and arbitrarily, his dealings with minor figures were even worse and less subject to question and complaint. Many merchants who tried to counteract Treskin's policies, who refused to be the obedient tools of his administration, suffered persecution, imprisonment, and exile. The fate of Sibiriakov was shared by Kiselev, Peredovshchik, Igumnov, and many others. [50]

Treskin's example was followed on a smaller scale by his subordinates in the districts. [51] The merchants, as a class, were not in a position to offer effective resistance to arbitrary action. In the first place, they could not rely on the support of the population, for their own activities had not endeared them to the peasantry and the natives. As a matter of fact, the peasants looked rather to the government to protect them against the merchant tyrants, as in European Russia they looked to the state for protection against the serf owners. In the second place, this merchant group, as we have mentioned, belonged more to the seventeenth than to the nineteenth century. The merchants were not educated or enlightened enough to seize upon the proper method of fighting the administration and defending their own interests. Instead of carrying their opposition to the administration on the grounds of national interest, efficiency, and more enlightened practices, they only complained against individual acts and persons. The same limited outlook which made them unable to make good use of their wealth to improve the social and cultural conditions of their fellow Siberians also prevented them from defending their interests in terms of national and popular needs. For this reason their complaints had all the appearance of slander and petty personal quarrels. It was not difficult for Treskin and Pestel to have them disregarded by the central authorities in St. Petersburg.

However, complaints continued to reach St. Petersburg, at times in a very devious manner. A group of Irkutsk merchants had finally mustered enough courage to write a petition denouncing Treskin's actions. The petition was carried to Alexander I by a merchant who, to escape detection by Treskin and Pestel, traveled by way of the southern steppes and managed to present this petition directly to the emperor while the latter was taking a walk. [52] This petition, and particularly the manner in which it was presented, proved to be the last straw; Alexander I ordered a thorough investigation of the situation by a Siberian Committee composed of the ministers whose functional jurisdiction included Siberian affairs.

The committee came to the conclusion that only a fundamental reorganization, such as had been intended for the last twenty-five years, could solve the difficulty. Before this could be undertaken, however, a new survey of Siberia had to be made and the most crying needs taken care of. Obviously, Pestel, the present governor-general, who had been residing in St. Petersburg for ten years, was unfit for this task. [53] A new man had to be chosen. Alexander I agreed with this conclusion of his advisers and appointed Speransky, at the time governor of Penza, as governor-general of Siberia with special instructions and powers to deal with the situation.

CHAPTER III

Laying the Groundwork for the Transformation of Siberia

1. Speransky--Governor-general of Siberia

PRIVY Councilor M. M. Speransky was not, in 1819, a new figure on the Russian political scene. Between 1808 and 1812 he had been among the most influential personages of the empire. Fallen from power and sent into exile in 1812, he had made the first step toward his political come-back in 1816 when he became governor of Penza.[1] In 1819 he hoped to be appointed senator and permitted to return to St. Petersburg. His nomination to the post of governor-general of Siberia seemed to him to be the emperor's way of keeping him away from the capital longer. The new commission, he felt, was only an honorable way of prolonging his exile. But he could take hope from the words of the nomination, which stated that upon completion of his mission in Siberia he would be recalled to St. Petersburg to assist in the drafting of a general administrative plan for the region. Speransky was therefore impatient to accomplish his work in Siberia: untangle the administrative confusion, correct the abuses, punish the guilty, and survey the country. As soon as he decently could, he reported the termination of his mission and impatiently waited for the imperial command to return to the capital at long last. As a result, Speransky's activities in Siberia seem to have been marked by an unwillingness to get to the bottom of all the difficulties and problems.[2] Not until his return to St. Petersburg had become a certainty did Speransky view the situation in its proper perspective and begin to work for the implementation of the general principles he had distilled from his observations.

In the rescript appointing Speransky, Alexander I had written:

I have already had repeated evidence that short-term inspections rarely attain their aim; in particular, one is even less justified in expecting their success in such a remote and vast region. This is why I consider it most useful to give you the title of Governor-general and to entrust you, as the chief of the region, with all the rights and powers pertaining to this position, and with a survey of the province's condition. On the basis of these powers, you will correct everything that can be corrected, you will uncover the persons who are given to abuses, you will put on trial whomever necessary. But your most important occupation should be to determine on the spot the most useful principles for the organization and administration of this remote region. After you have put on paper a plan for such reorganization you will bring it to me, personally, to St. Petersburg, so that I shall have the means of finding out orally from you the true condition of this important region, and of basing on solid foundations its well-being for future times.

This task, in Alexander's opinion, would not take more than one to two years.[3]

The main ideas in this rescript were much the same as those contained in the instructions to Selifontov seventeen years earlier, but this time the emperor's expectations were to be justified. Speransky was the most honest and gifted bureaucrat in Russia at that time, and the short term of his assignment would preclude the corrupting influence of Siberian administrative traditions from becoming operative. Speransky himself, when his return was temporarily postponed, was very much aware of this danger and warned his former chief and influential friend, Count Kochubey, that his staying in Siberia longer would cancel the good he had already done and prevent the successful fulfillment of the task of complete reorganization which had been entrusted to him. He could be effective only so long as he preserved the confidence of the people; and it became more and more difficult to keep this confidence as time elapsed and brought in its wake the usual grievances at unpopular decisions.[4]

Speransky's task, like Selifontov's, was twofold: first,

to straighten out the current disorder and bring to account
those guilty of misrule, abuse, etc.; in the second place,
to present an over-all scheme of reorganization to be based
on the data he would obtain on Siberia. We need not be concerned here with Speransky's fulfillment of the first task, as
this properly belongs in his personal biography; moreover,
all the available data on it were compiled over eighty years
ago in the 1,500 pages of Vagin's book already cited and more
recently summarized by A. Fateev. Our purpose here will
only be to indicate Speransky's attitude towards Siberia and the
change it underwent, in order to gain a better understanding
of the work of reform and reorganization which was carried
out under his direction.

Siberian affairs were by no means unfamiliar to Speransky.
As director of one of the departments of the Ministry of the
Interior between 1802 and 1806, he had come into contact with
Siberian problems and had taken part in drafting the limited
legislation based on the results of Selifontov's inspection. In
preparing his Financial Plan of 1810, he undoubtedly studied
with some care the role played by Siberia in the fiscal structure of the Russian state. But not only in his official capacities
had he become familiar with Siberian affairs. He had always
been a man of great intellectual curiosity, especially interested
in the natural sciences, religion, and philosophy. He followed
as closely as possible the publications and work of the Academy
of Sciences and the development and achievements of European
scholarship. We know, for instance, that during his governorship at Penza he read, among other things, the works of
Academician Pallas on Siberia and the Mongols.

Speransky was probably the first governor of Siberia to
promote scientific study of this area. He was the first Russian
statesman who attempted to base fiscal and administrative
regulations on correct statistical data. He kept a diary during
his journey through Siberia--curiously barren of political
matter--which contains almost daily entries on the climate,
the atmospheric pressure, the landscape, the physical resources, and the people. Speransky was the first governor
to visit the mines and factory of Nerchinsk--not only out of
humanitarian and administrative concern but also to satisfy
his scientific and intellectual curiosity. Where he could not
go himself, he sent others; he sponsored special explorations
and studies, such as a general study of the province of Iakutsk,
and an exploration of the roads to the Chinese border. He gave

assistance to Wrangel's expedition to the Bering Sea and the
Arctic regions, and even helped the eccentric Englishman,
John D. Cochrane, who had decided to cross Siberia on foot.
When a new ecclesiastic mission was sent to China, Speransky
saw to it that the occasion was used to collect as much information as possible about the Celestial Empire and Mongolia
and that a basic library of Chinese, Mongolian, and Manchurian
books was brought back to the School of Asiatic Languages in
Irkutsk. Speransky also made systematic efforts at learning
about the customs and problems of the native peoples, as well
as those of Siberia's nomadic neighbors across the border,
such as the Kazakhs and Mongols.[5]

The results of these investigations convinced Speransky
that Siberia's true wealth was still incompletely known and
had barely been touched. In particular, he suspected that the
eastern regions of the country harbored great mineral and
agricultural resources awaiting explorers and exploiters.
He endeavored to stimulate in the Siberian merchants an
interest in the potential wealth of these regions. With the
help of his friend and admirer, the Irkutsk merchant Basnin,
Speransky tried to organize a trading company of Iakutiia, but
was not very successful. Basnin's and Speransky's enthusiasm
was not shared by other Siberian merchants, and Iakutiia had
to await the discovery of gold later in the century to attract
the attention of the Russians. Convinced by his observations
that the economic life of Siberia, and the character of its
merchant activities in particular, rested on too narrow a
basis, Speransky wanted to introduce greater variety into
the trading life of Siberia. He wished to see Siberia and Russia
break out of their narrow trading field, which was limited to
exchanging Chinese tea in Kiakhta and bartering a few articles
and agricultural products over the southern Urals. He felt
that in Siberia Russia had an ideal location to open up the
Chinese market for Europe. Until her own industry was more
developed, Russia could easily play the role of middleman
between China and the West (especially England); to this end
Speransky proposed the lowering or even the abolition of
tariff barriers on goods in transit.[6]

Speransky dreamed too of a great future for Russian trade
in the Pacific Ocean. The Russian colonies and settlements
in North America, especially in California, could become
the source of much needed foodstuffs which Siberia would
import by way of the Pacific ports and the northern maritime

route over its river system. Even trade with China and the Philippines could be based on Siberia's coastal area. These considerations perhaps explain Speransky's favorable view of the Russo-American Company, whose monopolistic practices and plans were otherwise uncongenial to him. In passing, it might be interesting to note that Speransky was quite distrustful of American enterprise, in particular that of whalers and traders in the North Pacific, whose better commercial and organizational talents might provide "unfair" competition for the Russians. He was especially afraid that whalers and seal hunters might establish trading points and ports of call on the Siberian coast or the islands in the Sea of Okhotsk and penetrate from there into Siberia proper. Should the Americans be given a foothold, they would easily captivate the friendly natives; their energy and spirit of enterprise would drive them onward, and the power and security of the Russian Empire would be threatened in the heart of Siberia.[7]

These two factors--scientific knowledge of Siberian conditions and consciousness of the economic opportunities there--contributed to the change in Speransky's attitude towards Siberia. Although better informed than most of his contemporaries, in the government and out of it, Speransky had at first shared their low opinion of Siberia. To them Russia's possessions beyond the Urals were a penal colony, the dwelling place of escaped convicts and primitive, barbarian tribes, good only for providing furs and Chinese tea. Upon entering Siberia Speransky had written to his daughter, "Siberia is simply Siberia and has nothing in common with India," and then had gone on complaining about the absence of any natural beauty in the landscape or of pleasant traits in the inhabitants.[8] But in the course of his further travels, studies, contacts with people, and investigations of conditions, he began to change his mind. Though he clearly realized that Siberia was no "India," he saw that it too had a great deal to offer. He was struck by the great variety of natural conditions--climate, fauna, and flora; in Semipalatinsk, for example, he fancied himself in Central Asia; in Kiakhta he was almost in China. If the northern and northeastern districts seemed little more than barren and frozen wastes, the central and southern parts had all the makings of rich agricultural centers. As for the people, they too were not so hopeless as they had seemed at first glance. True, there was as yet little education and polish among them; the merchants were

quite crude both in their way of life and in their commercial
practices, and they could not yet play the role of enlightened
leaders of the country. But the common people were of a
different sort; they were hard-working, honest, enterprising
people, like the best to be found in European Russia, and it
was definitely not true that the majority of Siberians were
convicts. Not more than 2,000 convicts entered Siberia every
year, and they remained but a tiny fraction of the population. [9]
Now, if the doors were opened to the good elements of the
Russian peasantry, if the local population were ruled by an
honest and efficient administration, Siberia would soon cease
to be a colony and become an integral part--and not the poorest
at that--of the Russian Empire. Speransky believed that his
major task was to help to bring this about by instituting a
proper administrative system.

    But personal observations and experiences were not alone
in influencing Speransky's approach to Siberian problems.
Experiences and factual information are of little value if they
cannot be organized meaningfully within the framework of
basic principles and theory. Speransky, as a son of the late
eighteenth century, had not only an esprit systématique but
also something of an esprit de système. His education and
previous political activity had confirmed in him a predilec-
tion for theoretical constructions and formal solutions of
problems, which decisively influenced his approach to Siberia.
Nor should we forget that Speransky's political philosophy
underlay all his governmental work, even though he rarely
made it explicit in his official papers. [10] Speransky believed
that the primary role of the state was to give spiritual and
moral leadership to the people. The government and political
institutions should merely provide the indispensable and most
efficient tools for the preservation and development of the
moral and spiritual values inherent in the nation. That such
an attitude easily led to a conservative outlook we know from
the example of West European romantic political theory. The
conservative tendencies engendered by Speransky's political
philosophy were reinforced by bureaucratic training and
experience, as well as by his personal political timidity.
Furthermore, his ethical approach to politics misled Speransky
into overlooking the difficulties inherent in the application of
broad political principles and ethical norms to concrete social
and political realities by the exclusive means of formal
administrative regulations. As a result he rarely provided

hard and fast rules for carrying out the general aims set forth in the legislation. His idealism and his belief in moral progréss (which had a strongly religious, mystical tinge) prevented him from visualizing limited and immediate goals but always drove him to set goals for moral progress as absolute standards for the practical problems at hand. This feature of his political philosophy accounts for the seeming paradox that the immediate concrete results of the legislation he helped to bring about were not particularly notable but that nevertheless, in the long run, his work proved to be of great influence in guiding the development of Siberia.

Nor should we forget the historic period in which Speransky undertook his Siberian mission. In 1819 the Latin American colonies were in the midst of their struggle for liberation from Spain; barely half a century earlier a serious blow to colonialism had been dealt by the birth of the United States; Haiti had freed itself from the French during Napoleon's reign. It seemed that all colonies, especially settlement colonies, were destined to secure their independence within the very near future. Colonial empires had not long to live, unless they were willing to undergo a radical transformation, which was, of course, what actually happened. These events held the attention of all educated and politically conscious people of the time. A vast literature debating the pros and cons of empires, the means of safeguarding the economic and military (naval) advantages derived from the colonies without direct political control, was circulating among an eager public. A very popular book on the subject was Bishop Dominique de Pradt's Des Colonies, a two-volume work dealing primarily with Latin America, which went through many editions. [11] It is significant that several friends and acquaintances of Speransky sent him the book upon learning of his appointment to Siberia. This shows that the leaders of Russia still looked upon Siberia as a kind of colony (though more closely bound to Russia than the Spanish colonies were to Spain, if only because of direct contiguity), and that they were seriously concerned about its future relations to the mother country, especially in view of the growing interest manifested by Americans in the Pacific Ocean and the colonial revolts of the last fifty years. We have no way of knowing to what extent de Pradt's ideas helped Speransky to shape his own. But there is no doubt that the book proved to be of great interest to the new governor-general, for it gave scientific

support to, and developed the logical consequences of, conclusions which enlightened officials had slowly reached about
Siberia in the preceding quarter of a century.

Very briefly, de Pradt's argument was that the mother
country would be unable to keep its colonies of settlement
unless it were willing to grant them the same administrative
structure and link them organically through similar institutions, legal and social privileges, and close, mutually
beneficial economic relations based on freedom of trade and
enterprise. England had lost the United States, and Spain
was in the process of losing South America, because of their
insistence on treating the colonial settlers like inferiors,
especially in social and political matters. Moreover, the
governments at home had undermined their position through
restrictive legislation which had stifled the economic growth of
the colonies and made the connection with the mother country
unprofitable. Even if the gloomy predictions of de Pradt
were not as readily applicable to Siberia as to the American
colonies, the lesson could not be disregarded. The idea of
bringing about a more organic connection between the mother
country and the colony and more similarity in their social,
economic, and political structure was bound to appeal to the
officials in St. Petersburg, whose ideas had been tending in
that same direction since the latter decades of the eighteenth
century.

One of Speransky's well-wishers among the dignitaries
of the empire was O. Kozodavlev, at the time Minister of
the Interior. Upon learning of Speransky's appointment as
governor-general of Siberia, Kozodavlev sent him a copy of
de Pradt's book and along with it his own opinions on Siberia
which he had presented to the Siberian Committee a few years
earlier. It may be worth while to summarize the main ideas
of Kozodavlev's argument, for Speransky kept them constantly
in mind. In the first part of his short paper Kozodavlev pointed
out the necessity of sending a governor to bring order to
Siberia and to work out a plan of reorganization. This new
governor-general should be a high dignitary, preferably a
military person, in whose hands both the military and civilian
administrations could be combined. But the main task of this
dignitary would be to create a system which would stop the
excessive abuses of power by Siberian governors. In the past
the government had continually increased the functions of the
Siberian officials in an effort to put an end to mismanagement;

but with the increase in functions came a greater opportunity for abuses--it was a vicious circle.

To put an end to this system, Kozodavlev proposed to establish an advisory council to the Siberian governor-general.

> The establishment of the Superior Administration of Siberian Provinces, a council or commission whose members are partly appointed by the government and partly elected from among local inhabitants of various social classes, can limit the power of the governor, who as the president of this body would have a deciding voice only in cases when opinions are equally divided. [12]

In an emergency the governor could take temporary measures on his own initiative, but Kozodavlev wanted to introduce the principle and practice of participation in government and supervision of the local executive by a body containing some elected members.

Such supervision of the local executive could take place only if some other bodies or institutions were found capable of exercising this important function. "It seems to me," wrote Kozodavlev, "that in limiting the power of the local chief in Siberia it would not be useless to strengthen the power of the magistrates and city administrations." [13] The example of the Baltic provinces (Riga) showed how successful such a system could be. If the Siberian towns and cities were governed by elected representatives of the merchant class, the merchants would have the power and influence needed to supervise the local executive. Although Kozodavlev forgot that the merchants of Siberia were centuries behind those of Riga in education and civic consciousness, this plan offered an entirely new approach to the problem of controlling the authority of the emperor's lieutenant in Siberia. At first glance, it would seem that Speransky would have approved of this proposal and tried to implement it. But like most high bureaucrats Speransky had a very poor opinion of the Siberian merchant class; and, in the absence of a nobility, there was no other group whose members could be elected to responsible positions of councilors and advisers of the governor. Yet the idea of a council to supervise the power of the governor, a council organically connected with Siberia, was a useful suggestion. Speransky did not forget it, especially since it coincided with his feeling that under Russian conditions "collegiate" institutions were to be preferred, particularly on the local level.

After these preliminary considerations about Speransky himself and his approach to the problems of Siberia, we may turn to the work of reorganization and reconstruction which he directed. This important work covered a very broad field; it is quite obvious that one man alone, even when endowed with Speransky's amazing capacity for work, could not accomplish the entire undertaking by himself. Speransky was lucky enough to find able assistants like the future Decembrist G. Baten'kov who drafted important sections of the new statutes for Siberia. Furthermore, the reorganization did not take place without influential dignitaries and high officials having their say. In 1821 Alexander I established a special Siberian Committee to examine Speransky's report and to discuss the proposed legislation and work out its final details.[14] The sources accessible to us do not indicate the extent of the participation or specific contribution of each official and dignitary concerned; nor are we in a position to determine what kind of pressure, if any, was brought to bear on Speransky to have the proposed legislation for Siberia conform with the interests and desires of all those with a personal or political stake in the matter. The work of many, the statutes were in a sense the result of the collaborative efforts of the entire Russian government of the time and reflect the attitudes and ideas of St. Petersburg. This should be kept in mind by the reader in the pages to follow. But as we cannot with any degree of certainty determine the authorship of each specific provision, and also for the sake of brevity, we shall use the name of Speransky as a collective to denote both himself and all his collaborators, in Siberia and in St. Petersburg, who had a hand in drafting the statutes of 1822. Our decision finds further justification in the fact that Speransky was no doubt the most active and influential spiritus rector and chief author of the final legislation.

2. Siberian Society Comes of Age

As a result of the economic and social changes we have outlined earlier, Siberia was coming of age at the moment Speransky arrived to reorganize the administration. The

Siberian (Russian) people were no longer exclusively concerned with material achievements and were ready to shift
their interests and energies to the "higher things of the mind
and spirit." To this desire, Speransky was in a position to
give recognized institutional form and the favorable sanction
of the administration. In so doing, he stimulated and hastened
the full development of Siberia's cultural and social life. How
welcome such official support was to the Siberian intelligentsia
can be gathered from the frequent mention of Speransky's
efforts to provide opportunities for social and cultural contacts
in Siberia's cities. For this reason, that part of Speransky's
contribution to Siberian life which is not embodied in the
legislative acts of 1822 also deserves our attention.

On the basis of all contemporary evidence, there was no
such thing as Siberian "society" before Speransky's arrival
in Siberia. Potential members of a group with intellectual,
social, and artistic interests would have been the officials
(both military and civil) and the big merchants. The big
merchants, however, were in no position to become the center
of social life. With rare exceptions, they were still following
the tradition of the old Russian merchant class of avoiding
social and public life as much as possible. They lived in a
style which seemed to have remained unchanged since the
sixteenth or seventeenth centuries, before the accelerated
westernization of Russian society. Although educated in a
limited technical sense--almost all could read and write and
some were familiar with Oriental languages and customs--
the merchants had no cultural interests. A contemporary
traveler notes that although many of the Irkutsk merchants
were millionaires several times over, they lived, as their
Muscovite ancestors had, in a few small, dark, closetlike
rooms at the back of the house, slept on boards and trunks,
and ate the coarsest food. [15] Also they preserved the medieval
and Oriental custom of keeping the women out of public places
as much as possible. Vigel' relates with great astonishment
and amusement that for a New Year's party the very popular
wife of the governor of Tobolsk had finally prevailed upon the
merchants to bring their wives and daughters to the governor's
reception. The women dutifully came all dressed up in very
rich clothes, bedecked with jewels, but then sat like statues
along the walls of the room, refused to talk with any man,
and looked with boredom and disapproval at the dancing of
the officials. [16] Obviously such people could not become

centers of stimulating intellectual and social life.

Nor were the officials active promoters of social life,
as they were in European Russia. The Siberian officials were
for the most part a poor, half-educated lot who struggled
hard to keep their families alive and whose spiritual horizon
was rather narrow. Among the local officials, many had
been born and brought up in Siberia and still had the common
Siberian distrust of things intellectual. The conflict that had
raged between the officials and the merchants under Pestel
and Treskin precluded any drawing together to foster social
contacts. As a matter of fact, Treskin's policy was to keep
as much away from society as his position permitted.

Speransky's behavior and actions transformed this situation radically. He wanted to be in close contact with the
people and made himself accessible to everybody. He tried
to establish friendly relationships with both the merchants
and peasants. In his actions in Siberia he stressed public
relations; he used his moral influence, his powers of persua-
sion, his example of kindness in an effort to draw Siberian
society out of its shell. His immediate assistants were
well-educated young people whom he had brought along from
Russia (for example, Weickardt, Wild'e, Repinskii, Tseier).
Speransky encouraged the natural gaiety and sociability of
these young assistants and, with their help and active participation, organized dances, weekly social gatherings, and
frequent receptions. His popularity, the confidence people
had in him, and his ability to get along with all classes of
society contributed to the success of these gatherings. The
merchants were no longer afraid to meet and talk with the
governor-general and his colleagues. Speransky also helped
to break the barriers between officialdom and society by his
interest.in religious matters. He was active in organizing
Bible societies and other religious groups. These actions
helped to convince the Irkutsk merchants of the good intentions of Speransky, and they more willingly followed his
suggestions or requests to bring their families to social
gatherings. Contemporaries have all noted that during the
years of Speransky's residence in Siberia social life was
very gay and stimulating. [17]

Speransky also paid great attention to education. With
the help of his old schoolmate, P. Slovtsov, he founded a
series of secondary and primary schools. Moreover, he
stimulated interest in education by sponsoring voluntary

self-instruction groups on the model of the Lancaster Schools of Mutual Instruction. [18] He was also the first to realize that Siberia needed its own university and made some tentative plans which he transmitted to Kaptsevich, his successor in Western Siberia. However, it was not until 1888 that a Siberian university was founded. Speransky also helped to establish a local paper, although it did not survive for long after his departure, and until the middle of the century Siberia had no press of its own. At any rate, some intellectual interest began to awaken under Speransky's guidance, and within the next decades after his departure we see the development of intellectual life, cultural interests, and of an intelligentsia. [19]

The breaking of the monopolies of the big merchants and the end of bureaucratic tyranny and petty control led to a feeling of greater personal security among the people, which in turn fostered civic consciousness. If it was too late for the old members of the Siberian merchant aristocracy to change, their sons acquired a greater interest in things cultural. These wealthy heirs received an excellent education, traveled widely for pleasure as well as for business, kept in touch with intellectual developments in St. Petersburg, and associated with the educated officials. Soon they were to form an intellectual elite whose wealth was used to build up libraries and scientific collections, to finance scholarly expeditions, and to support local talents. Along with this increasing interest in cultural activities came an awareness that wealth should be used in a socially productive manner. Whereas in the eighteenth and early nineteenth centuries only a few wealthy individuals had ever thought of contributing money to public institutions--with the exception of donations for churches and hospitals--the younger generation after Speransky's time gave large sums for the establishment of civic hospitals, orphanages, schools, and public libraries. A good example of this new generation of Siberian millionaires was Basil Basnin, the son of Speransky's friend, who spent much of his time reading and studying, collected one of the better private libraries in Russia, and kept in close correspondence with many intellectual and scientific personalities of his time. He sponsored scientific expeditions and himself made observations and studies of Chinese customs. [20]

In the late 1820's and early 1830's the cultural development initiated by Speransky's governorship received an unexpected consolidation and further stimulation from the appearance in

Siberia of the elite of the Russian intelligentsia--the Decembrists. After the failure of their revolt on December 14, 1825,
they had been exiled to Siberia where they were welcomed
with great friendliness and sympathy. Upon completion of
their sentence of hard labor, they were settled in various
districts and towns of Siberia, and most of them became
cultural leaders in their communities. Probably the best
educated and most enlightened single group in Russia at the
time, with a very high sense of civic duty, they threw themselves heart and soul into the task of educating the Siberians,
of studying the land and the people, and of providing moral
and spiritual leadership. They established many schools,
helped their neighbors in medical and technical problems,
and systematically investigated Siberian life and nature. They
have left lasting memories in Siberia and can truly be called
the first enlighteners of the Siberian people. While some of
the Decembrists were also drawn into the administration,
they all maintained social contacts with the upper ranks of
the bureaucracy, particularly those settled near Irkutsk. [21]

With the help of a new type of bureaucrat that had come
to Siberia after the reforms of 1822, the Decembrists provided the core for most lively intellectual circles. Many
members of this new generation of bureaucrats were of
European Russian origin and had received their education
and first administrative apprenticeship in St. Petersburg
and Moscow. These new officials not only were better educated
than their predecessors but they also had a higher sense of
civic and moral responsibility. Siberia, for them, was no
longer a hunting ground in which to make a fortune but an
area entrusted to their care where they fulfilled those functions
of moral and spiritual leadership which--as Speransky had
so often said--were the true mission of government. Besides
attending to their official duties, they actively pursued the
investigation and study of the land and tried to give due attention to the needs and customs of the people they were
governing. As a German scientist observed in 1829:

> An diesen aufgeklaerten Kreis [in Irkutsk, with the
> participation of some Decembrists] schlossen sich von den
> Beamten und Offizieren der Ost-sibirischen Hauptstadt
> nur die zur letzten Generation gehoerigen.... Die neue
> Generation der Staatsdiener hat durch fruehzeitigen
> geselligen Verkehr und durch wissenschaftliche Anregung,

eine moderne Ansicht von ihrem Volke und vom Leben
gewonnen, und mit erfreulicher Sympathie zeigt gerade
diese in Sibirien der aeltesten und aechtesten Volkssitte
die ihr gebuehrende Theilnahme.[22]

Stimulated by these men, education became more and
more widespread, and from the middle of the nineteenth
century Siberia could favorably compare in this respect with
European Russia. All this contributed to the formation of a
new kind of Siberian leader: a man interested in the fate and
the history of the region and eager to obtain a good education
in order to be of the greatest help to his people and province.
This new Siberian leader was proud of his region, he vied
with the elite of St. Petersburg in intellectual and cultural
interests, he resented the fact that Siberia was still often
considered merely an area of exploitation. He believed Siberia
to be truly an organic part of Russia and in this belief he
only expressed the change in attitude towards Siberia that
had been in the making since the eighteenth century, had
been formulated by Speransky, and had received its administrative sanction in the statutes of 1822. As the Russian popular
song, speaking for a convict, expressed it: "Siberia, after
all, Siberia too is Russian land," and if this was the case,
then Siberia had to be Europeanized, while preserving its
positive distinctive features. This marked the beginning of
a Siberian regional consciousness.

3. Economic and Social Transformation

The transformation in the habits and cultural life of
Siberian society was but one aspect, and a somewhat intangible
one, of Speransky's governorship. The concrete and practical
outcome of his administration and his major contribution to
the future development of Siberia was the drafting of a series
of legislative statutes which remained the basis of the region's
administration until the end of the imperial regime. These
statutes, ten in number, were designed to provide a clear and
logical basis for all branches of Siberian administrative and
public economic life.[23] Unfortunately, the original drafts have
not been published, and therefore we do not know precisely
the original intentions of Speransky. We do know, however,
that there was very little discussion on most of the points

covered in the statutes; in only one instance, a minor one
as far as Siberian general problems were concerned, was
there sharp argument and Speransky's ideas did not prevail.
This was the proposal made by Speransky for a schedule to
free the "ascribed" (pripisnye) workers, i. e., the state
serfs who worked in the government factories and mines
or who tilled the soil to produce foodstuffs for the factory
workers (at times they combined both activities). Had his
proposal been accepted, it would have been the first instance
of serf emancipation by the government. No doubt the advisers
of Alexander I were not yet prepared to commit the government
openly to a course of eventual emancipation.

Besides setting up the administrative machinery which
prevailed with little change until the fall of the imperial
regime, the statutes also dealt with the problem of the transformation of Siberian economic and social life. As this
problem was the basis for all the specific regulations, it
is necessary to understand the intentions of Speransky and
the Siberian Committee concerning the economic and social
future of the region. Although many of the specific rules
drawn up proved less effective in practice than their authors
had hoped, they paved the way for the development of Siberian
economic resources in the decades to follow.

On the basis of the complaints by the Siberian merchants,
as well as the opinions of the Ministry of Finance, the government considered the creation of a healthier economic structure
to be one of the essential problems of Siberia. It was to this
field that attention was turned first. In laying a new basis
for Siberian economic life in accordance with the theories
current at the time, the first task was to break the private
monopolies on trade, and to abolish unnecessary bureaucratic
control in this field. [24]

To establish full freedom of trade became Speransky's
first concern. While still in Siberia he had prepared the
ground by restricting as much as possible the interference
and participation of officials in economic activities, interference and participation which had become common practice
in Pestel's time. [25] Executive orders issued by Speransky
during his stay in Siberia, as well as provisions in the final
statutes, abolished most of the detailed regulations of trade
which up to this time had been a mere pretext for bureaucratic
tyranny. [26] The Russian government at this time was not yet
able to break completely with bureaucratic supervision and

interference. But by the statutes of 1822 the chiefs of the administration (i. e. , governors-general, civil governors, district chiefs) were directed to exercise their supervisory powers for the encouragement and maintenance of freedom of economic activity. The importance of this concern can be gauged from the fact that at each level of the administrative hierarchy, the executive was particularly enjoined to safeguard freedom of trade. This was the function of the Main Adminis- tration (glavnoe upravlenie) in each of the two governor- generalships of Eastern and Western Siberia. The general provincial administration was to see to it that freedom of enterprise and trade was not restricted or violated on the district (okrug) level. The same obligation rested on the area administration (oblastnoe upravlenie). [27] To eliminate as much as possible the interference of officials and to prevent them from using their official position to bring economic pressure on individuals, one of the statutes prohibited officials from entering into loan relations with peasants and natives. Any claim arising from a debt to an official was to be declared null and void in advance and not acceptable for judicial action on any level. [28] As to the natives, in particular the Kazakh tribes on the border, their right to completely free economic activity (freely to sell and dispose of their produce and manu- factures) was specifically guaranteed. [29] The statute states in most emphatic terms that private trade and free enterprise are the basic means to the people's well-being and to the regular flow of food supplies. Only because of special Siberian conditions, which it was hoped would be only temporary, were the state granaries maintained as a precautionary measure for preventing famine. [30] This concern for the freedom of trade bore fruit very soon. Within the next few years after 1822 a series of new fairs and markets opened and boomed into very active centers, as for example the fair of Ishim in southwestern Siberia. [31]

Not content with guaranteeing this freedom of trade and enterprise administratively, the statute had provisions to encourage various forms of economic activity. To bring the whole area into closer trade relations with European Russia and to strengthen the economic bonds between the steppe and the old established districts of Siberia, mercantile ex- changes to and from these border regions were facilitated. Any Russian merchant, for instance, who had the right to trade in several provinces (this excluded peddlers and village

traders) now also received the right to trade with the steppe
areas through the established custom points. [32] Also, the
Kazakh Steppe was not considered the real state border of the
Russian Empire; therefore the border towns of Petropavlovsk
and Semipalatinsk were not considered ports, and caravan
trade was open to merchants of the second guild as well as
to those of the first. [33] To facilitate trade, the Administration
of Roads was to take particular care of, and give priority
to, those roads which were used intensively for the movement
of goods; such roads should be repaired before any others. [34]
It was a retrospective characterization of the attitude of
previous Siberian administrations that this point should be
the subject of a special rule in a fundamental statute.

To promote free commerce in the villages, peasants
were forbidden to interfere in the merchants' negotiations
for the hiring of horses, guides, and other temporary labor. [35]
Quite a few paragraphs in the statutes were devoted to the
handling of loan agreements. These rules put the legal aspects
of economic life into a more regular framework and facilitated
the recovery of money lent. For instance, verbal agreements
regarding loans were permitted, but they could not become
the basis for a regular lawsuit; if anyone wanted to make
sure that he would have the help of the authorities in enforcing
the contract, he had to draw up a written agreement. [36]
To speed up and facilitate the recovery of loans, all claims on
the nonpayment of debts were to be handled by the authorities
on the spot and did not have to be referred to the provincial
administration. [37] Finally, to prevent a legal suit from resulting in the complete ruin of the debtor, a minimum amount
of specified property, in particular agricultural implements
and hunting gear of peasants and natives, could never be
sold at auction. [38]

The Chamber of the Treasury (Kazennaia Palata) was
put in charge of the lands belonging to the state; it was to
survey them and transform them into state revenue items
(on a quitrent basis). These measures, the legislators believed, would enhance the productivity of peasant labor, as
they would relieve the peasants settled on state land of undue
government interference. [39]

In any case, the laws of 1822 expressed the feeling
that active economic progress was on its way in Siberia,
that there was an increase in the movement of goods--all
of which, with the proper government support, would lead

to a transformation in the way of life of most of the Siberian
people. That this was really to be the case can be seen from
a concrete instance reported in 1828 by the German scientist
and traveler, Erman, who noted that in Berezovo, in the
far north, a merchant had experimented with the planting of
wheat and that the success of this experiment might lead to
the development of a new agricultural area. [40] This could
have been done only after the bureaucratic fetters which
Treskin had put on the grain trade had been removed. In
those few areas in Siberia where a lack of arable land had
begun to be felt, the government saw to it that an adequate
and equal share of land was provided for each peasant; in
particular it safeguarded the full amount of communal land. [41]

The question of the state granaries required immediate
action by Speransky and later became the subject of a special
law (PSZ, 29, 133) in 1822. The principle followed by the
administration was to preserve the state stores of Siberia
as emergency aid to complement normal free trade in case
of need but in no case to allow the state stores to interfere
with the natural course of economic activity. [42] If possible,
the state granaries were to be used to encourage private
grain trade instead of introducing an exclusive monopoly
of the Treasury. [43] If the stores were established to support
trade and to help the people, there had to be some flexibility
in their location; for this reason the Main Administration
was given the right to change the location and number of these
stores in accordance with the development of agriculture. [44]
The grain stores were put under the direct supervision of
the president of the provincial administration (gubernskoe
upravlenie), i.e., the civil governor, and of his local representative in the district. This action was taken in the hope
that the stores would be established and operated on the basis
of their usefulness to the general population and cease to be
at the mercy of uncontrolled and narrow local interests. [45]

The state grain stores were also to have an important
part in the promotion of agriculture among the nomads.
While Treskin had used state stores and Treasury purchases
of grain to raise prices, thereby making agriculture a more
worth-while activity, Speransky wanted to use the stores
as a means of taking more direct action. He hoped that by
providing food in emergencies, by bringing in people familiar
with agricultural techniques, and by other helpful measures,
the stores and their administrators would stimulate agriculture

among the nomads. [46] He planned to establish state stores
and to construct permanent buildings for them in the steppe
area, but to maintain them only as long as free trade was
inadequate to the task and the poor were not provided for.
In no case were these grain stores to interfere with private
enterprise and trade. [47]

Special provision was also made for the establishment
of state fish stores in the remote areas of the province of
Iakutsk where agriculture was impossible and where fisheries
provided the staple. [48] Unfortunately, these laws were not
always adequately implemented, and even after Speransky's
time the state stores frequently remained the source of an
oppressive exploitation of peasants and natives by the bureaucracy. [49] Nevertheless, Speransky's statutes put an end to
direct bureaucratic interference, and the new organization
of the state stores provided incentive for the peasantry.
More than a generation passed, however, before the officials
lost the traditional view that only their interference could
lead to good results.

The improvement of the Siberian economy was directly
related to the settlement of agricultural colonists in that
area. [50] We have seen that several attempts at colonization
had been made by the government in the eighteenth century
and that, on the whole, they had failed. This failure had,
to a large measure, been due to the government's hesitant
attitude towards serfdom. The reign of Alexander I, however,
shows the first signs of systematic thinking about the eventual
emancipation of the Russian serfs. There was a gradual
crystallization of the idea that the state should take the lead
in slow and orderly emancipation by reforming the condition
of the state peasants. [51]

As the greatest serf owner, the state was capable of
influencing the attitude and actions of the nobility by its own
example. Most of the peasants in Siberia were state peasants,
and any transformation in their status would directly affect
the whole issue of serfdom. There is no doubt, as we can
see from various reports and papers written by him, that
Speransky too was aware of this problem. He was one of the
first Russian statesmen to realize that the state serf in
European Russia was facing a period of shortage of land.
This prospect was a revelation to his contemporaries, for
throughout many generations it had been assumed that land
was plentiful and only labor short. Foreseeing the imminent

decrease of available land, Speransky suggested that state
serfs, both in European Russia and Siberia, be given the
right to migrate and settle on free land in Siberia.[52] However,
the government was still unable to break away from its tradition of bureaucratic regulation and control, and although it
granted this right to migrate, it imposed various restrictive
rules (fulfillment of obligations, agreement of the fellow
members of communes) in spirit not unlike the Emancipation
of 1861. Only a few peasants could and did take advantage
of this law. It was left to the future Minister of State Domains,
Lieutenant General Kiselev, to put more substance into the
right of migration and bring about a greater movement of
colonization in the 1840's.[53]

In the absence of mass migration by state serfs, Speransky
concentrated his attention on the traditional method of bringing
people into Siberia, namely, the exile system. The system of
exiling people for settlement purposes--not as punishment--
dated from the seventeenth century.[54] But there had never
been any clear or specific rules for it, nor for the settlement
and disposal of the serfs sent to Siberia by their masters.
No records were kept, and no one really knew how many of
these unfortunate people came to Siberia, where they settled,
or what became of them. The official statistical survey of
1810, for example, frankly stated the ignorance of the authorities on this matter. This gave rise to shameless abuses and
ruthless exploitation and mistreatment of the exiles. Even
official records note the sad condition of the exiles, and
Treskin made efforts to have the government allot more
money for their support, at least during the journey, so that
they did not need to rely on private charity or theft. Under
such conditions the exiles could but rarely become useful
agricultural colonists, and most of them either escaped and
disappeared in the boundless spaces of Siberia or were caught
trying to escape and became forced laborers in state mines
and factories.[55]

A lengthy separate statute was drawn up to provide a
new approach to the exile system and to make use of the
possibilities of colonization which this system, for better
or for worse, contained. First of all, administrative exile
as a means of populating Siberia was ended forever (this did
not, however, in the least affect the administrative exile of
political offenders). From then on, exile to Siberia for forced
labor or for settlement or both became exclusively a form of

punishment inflicted by a court decision. No longer could a
serf owner send one of his serfs to Siberia because of some
personal caprice. [56]

Under the influence of the new ideas of penology introduced
by Beccaria, it was believed that a criminal should be given
a chance for rehabilitation; whenever possible, he should be
put in a position to become again a useful and productive
member of society. Thus for minor offenses a criminal was
sentenced to settlement as a peasant in Siberia with all the
rights and privileges of a peasant. For more serious offenses
a criminal had first to work off his term in some state enterprise and then would be required to settle as a peasant. To
encourage the establishment of families and households,
marriage between exiles was permitted freely, provided
the authorities were informed of the fact. [57] Further, to provide more incentive for the founding of families, all children
born to exiles (whether convicts or simple settlers) were
to be registered as peasants in the nearest community, and
they were free from all the legal limitations imposed on
their parents. [58]

The law of 1822 was intended to bring about a better
utilization of the labor of exiles which previously had been
wasted because of inadequate administrative procedures.
The Bureau of Exiles (Ssyl'naia Ekspeditsiia), set up as an
autonomous agency in Tobolsk, was to assign the convicts
to one of five categories according to their punishment and
abilities: forced labor in the mines, work in the chain gangs
on the highways, agricultural settlement, workhouses, and
finally, those who were incapacitated for productive work.
Exiles in excess of the needs in their category were to be distributed in the fertile areas of Tomsk and Eniseisk provinces,
while those too old to perform hard labor were to be sent for
settlement to the province of Irkutsk. [59]

Upon completion of the term of forced labor imposed
by the court (statutory maximum of twenty years) the convict
was free to settle near the factory or mine in which he had
worked and to remain there under simple police surveillance.
Presumably, he would engage in agricultural work in these
villages. Those too old or incapacitated for agricultural work
were also settled in villages where they had to be fed by the
community in return for light labor. [60] Should the former
convict have any preference for a specific area or village
in Siberia, he could settle there provided the community

was willing to take him in and the local authorities were informed. [61] Similar rules pertained to those assigned to highway repair crews; upon expiration of a five-year term, a laborer on such a crew could settle as a state peasant; if he had been a foreman for at least one year, he could also settle in a town. He could use his share of the crew's common funds for the first expenses of settling down; when he settled, his children entered the same social class as he, unless they had been educated at government expense. [62]

One of the problems arising in the process of settling former convicts was the possibility of a clash between them and the so-called old settlers. A series of rules in the statute on the exiles facilitated the absorption of former convicts into established peasant communities. To avoid burdening the community with taxes on a new member before the latter was able to pay for himself, the ex-convict was given an exemption from all taxes and dues for a three-year period. Should an exile pronounced incapable of heavy labor be taken into the household of an old settler, he could, with the consent of the community, petition for transfer into the category of state peasant. This petition could be acted upon by the local chamber of the treasury which did not need to take into account the original term of punishment. [63]

Forced laborers who had a family were to be given land allotments, in the same amount as the local peasants, in the neighborhood of the factories or mines in which they worked. In this way, their families could begin to till the land even before the end of their term of hard labor. [64]

A restricted number of convicts was to be organized into work groups in the provinces of Eastern Siberia. These work groups, maintained at the expense of the state, were to be used to prepare the country for future settlement by building villages, constructing dams, and carrying out other such projects. This was another way for the state to facilitate the settlement of free peasants. [65]

These good rules did not work out as planned. They had been drafted on the basis of the average number of exiles sent to Siberia in the first two decades of the nineteenth century, that is, about 1,500 to 2,000 persons a year. But immediately after the statute of 1822 was put into effect the number of exiles increased by leaps and bounds owing to a series of decrees which provided for the exile into Siberia of all vagrants, supernumerary personnel in military fortresses,

and other groups. Thus the yearly number of people sent to
Siberia rose to 6,600 in 1823 and to an average of 11,000 a
year between 1824 and 1827.[66] The statute had not been
designed to take care of such a great number of people, many
of whom were professional vagrants, i.e., individuals consti-
tutionally incapable of leading a settled life. These new exiles
found it much more difficult to become part of the Siberian
peasant community; friction between them and the old settlers
was chronic, and their usefulness to Siberia very limited.
Nevertheless, the statute had shown the way for a more
efficient and productive use of exile labor, and it had provided
for a better system of supervision and placement of these
unfortunate people. These efforts did not go completely to
waste, as not a few former convicts found a new home and
a productive role in Siberia.

One of the prerequisites for a productive agricultural
system was the elimination of the competition of unfree
labor.[67] Not for humanitarian reasons alone, therefore,
did the Russian government try to eradicate slavery in Siberia.
The struggle against slavery and the slave trade had been
a long, drawn-out affair. As early as 1728 the government
had ordered that freedom be granted to any slave who would
accept baptism.[68] In later years many other rules were
issued to facilitate the freeing of slaves and to prevent the
extension of slavery. In 1808 it was provided that slaves
bought or exchanged from across the southern steppe line
had to be given their freedom when they reached the age of
twenty-five. In 1820, during the governor-generalship of
Speransky, the government put more strength into this rule
by giving the slave owner 150 r. for each slave thus freed.[69]

The statutes of 1822 contained two clauses pertaining
to the curtailment of slavery. First of all, a work contract
could be undertaken only on an individual basis; in no case
could such an obligation be extended to the children or rela-
tives of the worker.[70] To prevent parents from selling or
hiring out their children, another clause provided that no
agreement for labor could be made in somebody else's name
and that no parent could undertake any obligations on behalf
of his children.[71] These rules were designed to restrict
indentured service to a minimum.

A special problem arose from the fact that the nomads on
the southern steppes, who lived on a very unstable economic
basis, could not support their children in times of famine.

At these times they tried to get rid of their children either by exchanging them for supplies on the "line" or by abandoning them in the frontier posts to the mercy and charity of the Russians. Such a situation encouraged the slave trade and led to all kinds of inhumane practices on the part of Russian merchants who took advantage of the natives' plight. Children of the steppe nomads were exported in great numbers and sold into slavery on the markets of southwestern Siberia.

The government had decided to put an end to this situation and to prohibit this trade in human beings in Siberia. Speransky, however, drew the attention of the Council of State to the fact that the southern nomads had to abandon or sell their children lest both parents and children perish from hunger. He argued that it was the government's duty to devise some way of taking care of those children if it were at all serious about its intention to stop the slave trade. He suggested that the local authorities be empowered to take in the children and find foster homes for them with the peasants in the agricultural districts of Siberia. In return for feeding and bringing up these children, the peasants would have the right to make use of their labor during a specified period of time. Upon the expiration of this period, the children, grown up by then, would be set free and given the right to settle wherever they wished. Shortly before his death in 1825, the emperor approved Speransky's suggestion. This solution of the problem was intended not only as a humanitarian measure but also as a means of fostering agriculture by providing peasants with more labor and by training the "children of the steppe" for an agricultural, settled life.[72]

Another important group in Siberia who could contribute to the development of farming in the area needed to be taken care of. These were the Cossacks, stationed either on the border or in the interior of Siberia. (Here we shall discuss only the Cossacks of Russian nationality; the native Cossacks are discussed in Part II.) Cossack units had existed in Siberia from the very beginning of the Russian conquest of that area. The Cossacks engaged in agriculture, trade, or handicraft during peacetime and were readily available for military duties in case of war or other emergencies. At all times they maintained their military organization and were under the authority of the high command of the army. In Siberia, besides regular military duties, such as the guarding of the border and the repression of uprisings, they were entrusted with various police functions.[73]

In the eighteenth century and in the beginning of the nineteenth century the Cossack formations (obshchestvo) had fallen into serious decline and were suffering great hardships. Illustrative of their condition is the following report of the commandant of the Saiansk fortress, dated June 30, 1746:

> ...and these Cossacks [of the fortress] have no rifles and also no sabres for their defense.... These Cossacks have come to this Saiansk fortress on foot and on the way, according to their own declarations, they have fed themselves with the "name of Christ" [i.e., by begging], and those who live in the fortress now are short of provisions and suffer great hunger, for they have not been paid their salaries.[74]

As a result, many Cossacks fled or settled in towns and villages and had themselves replaced by state serfs. Thus grew up the system of "peasant Cossacks" (vypisnoi kazak iz krest'ian) whereby peasants were impressed to perform the police and military duties of the Cossacks while continuing to bear the regular peasant's fiscal burden and without receiving any of the Cossack privileges and benefits in return. Theoretically this impressment was for a short period; but even for a short time such a system was ruinous for the peasants concerned. They tried to escape it by taking flight, and many Cossack posts and border forts were empty and of no practical military value.[75]

If there was any opportunity to make a living elsewhere or in any other way than by remaining in the service, the Cossacks took advantage of it. Thus, "it happened that Cossacks in active service would leave their posts to work for state enterprises."[76] More often, they took up trading or trapping.

Those who remained in the ranks of active Cossack units were overburdened with petty services which left them but little time to work their land and provide for their subsistence. The situation is well illustrated by the experiences of Governor Kaptsevich on his first inspection tour of the western sector of the Siberian border "line" in 1820. Kaptsevich

> ...saw wonderful land that was left untilled and Cossacks

who did not engage in agriculture at all. He expressed
his amazement at such a state of affairs. The Cossacks
told him that their ancestors had not engaged in agriculture, that they lived from hunting and trapping and
barter trade with the Kirghiz [i.e., Kazakhs], and that
the service, with its frequent and lengthy periods of
absence from home, did not permit them to have a permanent occupation. [77]

Speransky summarized as follows the main causes for
their plight: (1) they did not have clearly defined land allotments; (2) they did not receive adequate subsidies from the
government (for clothing, ammunition, etc.); (3) they did
not have easy access to responsible superiors and their
obligations were not clearly defined, so that often their local
superiors used their labor for personal profit; (4) they were
moved about too frequently and could not establish a secure
economic basis. [78]

To improve this situation a special statute was written
in 1822. Since we are not concerned with the details of the
organization of the Siberian Cossack troops, we shall note
only those features which reflected the government's attitude
and concern for the development of Siberia and which were
of significance for the region as a whole. First of all, the
Cossacks were clearly divided into two categories. On the
one hand there were the City Cossacks (gorodskie kazaki),
organized on a strict military pattern and stationed, as their
name indicates, in or near towns, fulfilling most of the
general police duties for the area. The City Cossacks were
confirmed in their appointment and duties by the regular
military hierarchy, but were then subordinated to the civilian
authorities of Siberia in all things except internal discipline
and supplies. [79] They do not concern us here. The other
category was that of Station Cossacks (stanichnye kazaki),
who lived in loose military formation in villages and were
used only for limited police functions and as a military reserve
in case of serious emergency.

Great attention was given in the statute to the Station
Cossacks in an endeavor to equalize their economic and social
status with that of the regular peasantry. Efforts were to be
made to increase the number of the Cossack stations, i.e.,
agricultural settlements. In so doing the administration was
to consider the need for settlement on the one hand and the

protection of empty or underpopulated areas on the other.
These settled Cossacks could then perform various government services without being much of a financial burden to the
state. [80] The Station Cossacks were allotted fifteen desiatin
per person near their station, and any lands which had been set
aside for them in the past were to remain in their possession.
Land which had already been made productive by their labor
was to remain in the permanent possession of those Cossacks
who had worked it, even if its quantity exceeded the fifteen
desiatin norm. [81] Finally, land should be set aside for the
Cossacks without waiting for a detailed survey of all Siberian
free land, in order to speed up the settlement process and
make the Cossacks self-sufficient as soon as possible. [82]

To bring the Cossacks closer to the regular peasant
population of Siberia, the internal organization of the stations
was patterned on that of the regular peasant villages. [83] In
judiciary matters these Cossacks were under the jurisdiction
of civilian courts and not of courts-martial. [84] Like the peasants and the natives, the Cossacks were given the right to have
minor disputes and unimportant complaints settled orally by
the head and elders of the station without interference of the
higher authorities. [85] To insure that the Cossacks would not
be called away from their regular work routine without due
cause, it was prohibited to make them perform police duties
or other services in areas more than 150 versts away from
their homes. Such services were to be performed by the
City Cossacks exclusively. [86] No Cossack belonging to one
station could be moved to another one, but he was also forbidden to join another non-Cossack community. Entire stations
could not be moved to other areas without their consent, and
in all cases children had to stay with their parents. [87] Thus
the constant moving about of Cossacks was ended, and they
obtained a more privileged status than the state serfs. Finally,
the Station Cossacks were not required to have special clothes
or uniforms, though they could wear a semimilitary dress if
they wished; but they had to have small arms of their own. [88]
To increase the incentives for economically productive labor
the Station Cossacks were given complete freedom of economic
activity, including the right to trade with the local population
and to carry on duty-free exchanges with the natives across
the "line." [89] Should City Cossacks wish to settle on the land,
they could be transferred to the status of Station Cossack
as complete units (kommanda) if three-fourths of the members

requested it. Those who refused to settle would then be transferred to other regiments. This transfer of City Cossacks
to the status of Station Cossacks was declared to be very
desirable, as it would decrease the state's expenses in maintaining them and would also further the development of
Siberia. [90]

Another step taken by Speransky to foster agricultural
development was his promotion of the general land survey
in Siberia. In 1823 it was ordered that the Chambers of the
Treasury of Siberia present data on the quantities of free
land available. This order was followed by a series of attempts
at making a general survey of Siberia. They did not bring
adequate results, and in 1837 there had to be instituted a
special bureau, the Siberian Survey. [91]

As a means of giving some incentive to the local bureaucracy and of fostering the settlement of an educated class
which would provide economic and social leadership, provision
was made for Siberian officials to be granted landholdings
(without serfs) in Siberia in recognition of their good services. [92] However, this plan failed, for Russian officials
hastened to return to European Russia, while native-born
officials saw in their transfer to European Russia a promotion
which they valued more than these land grants. Perhaps
another reason why this measure failed to bring the proper
result was the shortage of hired labor and the officials' lack
of preparation for, and interest in, managing landed estates
after having spent most of their lives in chancelleries. A
similar plan was put forth to take care of soldiers upon their
retirement. They were to be registered with the townships
(volosti) and thus become members of the peasant class. [93]

Special efforts were made to change the Kazakhs from
a nomadic to a settled, agricultural life. The following benefits
were provided for those who were willing to take advantage
of them: every Kazakh desiring to engage in agriculture was
to receive an allotment of fifteen desiatin of land. If in five
years this allotted land had not been put to use, it was to be
taken away and given to someone else. If, however, the land
had been worked, it could be transmitted to heirs like regular
real estate. To make these measures more effective by
inducing the natural leaders of the nomads to show the way,
the Kazakh sultans were to be given a triple land allotment
and the elders a double one. [94]

Speransky was more aware of regional differences and

problems than were any of the previous administrators. Thus he recommended that an end be put to efforts to have exiles and settlers engage in agriculture in areas which were obviously unsuited for it, as for example the Turukhansk district in the far north. He argued quite convincingly that these efforts, doomed to failure, were an unnecessary waste of valuable manpower. [95]

The government also took steps to develop an active money economy in Siberia. Currency had always played a subsidiary role in this vast area, for most of its economy was one of subsistence and barter. If Siberia were to become a more active and productive region, the use of money as a means of exchange had to become more common. To foster this development the government tried to transform various services and dues, heretofore paid in kind, into money obliga- tions and taxes. Even if the obligation could be met in kind (unavoidable in the more primitive and remote areas), the products had first to be assessed in monetary values. Thus, for example, the quitrent (obrok) had to be calculated in money terms even if it were paid in goods. [96]

The major burden that rested on the Siberian population consisted not so much in direct taxes, which were rather low compared to European Russian standards, as in the performance of various services for the state. Both as a means of fostering the development of a money economy and of freeing the peasants for their own work, special rules were designed for Siberia which changed all these service obliga- tions into money dues. [97] As a matter of fact, Siberia took the lead in this development, which remained a characteristic feature of its life down into the twentieth century. Services which previously had been performed on a personal basis by the peasants and peasant communities were to be performed by specially organized bodies supported through taxation. The tasks of keeping highways in repair and of transporting government officials and government supplies were to be taken care of by road-building crews and by special postal peasants, thus freeing the peasants from irregular labor drafts. [98] To insure that this new monetary tax would be dis- tributed fairly among individuals, the task of repartition was left to the villages and to the township (volost') community. [99]

Though in the long run some of the changes could not be maintained because of the difficulty in finding the necessary labor, these rules set a goal towards which the Russian and

Siberian administrations worked throughout the nineteenth century. The fiscal measures, as well as some of the rules governing contractual relationships, stimulated the greater use of currency in Siberia and helped the economy of the area to reach a higher level of maturity.

4.   Reorganizing the Administration

The administrative reorganization of Siberia, expressed in the major statute of 1822 (PSZ, 29, 125), was intended to promote and make use of the economic and social trends and plans we have just described. But the economic and social transformation of Siberia was not the sole aim of Speransky and the Siberian Committee. As a contemporary observer noted, the main idea behind the administrative reorganization was "to eliminate arbitrariness, to establish the rule of law, to improve the judiciary, to insure the safety of everyone, to develop trade and agriculture, in a word, make Siberia completely happy."[100] To Speransky and to most of his collaborators, it seemed that the task of government was to provide the necessary economic and political conditions for the social and moral maturing of the people. From his own observations during his stay in Siberia, Speransky was convinced that this region, perhaps more than European Russia in spite of its serfdom, needed to be guided if it were to reach a better status of moral and spiritual life and become a genuine asset to the empire. The presence of many exiles and convicts and the heterogeneity of the population made the ending of past abuses entirely dependent upon the achievement of moral maturity.

Speransky and his collaborators also aimed at establishing efficiency in the administrative apparatus and at providing for adequate control and supervision of the local authorities. In fact, Speransky felt that the corruption of the Siberian administration was not so much the fault of the individual officials as of the system. To prosecute individuals would not lead anywhere; what was needed was a general overhauling of institutions. As he wrote in a passage which is often quoted but which bears repeating because it best shows the tone of Speransky's work:

(1) Personal power easily transforms itself into abuse

and almost always it has the appearance of arbitrariness
[samovlastie]. Acting without public and lawful collaborators and for reasons known only to itself, this [personal
power] cannot, even with the purest of intentions, cover
itself against suspicions. In Siberia, where there has
never been and still is no public opinion, and where for
lack of a nobility it cannot arise for a long time yet, these
suspicions are even more telling. The very distances
reinforce them: for it is assumed that nothing ever
reaches the Highest Power [the emperor] because, in
fact, only little reaches it. The long habit of these suspicions and the experience of the frequent results of
arbitrary personal power have led the people there to
think that everything depends on the arbitrary decision
of the official; and they [the people in Siberia] have less
of a conception of legality than elsewhere. Until 1819
there was but one method of defense and resistance:
complaints and denunciations.

(2) Had even the personal power--personified in
Siberia up to 1819 by the Chief Administrator [governor-
general]--been limited by minute and precise rules, it
could have easily fallen into arbitrariness, for it was
too far removed from supervision and had no barriers
or restraints on the spot. Reliance on the personal
qualities [of the individuals] is no protection in this
case, for he [the administrator] falls into arbitrariness
gradually, imperceptibly, and not always with bad intentions. On the contrary, he is led astray with the best
of intentions, because of his very devotion to the good
and of his desire to reach it by the shortest or most
direct means. First, for the sake of cutting through the
procedure, he disregards minor formalities, then the
more important ones are affected, finally even the spirit
of the matter is opened widely to abuse. In such manner,
always in good faith, he destroys order, and believing
that he acts according to conscience, he is acting against
the law. [101]

The second part may very easily have been Speransky's
description of Governor Treskin, who, as we have seen,
paved the way to abuses and corruption in his efforts to

transform Siberia's economic and social character rapidly and in spite of local opposition.

As Speransky stated them himself, the general principles of the administrative reorganization were: (1) to transform the personal power of officials into a power vested in institutions; (2) to strengthen the supervision of local officials by vesting it in one central organization, to compensate for the remoteness of Siberia from St. Petersburg and for the absence of a mature public opinion; (3) to bring order into the confused relations between various administrative bodies; (4) to give to the local institutions organic unity and latitude for autonomous action without constant reference to central authorities; (5) to adapt the administration more closely to local circumstances and conditions; (6) to simplify and clarify the mode of operation of this machinery. [102]

In the opinion of Speransky and contemporary political leaders, Siberia was a distinct region with its own peculiar conditions and at the same time an organic part of Russia. The distinctiveness of Siberia stemmed from its geography, its diversity of climate and resources, and its mixture of peoples. The administrative divisions of the area had to take these facts into consideration. [103] Enlightened by the example of the British and Spanish colonial empires, which had failed to make allowance for the distinctiveness of their colonies (as had been clearly set forth in the popular book of de Pradt), the Russian government decided to take due account of these peculiarities. The area was divided into two governor-generalships to obviate the difficulties resulting from the tremendous distances; smaller administrative units were set up on a pattern which left enough freedom and flexibility to take care of special circumstances. [104]

Yet on the other hand Siberia was becoming an organic part of Russia; the aim of the new administrative system, therefore, was to work towards an identity with the European Russian pattern. Thus the provisions of the general statute on the provinces of 1775 were to remain in force unless specific mention was made to the contrary. [105] Identity with European Russia would come as a result of intensive settlement and development of agriculture, and therefore the administrative uniformity should start on the lowest level, namely the village and township. But this identity was still a thing of the future, and for the time being more care had to be exercised in meeting the demands of Siberia's peculiar

circumstances, while allowing for future changes. Thus the
Main Administration was given the right to classify the towns
according to their future transformation. [106] Further, the
Siberian "line" was not to be considered the permanent state
border, but with the spread of law and order into the Kazakh
(Kirghiz) Steppes, the regular administrative pattern of
Siberia would also be extended. [107] To take care of variations
in local conditions, the administrations of the two Siberian
governorships were given the right to establish district
administrations of four different types according to individual
needs. [108] Some large areas, because of their sparse population and their distance from the bigger centers, were to be
organized as separate units; these units were not to be intermediary links between regional and provincial authorities
but were to have the status of "simplified provincial administrations."[109] In due course of time, when these areas were
settled and better communications with them developed, they
could be promoted to the status of regular provinces. This
change was made in the second half of the nineteenth century;
and in 1887 one of the two governor-generalships, Western
Siberia, was divided into two regular Russian provinces,
Tobolsk and Tomsk, thus completing the formal process of
identification with European Russia in this part of Siberia.

Of immediate and greatest concern to the imperial government was the highest level of Siberian administration, the
office of the governor-general. Here the major problem was
to combine latitude of action, needed because of Siberia's
remoteness, with effective supervision and control to prevent
excessive abuse of power. Lack of supervision of the highest
authorities in the province was a problem common to both
European Russia and Siberia, but much more serious in the
latter. The difficulty arising from the absence of precise
rules and of a clear chain of command was described by
Speransky apropos of the discussion of the reorganization
of Russian local institutions in 1821. He wrote:

> Provincial institutions in the direct sense have no
> local supervision over themselves. The civil governor,
> as president of the provincial administration, cannot
> supervise himself nor the institutions equal to him.
> The procurator has only the right of making representa-
> tions. Supervision, with power to correct, belongs to
> the governor-general, according to the General Statute

[of 1775]. But there where this title does exist, his action, personal in character and not clearly defined, constantly wavers between arbitrariness and ineffectiveness. [110]

The solution designed for Siberia was to have the gover-nor-general assisted by a council, both council and governor-general forming the Main Administration with rather wide powers of executive decision. Taking up the idea expressed in the instructions to Selifontov in 1803, the Main Administration (glavnoe upravlenie) was instituted to supervise the local administrations for the entire territory and to make rapid decisions on emergency cases without needing to refer to St. Petersburg for instructions. [111]

The idea of having the governor-general assisted by a council was an adaptation of the old collegiate principle characteristic of Russian political life in the eighteenth century (and mutatis mutandis, in the seventeenth). We recall that O. Kozodavlev, Minister of the Interior in 1819, had advocated a partially elected council to assist the Siberian governor-general. Speransky claimed to agree in principle with the Minister of the Interior and indeed realized the necessity of having the decisions of the governor-general at least pass through the hands of a council. But very soon after his arrival in Siberia, Speransky began to express his doubts about the practicability of including elected members in such an advisory body. [112] In a rather lengthy paper, of which only excerpts are available to us, he gave his objections to an elected council as follows:

It would have been more correct to staff such a council [i.e., provincial council] with people not connected with the local administration. But, in the first place, it is impossible to form it with members of the nobility or the merchant class, because here in Siberia there is no nobility and only a few merchants. In the second place, to staff the council with officials from outside would have been contrary to the principle of economy in personnel. Moreover, when Siberia will have a greater population, when its wealth will become more available, and the benefits [to the people] will increase, then one will be able to form a council of its Main Administration from among people of the upper classes--but this will not change the present institutions very much. [113]

For the reader unfamiliar with Speransky's terminology
and the details of his political theory, it should be pointed out
that by upper classes he meant not the nobility (as most
historians have interpreted it) or even the wealthier people
(though they may be included), but meliores in the moral or
spiritual sense. However, he never gave any clear standards
for determining them, and one suspects that this was but a
means to avoid the entire question of elected representation
with which he had little sympathy. In letters from Siberia to
his daughter and friends, Speransky complained that this vast
region had no outstanding individuals of moral or spiritual
standing. He was appalled by the low level of cultural and
spiritual development which he observed even among the
better classes in the cities. He felt that several decades of
educational and social development were needed to produce in
Siberia a class capable of supplying qualified members for the
advisory council. In the meantime this council would have to
be composed of officials, in part selected by St. Petersburg,
in part nominated by the governor-general, though confirmed
by the central government.

As a result of these considerations, the highest executive
authority in Siberia was organized in the following manner.
The governor-general was to be appointed by the emperor and
responsible to the emperor personally. He was the lieutenant
of the monarch and as such he was the head of the Main
Administration which consisted of himself and the Council.
In some functions he was to act alone and independently, but
in some others, to prevent his overstepping the powers granted
to him, he was required to submit his measures to the Council
for information and advice. The governor-general's personal
function consisted in the administrative supervision of the
proper and rapid fulfillment of all measures, including those
issued by the judiciary. He was to inspect the region and the
various branches of the administration regularly; he was to
make recommendations for promotion and honors. Finally,
he had a qualified power of appointment and dismissal of
functionaries and, in case of special need, he could issue
temporary executive instructions subject to eventual confirmation by St. Petersburg. In all other things the governor-general
had to work in conjunction with the Council. [114]

The Council of the Main Administration (Sovet Glavnogo
Upravleniia) was to be appointed by imperial decree, three
members on the recommendation of the governor-general and

three members on the recommendation of the Ministry. In the absence of the last mentioned members, the presidents of the provincial court (gubernskii sud), of the chamber of the treasury (kazennaia palata), of the provincial board (gubernskoe pravlenie), and the civil governor (grazhdanskii gubernator) were to participate as members. For the discussion of specific matters the Council could invite the chief official concerned with that subject, such as the surveyor or the chief of engineers, to participate. The Council exercised general supervision over current administration; it examined the yearly reports of the governors, considered complaints by private individuals against the action of officials, and decided jurisdictional disputes between courts. In case of doubt regarding the execution of existing legislation, the Council gave its opinion on how the problem should be decided. Finally, it reviewed all matters pertaining to taxation, contractual obligations, supplies, recruits, etc. As mentioned earlier, the governor-general and Council could make changes in the borders of administrative districts under their jurisdiction. [115]

This Main Administration, however, could not introduce any new legislation or rules on its own; it had only the right to prescribe the manner of executing legislation handed down from St. Petersburg. [116] The relation of the Main Administration to the central government was ill-defined and somewhat confused. While the governor-general was the personal representative and appointee of the emperor, responsible to him directly, the Main Administration (of which the governor-general was the chairman) was directly subordinate to the Senate. [117] To make the confusion worse, the various functional bodies of the administration were considered as the local representatives of the major ministries involved (interior, finance, and justice). Theoretically, the Senate was the supreme coordinating body for the central ministries, but this relationship had never been adequately defined in the statute on the ministries of 1811. [118]

Except in the cases for which his powers were specifically enumerated, the governor-general could act on a matter only after submitting it to the Council. [119] However, the Council had only an advisory opinion; the governor did not have to take its advice, and the Council had no power to implement its decisions. Each member of the Council had an equal vote but, neither individually nor as a body, could it stop the execution

of any act by the governor-general. [120] It was the privilege of
each member to submit his separate dissenting opinion to the
central government in St. Petersburg, but as has been pointed
out, this was a privilege also granted minor officials to
protect them from prosecution if their superiors exceeded
their authority.

The role of this Council of subordinate officials was
very limited indeed. Eventually it deteriorated to such an extent that the Council became simply an institution for dealing
with a limited number of specific matters and lost completely
its original function of supervising and advising the governor-
general on questions of general policy. The Council was
abolished by Alexander III in 1887. [121]

Thus, in spite of the formal collegiate features, the
highest level of Siberian administration consisted of the only
slightly qualified personal rule of the governor-general. His
position of power was enhanced by the right of taking special
measures in emergency cases at his own discretion, provided
only that he prove their necessity later. [122] The governor-
general could be prosecuted only with permission of the
emperor himself. True, there were several ways of bringing
the governor-general to account for abuse of power: petitions
to the emperor or the Senate, not a very easy procedure, as
shown by the difficulties of the Irkutsk merchants under
Treskin's rule; reports by local authorities of illegal acts they
might be asked to perform; judiciary inquiries or decisions
revealing that crimes were committed in obedience to illegal
regulations issued by the governors-general; finally, inspections and special reports. [123] With some qualifications similar
provisions obtained in the case of provincial governors and
other subordinate officials. [124]

The autonomy of executive administrative action by the
Main Administration was preserved in several ways, but its
initiative was quite limited. If it was found that new legislation
would create serious difficulties or inconveniences if applied
locally, the Main Administration, having gathered the opinion
of all provincial agencies, could stop application of the legislation and report on it to the Senate. It would later act on the
basis of the final decision of the Senate. [125] In no case could
the Main Administration cancel or limit existing regulations.
It could not introduce any new laws or rules, it could not
establish new expenditures or demand from subordinate
agencies any payments not regularly provided for. [126] Besides

limiting the power of the Main Administration, these provisions had as their purpose the prevention of illegal exactions, which had been a traditional practice of previous governors-general.

Although the statute was also intended to establish the autonomy of the judiciary, this autonomy was not made complete. While a change of sentence of a lower court could be pronounced only by a superior judiciary body, decisions could be appealed to the Council of the Main Administration for errors of procedure. This right of the administration to intervene in the judiciary procedure was a lever which could be effectively used to restrict the independence of the courts. [127]

Siberia's administrative organization was hierarchical, in the form of a pyramid, whose local apex was the governor-general and his Council. For any deviation from, or change of, regular procedure, lower agencies had to request permission from higher authorities. [128] Superior authorities on any level, on the other hand, could cancel decisions taken by a lower agency if they found the latter contrary to law or merely inconvenient; general rules could be altered by the Main Administration only by special permission of the emperor. [129]

Below the Main Administrations of the two governor-generalships there were essentially three levels of administration: the province (guberniia) and the region (oblast'), the district (okrug), and the township (volost'). While the provincial organization paralleled rather closely that of the Main Administration, the other subdivisions were organized along much simpler lines. Each governor-generalship was subdivided into several provinces and regions. Remote and sparsely settled areas were organized as regions, which were on the same level as the provinces but had a much simpler organization. There were four such regions, one in Western Siberia (Omsk) and three in Eastern Siberia (Iakutsk, the Maritime Region, and the Troitsko-Savsk Frontier Region). A distinctive trait of the regional administration was that its chief officer combined military and civil functions (see Appendix III). These regional administrations were considered temporary arrangements to be replaced eventually by regular provincial administrations when the region had become more populated. [130]

The regular province (guberniia) had an administration which consisted of a civil governor (grazhdanskii gubernator)

and a provincial council (gubernskii sovet). The civil governor, like the governor-general, was appointed by the emperor
and directly responsible to him. He was the head of the
provincial administration and chairman of the provincial
council. Some functions he exercised alone--supervising
the administrative procedure, reviewing criminal cases,
inspecting his province, dismissing lower officials, con-
firming various elective officials on the township and village
levels, making recommendations for promotions, maintaining
contact with the military authorities stationed in his province,
and handling minor border problems. The provincial council
which assisted him was composed of the presidents of the
provincial board (gubernskoe pravlenie) and the provincial
court (gubernskii sud), the provincial procurator (gubernskii
prokuror), and the three chiefs of the police, economy, and
justice departments of the council. The last mentioned three
departments formed the civil governor's chancery and did
not directly deal with the population of the province. The
council was staffed exclusively by officials, very much on
the model of the ministries instituted by Speransky in 1811.
Like the Council of the Main Administration, the provincial
council considered complaints against the administrative
agencies, protected the rights of merchants and guaranteed
freedom of trade, decided on problems arising in the course
of implementing legislation, supervised the budget, government contracts, and the recruiting of soldiers. [31]

The administration of provincial affairs was organized
along functional lines. The three functions of provincial
government--police, economy, and justice--were taken care
of by the provincial board (gubernskoe pravlenie), the provincial chamber of the treasury (gubernskaia kazennaia
palata), and the provincial court (gubernskii sud). [32] The
provincial board, consisting of a president, one elder councilor, and three assistant councilors, was concerned with
purely administrative matters, or--in the terminology of the
time--police in the widest sense. This board had four departments: the first was in charge of the police in the cities and
districts; the second dealt with the promulgation of laws, the
registration of deeds, the keeping of archives, and the general
office; the third--trespassing on economic functions--dealt
with the budget of the provincial capital, the administration of
state property, public welfare, and enforced the collection
of taxes; the fourth was the Board of Exiles and Prisons.

Some autonomous agencies, such as the Board of Welfare, the Medical Office, the provincial architect, and the government printing press were also under the jurisdiction of the provincial board. [133] The provincial chamber of the treasury took care of economic matters. It consisted of a president and a varying number of councilors, depending on the size and needs of the province. The chamber of the treasury was subdivided into three departments: the first dealt with state lands, forests, factories, mines, and government contracts; the second provided money to the treasury, collected duties and taxes, and transferred money between government agencies; the third was the department of accounts and control. The chamber of the treasury also had general supervision of the Board of Recruits and the Office of the Provincial Surveyor. The chamber maintained direct contact and correspondence with the Ministry of Finance. [134] Finally, the functions of the judiciary were exercised by the provincial court (gubernskii sud), consisting of a president, one elder councilor, and three assistant councilors. This court considered civil cases on appeal and reviewed criminal ones. It also had jurisdiction over cases first tried in courts of equity (these were very restricted in Siberia, for there was no local nobility). [135]

Provisions for local differences were made in the next echelon of the administrative hierarchy, the district (okrug). There were three kinds of district organizations: the general type for ordinary districts; the so-called separate divisions for remote districts; and finally a type for underpopulated districts. Only the general district administration possessed a distinct institution for each of the functions of local administration--police, economy, and justice. The other types merged all three functions in an executive (police) body. The general-type district was in the charge of a district chief (nachal'nik okruga) assisted by a council of six members. These members were the police chief (gorodnichii) of the district capital, the district judge (okruzhnoi sud'ia), the land captain (zemskii ispravnik), the district treasurer, the clerk (pisar'), and the elected town mayor (gorodskoi golova), if there was one. The district chief was president ex officio of the council. Again it should be noted that, with the exception of the town mayor, all members of the council were appointed officials. The district chief was appointed by the governor, and it is not very clear to what extent the provincial council and the ministry participated in this appointment. The functions of the district administration (i. e. , the district chief and council) were of a general supervisory nature: the keeping of correct accounts, the inspection of the area, the control of the prisons and penitentiaries, the protection of the principles of freedom of trade, and the preliminary repartition of taxes and services. [136]

The police functions in the regular district, the executive part proper, were put into the hands of the land court (zemskii sud), which consisted of the land captain and two, three, or four deputies (zasedatel'), depending on the size of the district. At times the supervisor of exile settlements participated in the sessions of the court. The business of the land court was distributed among its members not according to subject but geographically, each land deputy being in charge of a section of the district. The land court policed the district, supervised the fiscal administration, kept account of the harvests and grain reserves, checked on tax evasions, and executed sentences of the court. The last two functions gave the land court, and especially the land captain, many opportunities to intervene in local affairs and to exert pressure on individuals as well as on official bodies. [137]

The economy of the district was under the jurisdiction of the district treasury administration (okruzhnoe kazennoe upravlenie), consisting of the treasurer, the supervisor of liquor sales, and the supervisor of the salt monopoly. The district surveyor was attached to it. Its functions were to collect taxes and to make periodic surveys of the economic potential of the area. The district court (okruzhnoi sud), consisting of the judge and two or three deputies and a clerk, was the first instance of both civil and criminal justice. [138]

The separate divisions, i.e. , districts far removed from the main area of settlement in the province, were administered by a land deputy (zemskii zasedatel') who was a member of the land court and was directly responsible to the land captain of the nearest general-type district. In his hands were concentrated all governmental functions for the area, such as general police, collection of taxes and tribute, protection of freedom of private trade, supervision of supplies, execution of court sentences, and investigations on behalf of township (volost') organs. This monocratic administrative institution had originated in 1783, when Irkutsk

province was organized and such special deputies were provided for remote districts. [139]

The underpopulated districts were usua'ly those whose
boundaries coincided with the area of movement of a nomad
tribe. These tribes were under the control of a land captain,
responsible to the district council of the nearest district.
The land captain had general executive and supervisory
functions in conjunction with the clan administration (rodovaia
rasprava). As the authority of the land captain was not always
clearly circumscribed, it was possible for him to interfere
unduly in the affairs of native tribes throughout the nineteenth
century. [140]

In conclusion we may note that the district was only a
bureaucratic link between the lowest subdivisions, to which
we shall turn shortly, and the provincial and main administrations. None of the administrative bodies on the district
level had any autonomy or initiative. They were merely inter-
mediaries which executed the orders of the higher authorities
or transmitted questions arising on the village and township
level. Even the district court merely initiated lawsuits which
were resolved on a higher level. The district court could
not review cases that had been first considered orally by
the village authorities. Such cases had to be brought to the
district court as if they were new ones for the court's decision
in the first instance.

The Siberian towns were theoretically on the same administrative level as the district. Although their organization
closely paralleled that of the towns in European Russia,
Siberian towns had much less autonomy. Quite a number of
economic and judiciary matters affecting only members of
the town community were delegated to town councils (gorod-
skaia duma) and elected mayors. These councils were not
truly representative bodies, for the legal and property qualifications for participation in elections were very high. The
government did not, however, freeze the situation of the
towns for all time. Siberian towns were classified into three
categories, and the assignment to one or the other category
could be changed by the Main Administration as conditions
developed. The three categories were: populated towns, towns
with medium population, and underpopulated towns. Towns in
the first category, actually cities, usually had an elected
council and mayor and an administrative setup similar to that
of a district. The functions of police, economy, and justice

were assigned to separate institutions. Towns in the second
category had a much simpler administration in which the
functional division was less pronounced and the power concentrated in the hands of a few appointed officials. Towns
in the third category had almost no self-government, and
practically all business was conducted by one or two officials. [141]

The lowest level of the administrative hierarchy for
the Russian population was the township (volost'). The township administration consisted of a township head or mayor
(volostnoi golova), one elder (volostnoi starosta), and one
clerk (pisar'). The first two were elected by representatives
from each village in the township, one elector for each one
hundred "souls." Only owners of property, in other words
heads of households, were eligible for the offices of mayor
and elder, provided they had served at least one term as
village elder. They were elected every year, but could be
re-elected. The clerk was also elected on the same basis,
but he could be an outsider because of the small number of
literates in the villages. All those elected had to be confirmed by the governor. Speransky had given the peasants
of European Russia a somewhat more important role by
stating in the regulations the specific reasons for which the
governor could refuse their choices. [142]

The responsibilities of the township administration were
left as they had been in earlier times and were much more
limited than those suggested by Speransky for European
Russia. As far as we know, this limited role had been proposed by Speransky himself and was not the result of any
pressure from his colleagues on the Siberian Committee.
The township administration in Siberia consisted only of the
three functionaries we have mentioned; there was no township
assembly or mir as in European Russia. The functions of
the township administration were very limited and purely
executive. It had general police power over the township,
took care of the repartition of dues and services among the
villages, cared for village supply stores (of which there were
only a few in Siberia), and executed the sentences of the
courts which applied to the villages. The only autonomous
function of the township administration was the trial of very
insignificant, petty cases, such as drunkenness or rowdy
behavior. [143] In European Russia this function rested with
the village authorities and not with the more remote township.

The township had only dependent, subordinate functions and, although its administration was made up of elected representatives from the peasantry, it remained at the mercy of the bureaucracy, whose obedient executive tool it was.

The statutes of 1822 devoted only one short paragraph to the village, which was the lowest social and geographic unit. This paragraph stated that the village (selenie) would elect one elder (starosta) and a varying number of assistants to the elder (desiatniki), but left their functions undefined.[144] It is difficult to see why the village was almost completely left out of the picture. The most likely explanation may be found in Speransky's general attitude toward the peasantry. Speransky believed that peasant participation in administrative activities should be permitted only after the peasant had reached a certain economic and moral level. He felt that in European Russia the most prosperous among the state peasants could be drawn into the general administrative scheme.[145] In Siberia, however, individual peasants might have reached a high level of economic well-being, but their moral and spiritual qualities were not equally developed. The Siberian peasant, as Speransky saw him, was frequently a former convict or a descendant of the lowest elements of society, who had not had an opportunity for schooling or an adequate religious life (as witness the tendency of Russian settlers to turn to idolatrous practices borrowed from Siberian natives). And wealth alone was not a satisfactory basis for social and political responsibility. This was an opinion which Speransky shared with all moderate and conservative political thinkers of his time. The Siberian peasant was not yet ready to participate in government but must be led toward that goal by the government. It may be added that in Siberia, as in seventeenth-century Russia, the prosperous peasant often engaged in trade and became identified with the merchant group; and we have noted the distrust of the monopolistic and "grasping" merchant class of Siberia evidenced by the government and Speransky.

The authors of the administrative organization of Siberia had made an effort at keeping separate the three functions of local government--police, economy, and justice. One of the principal aims had been to establish the judiciary as an autonomous body not subject to pressures and interference from the executive bureaucracy, but this division of functions[146] was not carried out consistently or effectively.

In particular, the judiciary, as we have noted, could not be freed from pressure by the executive as long as the procedural aspect of justice remained under the control of the governor-general and his delegates. [147]

The distinctive feature of this system, as noted by both contemporary and succeeding generations and often adduced to condemn Speransky, was its bureaucratic character. Almost all functions of the administrative, economic, and even social life of Siberia rested in the hands of the officials. Local society participated in an extremely limited way and only in matters affecting the towns or townships. The reasons for Speransky's decisions in this respect, as we have seen above, were twofold: on the one hand was the old bureaucratic and paternalistic tradition of Russian government; on the other was Speransky's skepticism of the ability of a crude and in many ways backward Siberian society to be of positive help to the administration. There was no local nobility in Siberia, nor was it expected that one would develop. There was no enlightened or even formally educated class except the bureaucracy itself. Even though the bureaucracy had serious defects, it could at least be improved under the proper system; and indeed it did show some improvement in the decades following the application of the statutes of 1822. [148] Until the population at large had matured sufficiently to participate in the administration, the bureaucracy had to be entrusted with the task of control and leadership.

Speransky's conception of the role of the Siberian bureaucracy corresponded to his fundamental political belief that the prime function of the state was to guide the nation toward moral improvement. He hoped that as this progress took place, the role of the bureaucracy would be restricted. At that time the councils which had been set up with each executive head--governor-general and provincial governors--would include not only bureaucrats but also delegates or representatives of the local population. Should conditions make this possible in the future, almost nothing would need to be changed in the statutes of 1822. Unfortunately Speransky had counted without the timorous caution of the government, without its almost pathological fear of the participation of public opinion in administration--a fear which made for even greater rigidity and bureaucratic control in later decades. Yet the fact remains that in spite of all these drawbacks the statutes of 1822 introduced to Siberia for the first time in

its history something which we can call the rule of law, a
Rechtsstaat. The basis for clear and orderly governmental
procedure had at last been established in Siberia, and even
though the practice continued to fall short of the aim, progress
was being made in the right direction. This was a necessary
condition for attracting free settlers and developing to the
full the economic potential of the region. Speransky could
indeed find some justification for his boast that, "I have
discovered the true political problem of Siberia. Only Ermak
can compete with me in this respect."[149]

For the imperial government the statutes for Siberia
marked a new departure in its approach to administrative
problems. As Prutchenko has so well shown, Speransky's
reorganization of Siberia was the first instance of a regional
approach to local administration. [150] Indeed, even if Speransky
was not the first to recognize it, he was the first to put into
practice the idea that in an empire as large and variegated
as Russia more attention must be paid to regional differences
and problems. This idea also led to a more scientific and
intensive study of regional conditions. If local administration,
the weakest part of Russia's political structure, was to be
improved and put on a par with the central administration, a
regional approach was imperative. The recognition of existing
differences and peculiarities and the basing of administration
thereon was the best method of counteracting the centrifugal
tendencies that border regions may possess and of preparing
the ground for a closer and more organic union with the core
provinces. For Siberia, therefore, an efficient and appropriate
policy had to be devised for the government of the many non-
Russian peoples inhabiting the region. The special statute
on the natives (which was, incidentally, the first attempt to
deal with the problem systematically and completely in a
legislative act) was an important part of Speransky's work
in Siberia. It is to a consideration of this statute and to the
conditions which produced it that we are naturally led in
our investigation.

PART TWO

Native Peoples of Siberia and the Russian Administration

CHAPTER IV

The Changing Conditions of the Natives

THE NATIVE peoples[1] had not, by 1800, been fully drawn into the main stream of Russian-Siberian life, and the government dealt with them as a separate problem. Yet the natives were affected by the changes occurring in Siberia in the eighteenth and early nineteenth centuries; the inner conditions of the tribes as well as their relations with the Russian population and authorities were undergoing a profound transformation.[2] This process was relatively slow, reflecting both the changes in the condition of the country and the shift of the government's attitude towards Siberia, and found its legislative expression in the statute on the natives of 1822 (PSZ, 29,126).

It is still very difficult to present a completely satisfactory account of this development. With few exceptions the historical sources on the natives of Siberia gathered by scholars and explorers in the eighteenth century (Müller, Fischer) deal with the period ending in the middle of the eighteenth century, i.e., just short of the intensification of the process we are interested in. Most of the material available for the period is of no direct use to us, for it is primarily ethnographic in character with relatively little information on the political and administrative pattern. Primary sources on native administration published in the historical and archeographical journals are extremely few and rare. It seems that even Soviet historians, who have been more interested in the history of these peoples than anybody before, have concentrated their attention on the early period (down to the seventeenth century) or on the eve of the Russian Revolution. If sources of local origin have been published in Siberia in any significant number since 1917, they have not been accessible to us. The materials we have access to are not very satisfactory for our purpose. First of all, they are very vague chronologically; the time of the events or circumstances is never made fully explicit. Furthermore, our sources seldom distinguish adequately among the various tribes. All too often they speak of Siberian natives in general without specifying what tribes or peoples they have in mind; this is particularly true for the small nomadic tribes of the north and the northeastern fringe area. Yet in spite of these limitations a few concrete observations can be made and preliminary conclusions drawn. They do help us to understand the pattern of the transformation taking place in Siberian life during the first quarter of the nineteenth century. They are a necessary as well as interesting complement to a study of Siberian administration.

The history of the subjection of these native tribes in the seventeenth century by the Russians has been told many times. It is a sad tale of cruelty, barbarism, and exploitation, especially for the primitive tribes of the northeast, and not unlike the often repeated, sorrowful pattern of colonial conquests. We need not recount this story here; the reader will find a general summary in English in Lantzeff's book and in German in the classical histories of Siberia written in the eighteenth century. But let us note briefly one item which has not received its due attention. Frequently, and particularly in its dealings with peoples with a higher form of social organization (such as the Buriats), Moscow repeated its practice of the fourteenth and fifteenth centuries, a practice which had been very successful in furthering the "gathering" of Russian lands by the Grand Duchy of Moscow and in paving the way for a social as well as political assimilation of these territories. In the treaties Moscow signed with the peoples it gathered in, there were clauses specifying that the subjugated nation would furnish men of service (primarily military personnel) to Moscow and that it would be in direct diplomatic contact with Moscow alone, all relations with other independent states being carried on through Moscow. In return for these obligations and the limitations on their sovereignty, Moscow left the conquered peoples complete freedom in their domestic affairs and even protected the authority of the local rulers or nobility. [3]

Such an approach had helped Moscow to establish control over vast areas without expending its military strength and had also allowed Moscow to limit the administrative personnel

for these far-flung territories. It was hoped that, like the
appanaged princes, the native nobility and rulers of Siberia
would be Russified and perhaps even take up service for
Moscow, thereby becoming the leaders in the process of
cultural and social, as well as political, Russification. That
this was not too wild an expectation could be seen from the
example of the Tatar nobility in the province of Riazan', who
had been eventually absorbed into the regular service class of
Moscow and had helped to pave the way for Russia's expansion
to the Volga. [4]

By concluding such treaties with the natives, Moscow
aimed at preserving the peace in the remote regions of the
empire and securing the maximum economic benefits from its
subjection of the natives to the fur tribute (iasak). Pursuing a
policy of leniency towards the Siberian peoples, Moscow did not
change in any way the legal and social structure of the tribes;[5]
it restricted the Church's efforts at imposing Christianity by
force and in general tried to be friendly to the natives. However, the mild and passive policy of the imperial government
was defeated by the actions of its agents in Siberia.[6] The local
representatives, the voevodas, the commanders of Cossack
groups, and others disregarded the instructions of Moscow.
They ruthlessly exploited the area and treated the native
population with great brutality. The collection of the fur
tribute every year was the pretext for expeditions deep into
the territory of the tribes, expeditions which were accompanied
by wholesale pillage and murder. Such practices provoked the
resentment of the natives who either fled as far from the
Russians as they could, or attempted to resist and revolt. In
any case, the voevodas and their assistants were actually
destroying the people who provided their own prosperity.
Moscow tried to take effective measures to put an end to these
abuses. It devised ingenious ways of preventing the local
administrators from bringing into Russia their ill-gotten
wealth; it continually admonished them to abide by the policy
of mildness and tolerance prescribed by Moscow and threatened
dire punishment in case of disobedience. All this was of little
avail, and the Russian officials continued to make fair game
of the natives in Siberia.

At the beginning of the eighteenth century there was
great need for a clear and general statement of the principles
regulating the relationships between the natives and the Russian
administration. Until then these relations had been left quite

vague, and when specific rules were stated they referred only
to individual cases. Now, however, it was felt that the Siberian
natives could be of more use to the government than they had
been before. The fur tribute had lost some of its importance to
Moscow, partly because its yield had decreased (owing to the
extermination of fur-bearing animals) and partly because of the
declining demand on the West European market. Also, Peter
the Great and his successors, concerned with the consolidation
of the borders of the Russian Empire and the security of the
trade routes, realized that the Siberian natives could also be
used for military and other services. In a way, this was
another application of the centuries-old practice of using the
subject peoples to maintain the strength of the state which had
conquered them.

This change in attitude towards the natives found its formal
expression in the instructions given by Savva Vladislavich,
Count Raguzinskii, in 1727-28 to the border commissars
Firsov and Likhachev. These instructions established the
basis of the government's attitudes toward the natives for
the entire eighteenth century, and it is therefore worth-while
to quote at some length the relevant passages.

1. As they [the natives] have proven their faithful service to the high imperial interests of H.I.M. in
providing transportation and postal service, in furnishing
guards, in reward of which H.I.M., always benevolent
to his loyal subjects, commands by his high decree that
all old judicial disputes initiated before 1720 be cancelled
and not be brought to trial...also, that it be made known
to the natives that small matters, such as disputes about
the kalym [marriage money], petty theft of cattle, beatings,
and so forth, with the exception of criminal matters and
murder, they--the loyal subjects--can try through their
own chiefs, and settle such matters through arbitration,
and need not let them come up for [regular] judicial
procedure and its delays. And when the matter is small,
let it be settled by the chief in each tribe, and if it is of
more importance, then let the three tribes elect two
headmen each, six men altogether, and their decision
is to be final, so that land commissars in the districts
and fortresses [towns] do not rob and ruin the natives
[in the process of trying] small cases. As for important
criminal affairs...they are to be brought before the land
commissar.

2. The natives can pay the iasak in money or in kind.

3. Because many natives have brought complaints that
the collectors of tribute, during the time of collection,
were ruining and burdening them with their exactions,
by decree of H.I.M. it is ordered: if a given clan or all
clans shall wish to collect the iasak of H.I.M. themselves
and bring it yearly to the treasury in the Commissariat
of Selenginsk or other districts... and to leave it there
and obtain a receipt from there, in that case tribute
collectors shall not be sent to those clans for whom the
chiefs will sign a pledge to bring the iasak for the entire
clan. This is done to avoid burdening the natives uselessly
and taking Russian servicemen from their duties. And
thus it is left to their free will, whether the natives will
pledge to bring the iasak themselves or whether the collectors should be sent there as before. [7]

These instructions established the principle that the
internal autonomy of the Siberian tribes was to be a reward
for the fulfillment of certain services. By implication, as
soon as these services stopped, the privileges of internal
tribal autonomy and self-government could be revoked too.
In spite of these instructions, however, there was one respect
in which the situation did not improve at all, namely, in the
collection of the tribute; the exploitation of the natives by the
administrators and merchants of Siberia continued. While
leaving the internal affairs of the tribes in the hands of the
tribesmen themselves, Raguzinskii's instructions did not
define the relationship between the Russian administration
and the natives, thus giving rise to administrative abuses.

In the eighteenth century the economic and social conditions
of the Siberian natives were steadily deteriorating, owing to
a series of factors which we shall attempt to describe briefly.
In the first place should be mentioned the obligations imposed
by the government on the natives. These were of two types:
direct taxes in the form of tribute, and services in kind and
labor. Direct taxes were almost exclusively restricted to the
iasak, the fur tribute. There were a few other small items,
such as grain deliveries and quitrent, but these affected only
a small number of settled natives. [8] By the beginning of the
eighteenth century the amount of iasak had reached a certain
level which did not change appreciably for over two-thirds of

the century. The amount required was not excessive, and since
the time of Peter the Great the natives had been permitted to
pay the tribute in furs or its equivalent in money. [9] But this
rather limited obligation turned out to be extremely onerous
because of the method of its collection. The collectors of the
iasak would undervalue the furs, set aside those of poor quality
for the government, and force the natives to deliver the best
at a lower price to themselves. The collectors, as well as
traders, would go themselves to the tribes and impose their
own prices and estimates, for the natives were in no position
to learn the actual market value of their furs. The peoples
who were no longer hunting and trapping, as for instance most
of the Buriat tribes, paid their tax in money and escaped this
type of exploitation.

With the disappearance of fur-bearing animals in some
areas and the decrease in the population of some tribes, the
iasak became a greater burden than had at first been intended.
The native tribes and clans were made collectively responsible
for meeting the assigned quota, so that as the number of
able-bodied trappers declined, the tribute lay more heavily
on the survivors. [10] These conditions were but little alleviated
by the fact that the government permitted the natives to pay
the tribute in money. Currency was rare in Siberia and was
particularly scarce among the remote tribes of hunters.
These people had very little trade, most of which was carried
on by barter, and they were quite at the mercy of unscrupulous
merchants who exploited their ignorance and weak economic
position. From this trade the natives could not earn enough
to meet the tribute payments.

An even greater burden was the labor service which the
government exacted from the natives. The sparseness of
Siberia's population and the tremendous distances led the
government--following the Muscovite tradition--to depend
on the local population for the transportation of officials and
government supplies and for the postal service. The postal
and transportation service, the so-called iam and podvody,
lay heavy on the peoples of Iakutiia and on the people near
Lake Baikal. The burden of these services increased in the
eighteenth century because the natives were required to transport the goods of the official caravans trading with China
(from the time of the Nerchinsk Treaty until 1762 when the
China trade was made free). In 1754, for instance, a Iakut
chieftain, recently baptized, sent a long and doleful petition

to Empress Elizabeth complaining that the obligation to transport the supplies for the military and civil authorities stationed on the shores of the Pacific Ocean was ruining his people. The Iakuts were losing their horses on the long and difficult trek from Iakutsk to the Pacific. He asked that some way be found to alleviate this burden. [11] What this service could at times mean can be gauged from the fact that, in 1804, 500 postal horses had to be ready at each relay for the transportation of the newly appointed ambassador to China, Count Golovkin, and his staff. [12] The lack of organization and the excessive powers and abuses of government officials further increased the burden of this service. [13] Whole villages were brought to the verge of ruin because the entire male population had to absent itself during crucial periods of the year, or because many of the horses had been killed or incapacitated by the hard usage they received. Such service also presented serious problems in the inner life of the clans, as is confirmed in several instances by the testimony of the natives themselves. [14]

So heavy was this burden that already in the late eighteenth century the government had remitted the iasak to those natives who would take up the postal service on a regular basis. This led to the formation of villages or settlements of natives whose main, if not only, occupation was the care of the iam. [15] But this change was not always for the better. Many natives were unused to a settled way of life, and it created serious stresses and strains within their social organization. Directly connected with the need of postal service had been the efforts of Moscow to have natives settle as agricultural laborers and to replace the iasak by a tribute in grain deliveries (the so-called "Tsar's plowing"). But this did not have much success, and throughout the eighteenth century only a few natives in Siberia continued to work the land on behalf of the state. [16]

The third service imposed on some natives from the end of the seventeenth century on, but more particularly in the eighteenth, was the formation of military units for the protection of the border. Throughout the century various decrees allowed or ordered the formation of local native military organizations. By the treaty of Burinsk (August 20, 1727) the care and protection of border signs and posts were entrusted to Buriat clans; soon thereafter another section of Siberia's border was put under the guard of the Tungus of Aksha. In 1760 Governor Jacobi--pursuant to a decree of the Senate--

organized a Tungus regiment of 500 men on the Chinese border,
under the command of their own chief, Prince Gantimur. In
1764 four more Buriat regiments were created, and in 1805
another Tungus regiment of 500 men. In 1800, for faithful
service, seven banners were conferred on the native units.
These military formations were known as "native Cossack
regiments," and like their Russian counterparts members of
these regiments continued to live in their clans, engaging in
their traditional occupations when free from military duties.
In the four regiments organized in 1764, the Buriat Cossacks
served for one year and then were free from recall to duty for
the following three years; this alternation continued to the end
of their lives or until they were incapacitated. The native
regiments were officered and commanded by their own clansmen; in theory the leaders were elected, but in fact--as with
the Cossacks of European Russia--the native nobility secured
the positions of leadership on an hereditary basis. In return
for their services the native Cossacks were freed from the
iasak. [17]

This military service was at times quite a burden and
often resulted in the deterioration of the economic status of
the clans involved. By and large the members of these military
formations received no salary, or a very inadequate one, and
had to find other means of subsistence such as cattle-raising
or trapping. The only benefits were some occasional gifts and
subsidies from the government and various privileges--
particularly honors or decorations--awarded to the nobility
of these clans.

As if all these difficulties were not enough, the Russian
government, in violation of its promises, failed to safeguard
the lands possessed by the natives from encroachments by
Russian settlers. In some cases the administration even put
heavy pressure on the natives to move to less fertile and
more remote territories to make way for prospective Russian
colonists. The Buriats, for instance, were made to leave the
fertile Ingoda Valley to make room for Russian peasants,
who did not, however, occupy it for some time. [18]

But the economic relations between the natives, the
government, and the Russian population of Siberia were also
developing in a way to necessitate a change in conditions. In
the first place, the Russian conquest cut off Siberia from its
old trade contacts with the south. [19] Whatever trade with
China there was in that period was a state monopoly or under

very strict government control. But of greater importance than this monopoly was the fact that the border between the Russian and Chinese empires had been shut tight, and for lengthy periods all contacts were interrupted. The natives could not sell their produce, especially valuable furs, to China directly. They also became dependent on Russian traders for their supply of essential articles, such as arms, ammunition, and ironware. This opened the way to unchecked exploitation of the natives by the Russian merchants. This exploitation had originated in the seventeenth century when the state favored certain privileged traders. [20]

Economically weak, ignorant of commercial techniques, without protection from the local administration, the natives found themselves at the mercy of these merchants. The traders sold things to the natives on loan, imposing an interest rate which at times reached 200 and even 300 per cent. [21] For instance, a certain loan made in 1688 could still not be repaid in 1822 by the debtor's descendants. A song, popular among the tribes of northwestern Siberia, tells still of the merchant who came around in the summer, bought all their catch of fish at low prices, and left them to the charity of government subsidies in the winter. [22] Another merchant in the Turukhansk area acted as if he were the God-appointed ruler of the natives, punished them himself, used their labor for himself or rented it to others, and demanded unquestioned obedience to his orders from the natives in debt to him. [23] The government tried to circumscribe the evil deriving from these unequal relations and prohibited the merchants from trading in the native villages and settlements. [24] Exchange with the nomads was allowed only in the towns and at the fairs. The more advanced natives like the Buriats sought to formulate rules of their own for which they requested government sanction and support. In 1800 the chieftains and elders of the Eleven Khori Clans reminded the government that a debt incurred by the clansmen, in particular the women, without the knowledge and permission of the elders, was illegal. They petitioned the government to refuse to recognize any debts incurred without the sanction of responsible individuals in the clan. [25]

These commercial relations which put the natives into permanent debt to the merchants also led to an extension of indentured service and even slavery. The large debts accumulated by natives could not be repaid by any means except work. At first individuals became the indentured servants of

their creditors; but when they were unable to work off the
debt entirely, their children too became indentured, and finally
entire native families fell into virtual slavery. [26] The constant
mention of this question in the decisions and proposals voted
by native assemblies indicates its urgency. The native tribes
attempted to stem this development and sought the government's
support in preventing the spread of hereditary indenture but
they were not successful in the eighteenth century. The government could not prevent this practice but kept it within some
bounds by making it impossible to transfer any such indentured
slaves from Siberia to European Russia. [27]

Many natives suffered grievously from repeated famines.
Their numbers decreased, especially in the northeast, while
their dues and obligations remained the same. The famines
and the increasing inability to feed all the people were due
only to a small degree to the restriction of native territory
through Russian encroachments. As a matter of fact, according
to our sources, such encroachment led to serious results only
in the western Altai Mountain region. [28] But the native hunters
of the north, pressed hard by their obligations and the demands
of Russian administrators and merchants, were moving away
into the remote corners of northeastern Siberia where it was
more difficult to find adequate subsistence. Furthermore,
many natives had become accustomed to a diet based on bread.
But native agriculture had not kept step with this new demand,
and in some instances climatic conditions precluded the growing
of grain. The natives had to buy grain at high prices from
merchants or from the state, thus sinking further into debt
and misery. [29] Under these conditions a crop failure meant
starvation, as occurred in the Turukhansk region in the
1810's. According to calculations made by Iadrintsev in
1892, in the Turukhansk area the native population had been
reduced by three-fourths between 1763 and 1816; many died
during the serious famine of 1809 and subsequent years when
the natives were driven to anthropophagy. On the island of
Kamchatka the population was 20,000 in 1744, but only 2,760
in 1823, and 1,951 in 1850. [30]

Finally, the mortality rate of many native peoples increased by leaps and bounds as a result of diseases brought
by the Russians--especially smallpox and venereal diseases--
just as the natives of South and Central America were swept
by disease after the Spanish conquests. In particular, the

smaller tribes in the north and northeast of Siberia (Ostiaks,
Voguls) were dying out rapidly.

This decline, however, did not encompass all the native
peoples of Siberia, but only those with a primitive hunting and
trapping economy. Data collected by Shashkov in the middle
of the nineteenth century and confirmed by later investigations
have shown that the cattle-raising and agricultural peoples,
such as some of the Buriats and Iakuts, actually increased in
number. For instance, in 1750 there were 21,642 male Iakuts,
35,070 in 1817, and 41,733 in 1839. A similar trend can be
detected among the Buriats who numbered 49,764 males in
1783, 58,730 in 1816, and 83,018 in 1839. This increase
offset the losses of the smaller tribes, and Siberia's native
population as a whole did not decrease but actually grew in
the second half of the eighteenth century. Of course, this
purely quantitative increase did not compensate for the virtual
disappearance of some nationalities and tribes.[31]

These circumstances were bringing about a gradual but
marked disruption of the old social system. The history of
this disruption is not our main concern, nor can it be easily
traced by a nonspecialist. The evidence is extremely hard to
come by and must be carefully weighed by competent anthro-
pologists and ethnographers. However, all historians and
students of customary law agree that the old clan system was
disintegrating; this process was especially marked among the
natives who were radically changing the economic basis of
their lives by taking up agriculture. The old-fashioned tribe
and clan were rapidly losing their normal social and political
functions. In areas where the natives had settled down to till
the land or where two peoples were coming into more active
and close contact by virtue of their military service obligations
or because they were beginning to perform similar functions
in the economic life of the region, the ethnic homogeneity of
clan and tribe was broken down. Thus it was noted that Tungus
and Buriats were mixing more and more, the Buriats entering
the Tungus clan, and vice versa.[32] As a result, the clan was
ceasing to be a social unit and was gradually changing into an
administrative and territorial one. Fostered by Speransky's
reforms, the process reached its maximum intensity after
1822, as we shall see later, but it had started before Speransky
in the late eighteenth century. Councilor Kulomzin noted that by
the beginning of the nineteenth century, the clan had preserved
only fiscal and administrative functions among the Buriats of

the Transbaikal region. Wherever the clan was preserved as an economic unit (obshchina), it did not coincide with the territorial one. [33]

Under the influence of the service obligations described earlier, as well as in a more or less conscious imitation of Russian manners, the chieftains and elders of the tribe were attempting to form a privileged nobility. Among the Buriats and Tungus, military service proved particularly conducive to this development, for the native military formations were under the command of the elders and chieftains, who in turn were treated by their Russian superiors not unlike regular officers. Government salaries or subsidies to the elders, whose positions had often become hereditary, as well as the authority they had as military superiors, tended to set them above the mass of the tribe. The Russian administration, eager to use the leaders of the native peoples as its representatives and delegates to facilitate its task of administration and to promote their closer integration into the Russian pattern, fostered this transformation of the native upper class into an hereditary nobility on the Russian model, though as yet not equal in rights to the nobility of the empire. Since the early eighteenth century, clan and tribal chiefs were given Russian titles, ranks (chin), decorations, subsidies, and pensions. The first titles of nobility--which gave their bearers functions of leadership in a given tribe--seem to have been granted by Peter the Great to the Tungus chieftain Peter Gantimurov. Gantimurov's descendants became hereditary nobles (dvoriane) and played an important role as the hereditary leaders from among whom were elected the chiefs of the Urulga Steppe Duma (the regional administrative unit for the natives established by Speransky in 1822.) [34]

The Buriat chiefs (taisha) received official recognition, special favors, and privileges from the time of the Burinsk treaty; the first letters patent to this title date from 1729 and carry a yearly salary of 20 rubles. The hereditary character of these functions and titles can be seen in the case of the Buriat Nazar Khubaev, who had been confirmed as chief taisha in 1787 and whose descendants occupied the same position until 1865. [35] The Buriat chronicler Vandan Iumsunov records that in 1805 the zaisany of the Eleven Khori Clans "were appointed titled councillors (tituliarnyi sovetnik) and they performed honorary functions among the Khori people and their descendants were found among the privileged." [36]

The members of this privileged native group had important functions within the Russian scheme of administration. For instance, the collection of taxes and tribute among the Iakuts was entrusted to the local princeling by a decree of 1763. [37] The administration used the elders as its agents and delegated all judiciary and administrative functions to them. Local Russian officials preferred to have the tribal chiefs settle all problems and discouraged the natives from appealing intratribal disputes to the Russian officials. On the other hand such a policy helped to preserve traditional laws.

The rise of a privileged group within the native community also led in some cases to a transformation of legal relations; in particular it fostered the development--encouraged by the Russians--of private real property and of specific rules for its usufruct and inheritance. [38] The Russians, while encouraging the development of private landownership, also favored the expansion of landed property among the native upper classes, especially among chiefs and leaders who received honorary titles, pensions, and decorations. For instance, the taishas of the Khori Buriats were given grants of land in 1744 and again in 1791, with the right to leave them to their descendants. [39]

Many rich and distinguished natives thus became more easily subject to Russian influences along social lines as well. In this respect the petition of the Iakut clan chief (toion) Alexis Arzhakov, submitted in 1789, is characteristic. In it Arzhakov formulated the demand that the Iakut leaders be given rights and privileges equal to those of the Russian nobility as the latter had been defined by Catherine's Charter to the Nobility (1785). [40] This Russification could lead only to a growing gap between the upper classes and the common tribesmen. A striking illustration of this rift was provided by the reign of the Buriat taisha Dymbyl Galsanov (1815-1822). Treskin's explanation of the cause for friction and dissatisfaction describes the situation quite clearly. The conflict between the ruler and his subjects, said Treskin, arose because "of [Galsanov's] youthfulness, tactlessness, authoritarianism, his overly eager abandoning of Buriat customs for Russian ones, his luxurious mode of life, and finally...his lack of respect for traditions." [41] No doubt this was a socially disruptive process, but it also led the native nobility to change its outlook on its own condition and on its relations with the Russians. More and more the native upper classes felt equal to the Russians, and they expected this identity to be formally recognized. [42]

But not in social and economic matters alone do we notice a transformation in the eighteenth century. The more advanced native peoples of Siberia were subjected to powerful new ideological currents. Of considerable importance was the influence of Christianity. The Muscovite authorities had made no serious efforts at Christianizing the natives, for it would have meant a decrease of the iasak. But in the eighteenth century the government of St. Petersburg manifested greater interest in the spread of Christianity. The reasons for the government's new attitude were not entirely unselfish and religious. A newly baptized native became a peasant in status, and he was often moved and settled as an agricultural worker either on state or--up to 1767--church lands. But the Russian clergy in Siberia proved unable to serve as effective moral and spiritual leaders, nor was the example of many Russian Siberians very effective propaganda for the Christian faith. [43] In some cases a rather narrow-minded and foolish insistence on the literal enforcement of dietary rules repelled the natives; for instance, the Iakuts had such difficulties because their diet was based on fish and meat and some milk products which they were not supposed to use during many fast days. As a result, only the poorest natives were willing to accept baptism, even then reluctantly, and their permanent adherence to the new faith could not be counted upon. [44]

The spread of Buddhism from Tibet proved to be of greater import, especially for the Buriats and Tungus. Buddhism started its penetration into the Buriat region in the seventeenth century and was well established by the middle of the eighteenth century. In the eighteenth century appeared native lamas who played the role of intellectual and professional leaders. As the relations with the Russian administration required more and more writing, the need grew for literate secretaries to the tribal chiefs. This function was readily performed by the Buddhist lamas. The Russians sponsored the training of local religious leaders so as to preclude a growing dependence on a foreign power, namely, Tibet. The instructions of Count Raguzinskii contained the injunction not to call in foreign lamas but to rely on native ones. [45] In later years the Russians sponsored the establishment of a chief lama (Pandita-Khambo-lama) at Gusinoe Ozero (1808) with wide ecclesiastical powers.

Although the government gave the official Buddhist clergy various privileges (on the model of the Tatar overlords of the past), it did not look with favor upon the development of lamaseries. The reason was obvious: as had already occurred to Peter the Great, more monks meant a smaller number of people capable of performing government service and paying taxes. In spite of the government's efforts, which were probably not very consistent, the number of monks grew from 617 in 1774 to 2,500 in the early 1820's in nineteen big monasteries.[46]

Buddhism as a cultural force and its monasteries as an economic and social factor exercised a great influence on the way of life and outlook of the natives. In the early nineteenth century most travelers commented favorably on the literacy and the high moral and spiritual standards of the Buriat people. The necessity of supporting a greater number of monasteries, monks, and clergy also encouraged the development of agriculture among the Buriats.[47] Although the primitive tribes of hunters and trappers in the northeast remained backward, it was becoming increasingly difficult to treat peoples like the Buriats as if they were savages without regard to their cultural and social needs. Furthermore, the spread of Buddhism made Russification and Christianization more difficult and helped foster national consciousness, which in turn underlined the necessity for new administrative provisions to guide the relations between the Russian government and these people.

As a consequence, the old-time customary and legal relations between the Russian conquerors and the Siberian natives were in great confusion. The poor and backward tribes of the far north and northeast were undergoing a very serious economic crisis which undermined their traditional patterns of occupations and livelihood and led to their slow but steady decline in numbers. On the other hand, such peoples as the Buriats were maintaining their numbers and even improving their economic conditions by taking to new and more profitable pursuits, but their traditional social fabric was being subjected to serious strain and deep-going transformation. Within these tribes the old social system was breaking up and the traditional economic base was changing, opening the way to internal friction and difficulties. This unsatisfactory situation, coupled with the new attitude towards Siberia we have described in the first part, led the government to take steps to improve the circumstances of the natives and to clarify its relations with them. The increasingly frequent inspections and revisions-- although none led to significant practical results--were clear evidence of the government's growing concern.[48]

CHAPTER V

A New Approach Toward Native Administration

AS IN MANY other fields of government, the accession of Catherine II initiated a new approach to the problems of Siberia. To the practical tasks of administration Catherine and her advisers brought an ideological framework which helped them to see the problems more clearly and find ways for their solution. The ideological basis of Catherine's approach to the Siberian natives was her acceptance of the fashionable concept of the "noble savage." From this concept it followed that it was the duty of government to recognize the peculiar features and customs of native peoples and to preserve their moral and social qualities. Such an approach could have great value in creating a more effective administrative organization in which the positive traits of the natives could be made to serve the government's purposes rather than to provoke resistance.[1] Catherine could take no immediate steps in this direction, however, as she had no adequate information about the various native peoples and no precise ideas about the differences between the social organization of the various native tribes, the variety of their economic foundations, and the special needs of each particular tribe and people.

These considerations found their expression in the mission of Major Shcherbachev in 1763. He was instructed to ascertain more accurately and completely the true situation in Siberia, the number of the natives, their tribal arrangements, the amount of tribute exacted from them, etc.[2] The information gathered by Shcherbachev was to form the basis for new instructions and for new quotas and rules for the collection of taxes, performance of services, and the government of the natives. One outcome of this mission was a census of the taxable natives. The census showed 186,000 "souls," indicating roughly a total native population of 450,000.[3] These natives were to pay the rather moderate ia sak of 165,000 r. a year. This amount remained fixed until Speransky's new census, though in the meantime the number of some native peoples had changed appreciably. Another result of Major Shcherbachev's mission was to reaffirm clearly the principle of inner self-government of the native tribes, and to permit appeal to Russian authorities only if there was a conflict between tribes or if the litigants were dissatisfied with the decisions of their chiefs.[4]

But beyond this rather limited formal achievement Major Shcherbachev's work initiated a series of measures for the solution of the economic and administrative problems of the natives. These measures were introduced at various times over a period of about fifty years, from the early years of Catherine II's reign to the governorship of Speransky. In the majority of instances these changes (though perhaps not the specific form they took) were also desired by the natives, their desires being manifested in petitions and decisions of tribal assemblies which came to the attention of the government.

The first need was to check the shameless exploitation of the natives by the merchants. The instructions of 1763 prohibited the merchants from entering the territory of the tribes except at the time of the yearly market.[5] In 1766 the governor of Irkutsk, Frauendorf, proposed that all loans concluded by the Buriats with Russians be declared null and void unless they had been authorized by the tribal chieftains.[6] The intention to restrict the freedom of Russian traders in native tribes found its expression in a code agreed upon by a tribal assembly, the Khep Toktagal of 1800. This code fixed a maximum interest rate on loans, prohibited trade on credit, and specified that children of indentured servants could not be compelled to work to redeem their parent's debts, even if on the death of the parents the debt had not been repaid in full. Indentured servants had to be given a minimum subsistence salary of 15 r. a year and clothing, and their tax obligations had to be paid by those making use of their labor.[7]

Efforts were also made to alleviate the burden of services in kind, particularly the postal and transportation service. Thus as early as 1789 a private petition of a Iakut princeling to the Council of State requested that the Iakuts be freed from the postal service obligation which should be turned over to

the Russian settlers. [8] In 1816 there opened a new period for
the natives of the Iakutsk region when the performance of the
postal service was put on the basis of freely-agreed-upon
prices. [9]

Another important problem was to cut the heavy toll
exacted by the periodic famines, not only out of humanitarian
concern but also to put an end to the necessity of feeding many
natives from treasury resources. The best way of obtaining
this result seemed to be to develop agriculture among the
natives. Catherine II had given great quantities of land in
permanent possession to those few natives who had already
settled. However, the measure did not have a widespread
effect, for its application left much to be desired. [10] In 1784
a decision of the Council of State reinstated the rights of native
princelings and chieftains to the land which had been granted
to them by imperial acts in the past. [11] In 1788 permission
was granted to the administration to give land to those Kazakhs
who entered the Russian Empire, without requiring special
approval by the authorities in St. Petersburg. [12] At the same
time the government tried to promote the settlement of Kazakhs
by building permanent houses for their sultans. Despite these
inducements the Kazakhs found it more profitable to continue
their cattle-raising economy, the produce of which was in high
demand in both Central Asia and Western Siberia. As it turned
out, only the poorest among them, those who had not enough
cattle to secure their subsistence, proved willing to settle
down as tillers of the soil. [13]

The initiative in improving agriculture often came from
the natives themselves. In this, the Buriats, who had become
acquainted with agriculture even before their conquest by the
Russians, led the way. In 1792, for example, the Buriats of
the Khori region requested subsidies and seeds to start agriculture. This request reached the Council of State, which on
September 27, 1792, set aside 20,000 r. for this purpose,
giving the following reason for its decision:

> The council is of the opinion that the establishment of
> agriculture among these natives [inovertsy], by giving
> them a better means for finding their subsistence and
> by decreasing the dearth of bread that occurs in their
> region, is, of course, a most worth-while enterprise
> and one which should be supported. [14]

In 1808 the limits of the rights of the natives to their lands were fixed for the first time. As we may recall from the first of these studies, the Council of State had decided to allot 30 desiatin per soul with full rights to the minerals that might be found beneath the surface. By the law of August 22, 1818, issued in connection with the Buriats' claims, the Council of State decided to consider all land tilled by the natives as state lands in the possession of the natives. This was a much more liberal attitude than that taken previously, and it provided a more secure foundation for the possession and exploitation of these territories by the natives. [15]

The results of the spread of agriculture among the Buriats of the Baikal region began to be noticeable by 1800. In the 1780's Buriat-grown grain was brought to the markets of Irkutsk province, and in 1787 the shulenga of the first Buianov clan of the Kuda Buriats was ordered to make grain deliveries to the state distilleries. [16] At the end of the eighteenth century the Khori Buriats were supplying the larger part of the wool for the state textile factory on the river Tel'ma near Irkutsk. The director of this factory, O. Novitskii, petitioned the government that the Khori taisha be given the rank of staff officer in recognition of his people's contribution to the enterprise. When this failed, he attempted to have the Khori Buriats attached to the factory and to have the factory managers become the natives' protectors and judges. Although Novitskii's proposals were rejected, they show the role played by the Buriats in the economy of the region and the efforts made by local administrators to bring their legal and administrative position into harmony with their new economic function. [17]

The absence of clearly defined rules and the increasing difficulty of the administration resulting from the change in conditions were acutely felt by the natives, especially the more advanced ones like the Buriats and Iakuts. They expressed the desire for a reorganization of the relations within the tribes and between the tribes and the Russians. At the very start of the nineteenth century, the Kalmyks, through their chieftains and clergy, petitioned the Russian government for a revision of the regulations of 1640, which were still the basis of their political and legal organization. In 1802 the College for Foreign Affairs was instructed to take up these matters. Eventually a special congress of prominent Kalmyks was convoked, which passed resolutions amending the regulations of 1640. The resolutions were examined by a special government commission in 1827 but never received legislative implementation. [18] The Buriats on several occasions indicated that since their exit from Mongolia several centuries before, they had had no rules for their internal government and in particular no rules determining their relations with the Russians. [19] Though this was somewhat of an exaggeration, the natives did feel a lack of clear regulations.

The instructions given to Major Shcherbachev in 1763 had provided only for a few preliminary rules to govern the relations between the Russians and the natives. They had never been fully worked out and developed. These instructions, repeated in 1783 and again confirmed in 1803, provided that in all civil cases and in relatively minor criminal ones, the native courts or judges (chiefs) would make the decision on the basis of the customary law of the tribe concerned. Only serious criminal offenses were to be dealt with by the Russian authorities. [20] For some of the tribes, such as the Northern Buriats, the Russians had set up a general administrative scheme. [21] As Speransky pointed out in his survey of Siberian conditions, the rules and customary laws of the tribes and clans were all oral, sometimes contradictory, and not always well defined and universally accepted by the natives themselves, and the punishments were at times too cruel and out of proportion to the offense. As a result, there were constant conflicts among the natives, and many complaints were brought before the Russians, who judged them according to Russian standards, which often conflicted with the natives' ideas of justice. [22]

As early as the eighteenth century, several attempts were made to solve the administrative difficulties. Most of these efforts consisted in finding out the existing rules governing the affairs of the tribe and its relation to the Russians. The natives themselves were asked to provide the necessary information, and on the basis of this information and the desires expressed by the natives, the government then tried to take some action. This bureaucratic approach had its origin in the reign of Catherine II. [23] To limit the arbitrariness of the native judges and the abuses brought about by their uncontrolled actions, the Russian government "...in the eighteenth century formed for their direct administration tribal bureaus [rodovye kontory] composed of zaisans under the chairmanship of the chief taisha, and subordinated to the land court." [24] In 1788 the Council of State ruled in the case of Kalmyk chieftains

that they could be demoted only as a result of specific complaints and a decision of the court. A similar principle
doubtless was put in force for other tribes.[25] To avoid confusion and conflicting jurisdictions, it was clearly specified
in the steppe code of 1808 that no case could be appealed to
Russian or superior courts while under consideration by a
lower authority.[26] The frequent repetition of this rule in
various administrative orders and legislative reminders
seems to indicate that it was not observed very closely.

Although it is difficult to determine the facts precisely,
there can be no doubt that Chinese practices were of influence
not only in the customary laws of the various tribes (as has
been shown by Riasanovsky) but also in the relations between
the natives and their overlords. This is easily understood if
we remember that the peoples of southeastern Siberia had
been subjects of the Mongols and Chinese before their conquest by the Russians; the Baikal Buriats, for instance, had
been tributaries of the Khalkha Mongols in the seventeenth
century.[27] That this influence did exist is also indicated
by the fact that when the Russian administration gathered
materials for the compilation of a code of the steppe, many
Chinese legal sources were consulted.[28] It is interesting to
note the similarity between the rules for the Kazakhs drafted
under Catherine II and some of the provisions of the code of
1789.[29] Whether this was an instance of the Russians bor-
rowing directly from the Chinese or adapting themselves to
Kazakh traditions developed earlier, when the Kazakhs were
in closer contact with China, the present writer is not in a
position to decide.[30]

In any case, the last decade of the eighteenth century witnessed an intensive movement to codify existing administrative
rules and the customary law of the natives. A compilation of
the regulations issued by the Russians in Iakutiia, the so-
called iasak excerpts (iasachnye vypiski), had been started in
conjunction with the mission of Major Shcherbachev.[31] Later,
in the first two decades of the nineteenth century, a series
of tribal assemblies was called to compile and agree upon the
contents of the customary law. Government orders were issued
clearly setting forth the purpose of such tribal meetings, one
of which is quoted here at some length:

Order of the Land Deputy [zemskii zasedatel'] M.
Karamzin to the Chief Taisha of Balagansk, Andrei

Nazarov: The Land Court of Irkutsk, by its order of
March 21 of this year, under No. 4696, pursuant to a
similar order from the Provincial Administration, has
prescribed to me to collect immediately the most reliable
data, so as to be fully informed about the methods which
guide the native chiefs in the decision of [judiciary] cases.
In the first place: how did native chiefs act in former
times in trying their subjects? also enumerate completely
and accurately all those cases and the contents of judiciary
inquiries, as for example: big and small theft of cattle,
disputes, nonpayment of the kalym [bride price], etc.;
and also indicate in all detail the rules by which they
[native chiefs] were guided and still are guided. In the
second place: how is all this done at the present time
and specifically what does the power of the clan chief
consist in? At the same time gather from all the native
communities their opinion based on resolutions of tribal
assemblies and common consent, how they think it most
convenient and consonant with present conditions to establish their judiciary for petty cases in the future..., i.e.,
[whether they want] things to remain on the old basis or
have them established on some other convenient basis.
In the third place, find out about the degree and manner of
punishment inflicted on the guilty until now. In pursuance
of which I command your honor [blagorodie] to compile in
the immediate future the data in the above order and to
forward them to me with the necessary additions and
explanations. Any delay will subject you to prosecution.
28th day of March, 1818.[32]

Other tribes followed suit. The material gathered at these
tribal assemblies, of historical character and expressive of
the wishes of the natives, was forwarded to the authorities
and used later by Speransky and his aides. This movement
for codification was continued with government sanction and
eventually led to the drafting of the Code of the Steppe in
1841.[33] Although this code did not receive legislative sanction,
it nevertheless played a great role in the legal and administrative life of the Siberian natives until the Russian Revolution.[34]

    In summary, it can be said that from the accession of
Catherine II onward, there had been a decisive change in the
economic, social, and political conditions of the natives. In
this process of transformation and change two divergent trends

can be detected. On the one hand there was a deterioration of conditions among the primitive trapping and hunting tribes of the far north and northeast, who fell victims to the ruthless exploitation of merchants, officials, and new settlers. Instead of profiting from the contact with a more advanced culture, their energies and fitness for survival were sapped by the ills attending these new contacts. Pushed into the remote corners of Siberia, these peoples declined in numbers and became the stepchildren of the empire, roaming forlornly and aimlessly in the tundra. On the other hand, an equally important but more positive transformation was taking place among the more advanced, socially better organized peoples of the south-eastern areas of Siberia. These natives, who formerly had been hunters, trappers, and nomads, were slowly settling down to a more regular and productive way of life. Partly under pressure from the Russian administration, these peoples began to take to agriculture and to participate in the general economy of the region.

In both instances the change in the traditional economy and the natives' way of life resulted in a profound transforma-tion of social relationships. More striking were the changes occurring among those natives who were settling on the land and taking up agriculture, thereby drawing closer to the Russian population of Siberia. This social transformation, taking place in less than half a century, went so far as to threaten the traditional family and clan relationships, both economic and political. It was not surprising that the natives felt somewhat disoriented and were looking for a new formu-lation of their relationships; this search, in turn, directly affected their position vis-à-vis the Russian administration. Inasmuch as the settling of natives in agriculture was pro-moted by the government as part of its program of expanding Siberia's economic potential, it was imperative for the Russian authorities to work out administrative rules more consonant with the changed conditions, especially with the progressive Russification of the leaders of the more advanced peoples like the Buriats, Tungus, and Iakuts.

Although the efforts which were made in this direction in the latter part of the eighteenth century were for the most part unsuccessful, these attempts, the experience of trial and error, left some impression and facilitated the task of Speransky and his advisers in the early 1820's.

CHAPTER VI

A New Administrative System for the Natives

MUCH attention was paid to the conditions and future of the Siberian natives in the laws of 1822, as we have had occasion to mention in the first part of this study. In the following pages we shall limit ourselves to a description and analysis of the special statute on the natives which deals with administration.

By and large, Speransky combined and elaborated the trends that had become manifest before his arrival in Siberia. He resumed Catherine's humanitarian protection of the native customs and way of life. But at the same time, he favored a synthesis of the cultural and spiritual values and of the economic and social ways of life of both the native and Russian populations in Siberia. He considered that Siberia was already a Staatsgemeinschaft, and he wanted it to become also a Kulturgemeinschaft. It was only natural that such a goal would focus Speransky's primary attention on those natives that could easily be integrated into the social community of Siberia, i.e., the settled tribes and the more advanced, economically differentiated peoples like the Buriats.

More than any previous governor he actively cultivated social contacts with the natives and tried to study their customs, religion, and history. Not that these contacts and studies always led him to approve of the natives' way of life. To his daughter, for example, he described his disgust at the behavior of the wild Kazakh tribes at their festivities which he witnessed on the southern border.[1] Naturally enough, it was the more advanced culture and religion of the Buriats and the Buddhist priesthood that attracted him most. He went out of his way to visit Buddhist monasteries, and in each he spent long hours talking with the monks about their religion. He secured the participation of the lamas in the establishment of branches of the Bible Society in eastern Siberia, and organized a nondenominational religious group in Irkutsk. [2]

Although Speransky was very much interested in the propagation of Christianity, he felt that the moral values of Buddhism were very close to those of Christianity and therefore it was not necessary to press for conversion. [3] The Christian missionary should, therefore, be a leader not only in the religious but also in the intellectual, cultural, and social development of the natives. It was a misfortune that the Russian clergy had not understood this earlier and that it was not prepared to take upon itself this leadership. For this reason, Speransky welcomed and supported the work of the English missionaries in the Baikal region. These English missionaries, sent on behalf of the English Bible Society, did not press for baptism but rather tried to develop in the natives all their cultural, economic, and moral potentialities. To achieve this, they studied the Mongol language and established a Mongol printing press; they acted as advisers and teachers of agriculture and medicine. There seems to be no doubt that they played an important role in the development of the Buriats in the nineteenth century by helping in the education of a group of intellectual leaders. Speransky's attitude toward this activity was quite different from that taken later by the suspicious government of Nicholas I. Speransky helped the English missionaries as much as possible, made loans to them, helped them to secure title to the land they occupied, and in general protected and helped them in all the ways he could. These missionaries also contributed to the development of agricultural techniques among the Buriats, and this aspect of their activity was, of course, more than welcome to Speransky. [4]

Speransky was also concerned with spreading education among the natives as well as among the Russians. Some steps had been taken toward the development of a native school system before his arrival in Siberia. He stimulated this movement and supported it in all ways possible. Although his successors in Siberia displayed little interest in education, the seed he had helped to plant did not die, and throughout the nineteenth century the natives, in particular the Buriats, continued to support their schools and to further education. [5]

The main problem Speransky had to face was the need for

clarifying and defining the administrative and legal systems governing the lives of the natives. The statute that he drafted for this purpose played a great role in the development of the natives and was maintained as a guiding document throughout the entire nineteenth century. [6] On the one hand, Speransky and his advisers wanted to preserve the customs of the natives wherever possible and secure the autonomy of the internal life of these tribes. On the other hand, they wanted to leave the way open for the economic and social transformation which they felt was bound to occur. In their view, the economic and social transformation would bring the natives closer to the Russian population of Siberia and in the long run would bring about an organic Russification.

Speransky did not use the phrase "organic Russification," but that was clearly his goal. If he were asked to explain his policy, he would probably have answered something like this: "It is the task and function of the state, the Russian state in particular, to provide leadership and guidance to the peoples inhabiting the empire, to raise their spiritual and moral, as well as material, culture. Each of these peoples has values and traditions of its own which are worthy of preservation and incorporation into the one imperial-national culture. In this process, the Russian people have a very valuable spiritual contribution (Christianity) to make, and they also must give leadership to the social and economic evolution of other peoples. The history of the last decades shows that the natives are slowly following in the same path as their Russian conquerors and neighbors; they too settle down, start tilling the soil, and participate in the economic exchanges of the region; many of them eagerly accept the social institutions of the Russians. This process should be fostered by the government as much as possible."

But to this Speransky would immediately add (in distinction to the makers of Russian policy under Alexander III and Nicholas II), "No violence should be exercised to bring about the final result. The natives have to come to it by themselves, through the operation of a changed way of life, a different and new pattern of occupations and economic activity. Only then will the process be truly organic, i.e., not imposed artificially, against the wishes of the peoples concerned and in violation of their traditional spiritual and social values. A Russification mechanically imposed from above would be both futile and cruel, whereas an organic amalgamation into the all-Russian community would benefit both the native peoples and the Russians." This amalgamation was very desirable to Speransky and to the government in St. Petersburg, and if the law of 1822 contained any innovation of principle, it was in the attempt to facilitate this process. Clearly enough, in 1822 such a program would apply primarily to the advanced peoples --the Buriats and some of the Tungus and Iakut tribes.

On the preceding pages we have stressed the need for order and clarity in the internal structure of the tribal societies. But this need was not felt by all tribes alike. Some thought that their internal organization was quite satisfactory and expressed their wish to maintain its essential features. In this respect it may be worth while to quote at length a description of the customs of the Buriats of the Ida, Tunka, Balagansk, and Kuda districts.

> According to the ancient Buriat customs and on the basis of legislation [according to a footnote this refers to the instructions of Count Savva Vladislavich], they consider the following matters reserved for their own judiciary action in avoidance of formal transactions in courts from which they believe they may suffer delays, burden, and ruin, because of their way of life, old traditions, and lack of education: (1) all kinds of theft, robbery, and swindle of no greater value than the property of the guilty; (2) quarrels, fights of all kinds which did not result in death, serious illness, or the maiming of limbs; (3) division of inheritance, payment of debts, kalym, etc., in an amount not greater than the wealth of the parties; (4) violation of peace and order in the community, short absences, drunkenness, laziness, etc.... The power of native clan chiefs: (1) the power of the chief taisha consists in the execution and supervision of laws and ordinances of higher authorities; in the preservation of law and order among the people entrusted to his care; in the supervision of the justice and honesty of the actions of clan shulengas and elders; in compelling these latter to perform the obligations of blameless service; in the accurate and full execution of orders of superiors...; in making every effort to provide his subjects with a better and more peaceful (orderly) way of life; in improving their agricultural establishments and, by means of laws and old customs, protecting the

free life and property of everyone, without favoritism,
from all exactions; and, on the basis of the power given
to him, in restraining his subjects by means of appropriate punishment from all kinds of crimes, disorders,
laziness, and maladministration; (2) the power and obligations of the other chiefs consist in these same matters as
for the chief <u>taisha</u>, in the capacity, as it were, of his
assistants or local clan chiefs over their own clansmen. [7]

Even though this statement was made after 1822 and cannot
therefore be taken as an entirely reliable description of the
Buriat customs of an earlier time, it gives some indication
of the foundations on which Speransky built his regulations.

But not all the tribes were in so favorable a position as
the Buriats. As Riasanovsky, the best student of this question,
has noted, in the beginning of the nineteenth century there
was "a lack of precision in jurisdictional competence and in
judiciary instances, a lack of rules of judiciary procedure,
no separation between the courts and the administration, no
codification of legal customs..."[8] All this Speransky wanted
to correct. As he said, it was not a question of changing the
essence of the power of local agencies but of adapting them
to the actual needs of concrete problems. He based his statute
on the natives on five principles: (1) divide the natives into the
three categories of settled natives, nomads, and vagrants; (2)
for the nomads and the vagrants, the administration should be
based on their old customs, but these had to be better defined
and organized; (3) the police functions of local authorities
should be of only a general supervisory nature, the internal
autonomy of tribes should be left untouched; (4) freedom of
trade and industry should be protected; (5) taxes and tribute
should be made proportional to the abilities of each tribe and
be imposed at regular intervals (so as to preclude the earlier
situation of the tribute's remaining unchanged for almost a
century). [9]

The settled natives were classified as state peasants. [10]
Their territorial possessions were confirmed, and should they
lack land, they could be alloted extra portions of unoccupied
land. If there were enough of them, the settled natives could
form a separate township in which their language would be
used for official purposes; in all other respects they were,
administratively speaking, identified with the Russian peasantry. [11] However, Speransky and Baten'kov (the coauthor of

the statute on the natives) failed to give either a list of settled
natives or, which was even more strange, a set of clear-cut
criteria by which to differentiate a settled from a nomad
people. [12]

For all practical purposes, the statute pertained to the
nomads and vagrants. These were characterized, in the
words of the law itself, as follows: (1) uncertainty of place
of residence; (2) level of civic education; (3) simplicity of
customs; (4) particularity of customs; (5) methods of finding
subsistence; (6) difficulty of communication; (7) lack of currency for exchange; (8) lack of means to sell the produce
of their hunting and fishing on the spot. [13] Obviously their
administrative setup had to be different. But the government
was not to interfere more than necessary, and in all civil
cases the natives should be left every means of arriving at
a settlement on the basis of local customs. The criminal
cases were limited in number and type, and only these types
of criminal cases were to be brought before the Russian
authorities. [14]

Nomads, of whom the statute provided a partial list
[Par. 83] were equated to the peasants but had their own
administration and rights. [15] They always kept these rights,
and even if they desired to become settled, they could not be
forced to become peasants (i.e., serfs). They were under
the jurisdiction of the laws of the steppe which were to be
codified eventually. All judiciary matters except for five
specified types of criminal cases (rebellion, premeditated
murder, pillage, counterfeiting, and stealing of state property)
were considered civil suits and were to be tried according to
the tribal customs. [16] The vagrants had the same rights as
the nomads, but their administration was simpler. Also their
territory was not to be rigorously defined; they were to be
assigned large tracts of land within which they had complete
freedom of movement. They did not pay a share of the local
dues. [17]

The administrative organization set up for the nomads
was based to some extent on the existing clan structure. Each
encampment, or ulus, of fifteen families or more formed a
clan administration (rodovaia uprava). This administration
consisted of one elder (starosta), whose position was either
elective or hereditary, depending on the custom of the tribe,
and one or two elected assistants. These assistants were to
be elected from the better and most honored members of the

clan. Within the clan the elder might preserve his traditional title (such as kniazek), but the possession of such a title did not affect his relationship to the Russian administration. The clan administration was to transact its business orally, both in providing information to the district administration and in executing its instructions. The vagrant natives had a similar but simpler organization. Their clan administration consisted only of one elder who conducted all affairs orally. [18]

The clan administration performed the general and direct police functions in the clan. The elder could punish for small misdemeanors according to the customs of the clan. No other member of the clan could inflict any punishment without specific instructions from the court. All regulations and orders from superior authorities were executed through the elder and the clan administration. Since the clan was considered as a single tax unit, the clan administration determined the distribution of the tax burden among individuals. The elder might present petitions on the needs of the clan; he informed the higher authorities of any extraordinary happenings in the clan and always had to know the exact number and composition of the clan. The elder gave permission for absences exceeding two days, saw to it that supplies were provided for the bad season, and was the agent for all dealings with the state concerning provisions. [19] While in a sense the clan administration was on the same level as the Russian village, the clan had a greater degree of autonomy and more administrative functions.

Several clan administrations constituted a native administration (inorodnaia uprava). Like its Russian equivalent, the township, the native administration consisted of a head (golova), two elected elders, and one clerk, if a qualified person was available. The position of head of the administration was elective or hereditary, depending on the local custom. Vagrant tribes did not have a native administration.

The native administration had complete authority over the clan administrations. It inspected the clans to see that they were properly governed, confirmed the petitions on individual clan needs, and kept a census of the population. It executed the ordinances of superior authorities, enforced the payment of taxes, and maintained law and order in the area. It was to protect the rights of the natives against external interference and to conduct investigations in special cases. The native administration was directly subordinated

to the land police, from whom it had to request special instructions before taking action, except in specified emergencies.[20]

The land police (zemskaia politsiia) was the link between
the native administrative institutions and the Russian administration. It consisted either of the individual land deputy
(zemskii zasedatel') of the separate districts or of the district
land court (zemskii sud).[21] The land police transmitted all
regulations from above and issued limited orders on its own.
The native administrations were entirely subordinated to it
and had but little initiative of action left to them.[22]

In spite of the use of terms like clan, the native administration was not really based on clan and family groupings.
Because of the changed conditions which we have described
earlier, the clan structure was in decline in the eighteenth
century. The clan was becoming a territorial and administrative unit, no longer resting on traditional family ties. This
trend was now legalized in effect by the statute, and the
artificial character of the clan was shown by the fact that
new "clans" had to be created to comprise small, unattached
groups of natives, as for instance the sbornyi rod ("mixed
clan") near Irkutsk. The historian of the Buriats, Kudriavtsev, was quite right in noting that the clan had become an
administrative unit equivalent to the Russian township (volost')
and the ulus to the Russian village commune (sel'skaia obshchina.[23]

The natives had a third institution, the steppe duma
(stepnaia duma), which was on the same level as the district.
This institution replaced the old kontora of the eighteenth
century and the zemskaia izba of the seventeenth. A steppe
duma was composed of the principal clan chief (glavnyi
rodonachal'nik), such as a taisha, and deputies elected from
the ranks of the native nobility or prominent individuals.
The duma carried on its business in writing and had its
own clerk. Its functions, primarily economic, were similar
to those of the dumas in the towns: it kept a permanent census
and also account of the monies and common property. It
was to promote agriculture and economic productivity, had
general supervision of the supplies of the natives, and could
petition superior authorities regarding economic needs.
All its prescriptions were to be carried out through the
heads of native administrations and elders of clans.[24]

Judicial proceedings among the natives were conducted

in the following manner. A case was first taken up orally,
and only if no decision or satisfactory solution could be
reached by the natives themselves could they initiate regular
judicial proceedings in writing through the Russian courts.
Only the five types of cases classified as criminal (see p. 117)
had to be referred directly to the Russian administration.
In civil cases the clan administration acted as an oral court
of the first instance. Those natives whose custom was to
proceed by arbitration might do so, but the decisions arrived
at by arbitration could not be appealed; if arbitration failed,
the case had to be either dropped or initiated anew. The
court of the second instance, in particular for cases between
members of different clans, was the native administration.
The oral court of the third and final instance was the land
police. The major function of this body was to put an end to
misunderstandings between natives and to reconcile them on
the basis of the laws of the steppe and of custom. No matter
was to be brought before the land police without a request
from the native plaintiff, so that the land police had no right
to initiate any action on its own. If no agreement could be
reached by the land police or if one of the parties was dissatisfied by the decision reached, appeal could be made in
writing to the regular Russian district court. The dumas of
the steppe had no judicial powers, but they could act as
arbiters if they were requested to do so by the two parties. [25]

The native elders and chiefs were not to receive any
specified salary for their services, unless the custom of the
steppe provided that some specified revenues be set aside
for their use. This meant that the poorer members of the
clan were rarely able or willing to serve as elders or chiefs,
even if the tribal customs permitted their election. Recent
(particularly Soviet) historians of the peoples of Siberia have
stressed--perhaps unduly so--that the statute of 1822 consoli-
dated the dominant role played by the native nobility and
fostered the tendency to make local administrative functions
hereditary. The clerks (especially in the dumas) did receive
a salary which was set by the provincial authorities. This
expense as well as the expenses for buildings and other necessities of administration were borne by all members of the
clan. [26]

The elders and elected chiefs were confirmed by the
civil governor or the chief of the region. The principal chief
of the clan (glavnyi rodonachal'nik) was confirmed by the

governor-general. The reasons for which confirmation might
be withheld were specifically enumerated: bad conduct as
proven by a judiciary decision, disapproval of the individual
by more than one half of the members of the clan, and proven
bad character (although the methods of proof were not specified). In these cases a new election was obligatory. Any of
the elected native chiefs could be demoted or unseated by the
same authorities that had the power of confirmation, and also
only under specific conditions: commission of a crime, abuse
of power as proven by a judiciary decision, and petition by
the majority of the members of the clan.[27]

The chain of command of the native organs of administration was as follows: the clan and native administrations were
directly subordinated to the land police (i.e., the district
land court or, in separate districts, the land deputy). Through
the land police, they were under the district administration
and all the agencies above it. The duma of the steppe was
directly subordinate to the general district administration
and to the agencies above it. While the district administration was immediately superior to the native bodies, the
district clerks had no direct control over native affairs and
could intervene in them only through the collegiate bodies
of the district.[28]

The protection of the natives from the direct and constant
interference of individual officials was one of the notable
accomplishments of the statute. The natives had more local
autonomy than the Russian villages and townships into whose
affairs the ispravnik or zasedatel' could meddle rather freely.
The settled native traders of Central Asiatic origin (Bukhartsy)
living in those towns where they were a large minority could
form their own ratusha and have their own oral court of justice
conducted in their own language. In any case, the natives
living in the towns had the same status as the Russian town
population, and if there were more than twenty of them they
could elect their own elder.[29]

To enable the natives to fulfill their obligations, their
taxes had to be determined very precisely and ahead of time
in as simple a fashion as possible. The labor services required of them for state transportation and communication
were to be restricted to a minimum, and the Russian authorities were to make annual inspections to supervise the fulfillment of this condition. As a further protection for the natives,
it was provided that natives could be imprisoned only for the

most serious offenses; thus, preventive imprisonment, often a source of exactions and abuses, was eliminated. No witness could be called if he had to make a journey of over three days walking.[30]

For the convenience of the natives the governor was to establish yearly fairs, either in the towns or in the villages or encampments. Wherever there was no fair or where one could not be established on account of the sparsity of population, its place was taken by a suglan or mir,[31] where the natives would come to pay their taxes and tribute. The suglans could be transformed into regular markets or fairs if the natives wished it. At the fairs and suglans the natives elected an elder who maintained law and order, exercised police functions, and took care of all disputes. Taxes were to be collected only at the fairs or suglans; no fiscal agents were to be sent to an ulus, or encampment, except when the elder had not delivered the tax for over two years. To safeguard the interests of the natives, taxes were not to be collected until the end of the fair, and local authorities were to see to it that the prices of articles sold at the fairs were not forced down. To protect the natives from being cheated on the value of their goods, only ordinary furs were to be appraised at the fair; valuable pelts had to be forwarded to the provincial or regional capital for appraisal. In line with the government's efforts to increase the use of currency, dues in kind were to be calculated in currency and if possible converted into monetary payments on the basis of an average price fixed by the provincial council (again to avoid arbitrary action of individual governmental agents).[32]

The law of 1822 also had provisions for the protection of the economic potentialities of the natives. Special emphasis was given to freedom of trade. In his general consideration of native administration Speransky pointed out that the previous restrictions on the free movement of traders in native settlements were no longer necessary, for with the expansion of trade competition would grow too; the natives would acquire better knowledge of commercial practices and be in a better position to defend their interests.[33] Obviously, this pertained primarily to the more advanced peoples of Siberia, who were beginning to have an important part in the region's economy; again we find the Buriats and Iakuts benefiting most from this provision. The principle of freedom of commerce, except for

the prohibition of the sale of alcoholic beverages, was re-
emphasized by strict regulations.[34] The natives were given
greater freedom to move; often only the verbal permission of
the clan chief was necessary. They could bring their produce
to the market themselves, thus avoiding the buying monopoly
of the itinerant merchant.[35] This provision also reflected
and satisfied the new conditions and needs of the Buriats and
Iakuts. The land possessed by the natives was guaranteed
against encroachments by other tribes and Russian settlers;
the land belonged to the state but was given in permanent
possession to the natives. Taxation schedules were fixed
especially for the natives, and no new tax was applicable to
the natives except by personal command of the emperor.[36]

The state was to sell the natives those articles which
were essential to them. The price level for articles of prime
necessity would therefore remain low, but in no case should
these sales by the state restrict or prevent free commerce.
The state was to sell only grain, salt, powder and shot,
articles mostly needed by the hunting and trapping primitive
peoples of the far north who often did not have the means of
buying them on the open market. The state stores were not
to retain more than 6 per cent profit, and in case of real
need the profit was to be foregone entirely. State stores were
not allowed to make any sales on credit, though the natives
were allowed to pay either in currency or in kind. In all other
respects the rules applicable to state granaries applied here
too.[37]

There were also a few provisions of a social and cultural
character which deserve some mention. The natives had
complete freedom of religion and the right to change legal
status (become city dwellers, peasants, etc.). With permission of the governor they could establish schools in which
their own language was used, but they also had the absolute
right to attend Russian schools if they wished. They were also
given the privilege of petitioning the government directly.
The missionary activities of the orthodox clergy were to be
very mild, and in no case were conversions to be forced.
The authorities of the district were particularly charged with
enforcement of this rule. Newly baptized natives should not
be punished harshly or prosecuted for errors in ritual and
diet; this restricted the disciplinary powers of the clergy
over the newly converted. The titled personages among the
natives could preserve their titles and prestige within their

tribes. But the authorities were to recognize such special
status only when it was based on an actual administrative
position or function. Native noblemen were not considered
members of the nobility of the empire except in specified
cases. These last points were intended to maintain the local
nobility's power and prestige but at the same time make their
identification with the Russian nobility dependent on their
actual political and administrative role.[38] As a matter of fact,
the native leaders, especially those whose positions had
become hereditary, tended to consider themselves on a par
with the Russian officials. The often quoted Shashkov remarked
apropos of the Buriat taishas: "They consider themselves
functionaries [chinovnik] and oppress the natives often only
to show their official position. They make efforts to imitate
the Russians in the outward forms of their lives."[39]

   In the minds of Speransky and his collaborators, the law
of 1822, which gave judiciary autonomy to the natives, was to
be supplemented by a code of the steppe. For this purpose
the provincial and local authorities were ordered to collect
all necessary information on the prevailing customs and customary laws. The materials so gathered were to be forwarded
to St. Petersburg where a special commission would put them
in order, eliminate the contradictions, fill in the existing
gaps, and draw up a code on which both native and Russian
judiciary officials could base their decisions. The gathering
of this information proceeded in a very haphazard and uneven
manner.[40] In some provinces the local administration took
great pains to collect the data as precisely and completely
as possible. In others it merely obeyed the letter of the order
and sent in a very superficial and uncritical collection. Moreover, as has been noted by Riasanovsky, the natives, when
questioned by the administration, often adapted their answers
to what they thought would be pleasing to the Russians and
exaggerated the role of Western, particularly Russian, elements in their laws and customs. In spite of these limitations,
however, the commission in St. Petersburg assembled an
imposing amount of data, and the resulting collection of
customary laws is an invaluable source of information on
the social and political conditions of these tribes at the beginning of the nineteenth century. It concluded, both logically
and historically, the efforts at codification which started on
the initiative of the natives themselves in the last two decades
of the eighteenth century.[41]

The code of the steppe was not completed until 1841, and conditions were such as to preclude its legislative implementation or imperial approval. In this respect it shared the fate of the other efforts at codifying local customary law (for West Russia, Southwest Russia, and Lithuania) undertaken by Speransky in the 1830's. We need not repeat the account of this failure, as its history has been fully and ably summarized by A. Nol'de who also gives a more detailed account of the regional variations in the collection of materials and a list of the Chinese and Mongol sources which were consulted. The draft of the Code of the Steppe, as completed in 1841, was printed in fifty copies which were circulated only among a few officials. [42] But in spite of this limited circulation it reached the authorities in Siberia and even the natives. As Riasanovsky points out, this code, though it never became official, was applied in judicial practice not only by the native courts but even by the Russian judges throughout the nineteenth century. It was so much alive that in 1918 it was copied almost literally for the codes promulgated by the revolutionary authorities of the various Siberian nationalities. [43]

By becoming the practical guide for judiciary decisions, the steppe code of 1841 also helped to level the distinctions in the customs and laws of the various tribes. It thus played an important role in speeding up the process of making uniform the ways of life and the social and political relationships of the Siberian peoples. By creating a unified terminology, by introducing more principles of Russian law (particularly in regard to property), the code helped to bring the Siberian peoples closer to Russian culture and to foster the community of culture which had been Speransky's goal.

The general features of the statute of 1822 remained the basis for governing the natives until the end of the century and even later. By this statute limits had been placed on the Russian local administration, and its interference in all judicial matters had been quite effectively restricted. A balanced estimate of the basic characteristics of the judicial provisions of the statute is given by Riasanovsky in the following terms:

It established clearer limits to the jurisdiction of native courts, it set up a system of judiciary instances, of firm terms for appeals, it introduced a few general principles of judiciary procedures, and a few other things. But the system of the statute was not devoid of serious defects: the union of justice and administration,

a great number of institutions, lack of acquaintance of
higher authorities with the customary law of the natives,
absence of detailed procedural rules and of a code of the
material customary law, etc. [44]

In administrative matters the Russians maintained their
dominant role, and the natives had wide discretion only in
applying the policy set by Russian officials. However, the
lack of distinction between judicial and administrative functions
in the native system, as well as the pattern of subordination,
left the door open to intervention by Russian officials. In other
words, while the statute did put effective barriers against
arbitrary interference by individual officials, it did not protect
the natives fully against the collegiate bodies of the administration.

Another characteristic aspect of the statute was the
dominant role assigned to the "better" among the natives,
whether they were hereditary nobility or elected wealthier
members of the clan. In this respect Speransky was not only
bowing to existing conditions but also following the basic
principle of his political philosophy. In Speransky's view,
only those whom he considered the "better people," economically, and even more important, spiritually, could be given
positions of responsibility. Yet we should also note that these
"better" people were also those who were more Russified,
or tending to become so. In this way the native aristocracy
was to play a guiding role in the progressive and organic
Russification of the natives. [45]

The statute, however, presented serious difficulties in
its application. First of all, the boundaries of the natives'
territories were not specified by the law, nor were any clear-
cut rules established for determining them. It is true that a
final decision on boundaries would have had to wait for a
complete survey of Siberia--something that was still far off.
But even had this survey been completed, the native lands
would still not have been clearly protected against possible
encroachment from neighboring tribes or the Russians; and
this was particularly serious in view of the government's
policy of stimulating colonization. Inasmuch as no absolute
native title to the land was recognized and the vagrant natives
had no definite territory with recognized borders, the state
could always change boundaries and ratify seizures by the

Russians without leaving the natives any formal method of recourse. [46]

Another difficulty, not foreseen by Speransky, developed immediately. The three categories of settled, nomad, and vagrant had been set up to safeguard the customs and ways of life of the natives. However, the law had not clearly specified the standards to be used for placing a tribe in one or another of these categories. In its haste to put into effect the provisions of the statute of 1822, the Russian administration did not enter into a serious and detailed study of the natives' actual way of life but based its decisions on superficial features. For instance, the Ostiaks of Berezovo were not differentiated from those of Obdorsk; both were classified as nomads, although the Obdorsk Ostiaks were fishermen. The schedule of taxation based on the category of nomads proved extremely difficult for the fishermen to meet. [47] The desire to promote agriculture and to increase as much as possible the number of settled natives (who paid more taxes) led the Russian local authorities to classify the natives very readily as settled, even when there was little basis for such a decision. For example, the Tatars of the Baraba marshes, who had a small amount of land for grazing the horses they used for postal service, were classified as settled natives and burdened with the regular obligations of the peasantry even though they still derived most of their income from hunting.

Since the taxes on the peasants were much heavier, many natives who were transferred to the category of settlers exchanged a relatively easy burden for heavy fiscal obligations which they were unable to meet. Thus in 1824 and 1832 the natives of Tobolsk province could pay but 60 per cent of the total required. Before 1824 they had been paying 1.50 rubles per soul, but after their reclassification they had to pay 11 rubles per soul and sundry dues amounting to a total of about 20 rubles per soul. Small wonder then that they were petitioning for a change in their classification. [48] The arbitrary inclusion of natives among the settled population did not result in promoting agriculture, as had been intended. These peasants-against-their-will were not able to adjust themselves to a settled life; the tax burden was too great for them to carry, and their condition deteriorated instead of improving.

As could have been expected on the basis of some of the observations we have been able to make previously, the worst sufferers from the new classification and the resulting

economic transformation were the more backward peoples,
the hunters and trappers. They were in no position to bear
any increase in their tax load, and their way of life and social
organization were so primitive that the new statute was not
fully applicable and could not adequately protect them against
the exploitation of merchants and officials, who in these
remote regions were not kept in check by a collegiate board.
The statute of 1822 had but little effect on the primitive and
backward peoples who could not be fitted readily into the
scheme of ulus, clan, and steppe duma organizations. [49]
Conversely, the statute benefited the more advanced peoples,
such as the Buriats and the Iakuts. For them the law of 1822
was an important landmark in their progress towards fuller
integration into Siberian society and more active participation
in the economic development of the region.

However, the natural and slow improvement which might
have taken place through the extension of self-government
and autonomy was stifled by the subsequent policies of rigid
bureaucratic control pursued under Nicholas I and Alexander
III, while Alexander II was too much absorbed in the problems
of European Russia to pay much attention to the needs of the
Siberian natives. Thus by the end of the nineteenth century the
circumstances of most Siberian natives were not greatly
improved, although the more advanced peoples had slowly
transformed their ways of life--economic, social, and cul-
tural--and had moved farther into the orbit of Russian civilization. Yet whatever may be said of the well-organized and
advanced peoples, their more backward neighbors in the
northeast remained the stepchildren of the empire.

CHAPTER VII
Conclusion

COMPARED to Russia proper, the vast Siberian subcontinent was still living in "Muscovite" times in 1800. Though clad in European dress and bearing Western-sounding titles and ranks, the Russian administrators of Siberia were more akin to the old voevodas than to their colleagues in St. Petersburg. Siberia's Russian population lived in the same manner as had their ancestors of Central Russia in the reigns of Tsars Michael and Alexis. Some of the natives were slowly being pulled into the orbit of Russian society and culture, but many of them--especially the primitive peoples--were still living in isolation from the Russian world, exploited by it, and in sulking opposition to it. Their situation was like that in which the Finnish tribes of North Central Russia found themselves in the Middle Ages after the Russians had moved into their territory and settled there. The relations between the Buriats and the Russians, on the other hand, might be compared to those which prevailed between the Russians and the Tatars after the fall of the Golden Horde, while the Kazakhs were to southwestern Siberia what the Crimean Tatars and Turks had been to the southern Russian provinces in the seventeenth and eighteenth centuries.

The second half of the eighteenth century had brought about many social, economic, and administrative changes in Siberia, and by 1800 the region was in dire need of a reorganization of its social and administrative structure. The question was only how and to what end. The merchants, clinging to an old-fashioned seventeenth century outlook on trade and industry, wanted a transformation in the spirit of the social and economic legislation of the Muscovite state:

129

monopolistic privileges and the establishment and consolidation
of serfdom and other forms of bondage. The natives did not
know clearly what they wanted, but they knew that their
present situation was not tolerable à la longue. They needed
a new definition of the principles guiding the relation between
their traditional customs and the requirements of the Russian
administration. The Russian bureaucracy too was aware of
the need for change but was divided on its direction and
method: on the one hand, Treskin and Pestel followed a
policy of strict étatisme and bureaucratic despotism; on the
other, Kozodavlev, the agents of the Ministry of Finance,
and Speransky wanted to apply to Siberia the ideas of late
eighteenth century enlightened despotism, economic liber-
alism, and humanitarianism. The solution eventually worked
out was, in a sense, a compromise between bureaucratic
control and the demands of economic freedom and humanitarianism.

The legislation enacted in 1822, based on the new situation
that had developed, made use of the experience acquired
from past trials, errors, and haphazard measures and capped
trends which had crystallized during the late eighteenth
century. The slow and inchoate transformation that had
disrupted earlier practices and norms was finally brought
under control in a regular legislative order. Thereby, the
emerging pattern was clarified; and purposeful action, based
on known rules with predictable results, became possible.
A return to previous conditions had been made impossible,
however inadequate the application and implementation of
the new legislation. Speransky and his collaborators did more
than put the stamp of official approval upon certain existing
trends and bring sense and clarity into a chaotic situation.
The very act of clarifying the basic character of Siberia's
recent evolution, of harmonizing each part of its life with
the whole, rendered the people of Siberia and the government
of Russia conscious of a pattern of development, a pattern
only dimly perceived heretofore by a few and never acted
upon consistently. Along with the awareness of this pattern
came the belief in a new and different future for Siberia.

Of greatest significance was the new attitude towards
the economic potentialities of Siberia. Before the middle
of the eighteenth century, Siberia had been viewed only as
a source of furs; after that period it was increasingly valued
as an area of potentially vast agricultural resources. The

officials of Catherine's time and Governors Pestel and Treskin
thought it possible to develop agriculture and attract peasant
settlers by despotic and bureaucratic methods; but their results
were not very satisfactory. Speransky first realized clearly,
and attempted to act upon this insight, that agriculture pros-
pers best where the individual is given wide opportunity to
develop his initiative and enterprise. For maximum development of a solid agrarian economy, the population must be
allowed to make its own decisions on economic matters and be
given a choice in disposing of the fruits of its labor. It was
therefore desirable to allow as much economic autonomy
as possible, and the administrative structure had to be
geared to this new approach. Speransky also believed that
the development of the region's economy would be conducive
to an advance in the spiritual and moral level of the people.
Participation by the natives in a stable economy would, he
believed, lift them to cultural equality with the Russian
population. In spite of the limitations and drawbacks in the
application of the new laws, the promotion and safeguarding
of free economic activity by the new administration were
the major contributions of the statutes of 1822. They encouraged a new outlook and gave new direction to the region's
energies and resources. In so doing, the reforms of 1822
helped to open Siberia as the future agricultural and industrial
"frontier" of Russia.[1]

Speransky, nurtured on romantic "historicism," had no
wish to destroy the traditions and customs of the people.
Nor did he wish to alienate them by forcing them into new
ways. He felt, and history seems to have vindicated him,
that more thoroughgoing reforms could be accomplished
with the participation of the people than without it. He rejected
the reliance which Pestel and Treskin had placed on a clear
and radical break with tradition to be carried out through
harsh and authoritarian means. Instead, he hoped to awaken
the people's civic consciousness and to secure their willing
acceptance of the government's leadership. It was the only
sensible approach, Speransky believed, if the state were
to continue as the spiritual and moral guide of the nation.
Hence the importance he attached to the government's social
and cultural activities and to its fostering of private initiative
in economic matters. In the school of social, cultural, and
economic experience, the individual would reach spiritual
and moral maturity. In the long run, perhaps, this would lead

to the participation of the spiritually mature and economically successful individuals in the administrative and political life of the country. Such was Speransky's ultimate goal.

The legislation of 1822 therefore assigned to the bureaucracy a passive background role in the economic life of Siberia. The administration and its agents were relegated, as much as conditions permitted, to the spheres of government and politics in the strictest sense. Yet Speransky proved incapable of breaking completely with the old tradition of bureaucratic guidance in which he had grown up and risen to prominence. This tradition, neatly fitting into the practices of enlightened despotism, allowed the officials to retain their role of active moral leadership. The despotism of the individual bureaucrat, however, was tempered by the collegiate boards which were set up to assist and restrain him.

As a result, the people's range of social and cultural activity and of private initiative in economic matters was immensely widened; they were freer to develop their own way of life. The foundation was laid for the development of a new kind of man, the "Siberian man" of whom later "regionalist" writers loved to speak in such glowing terms. The new laws also helped to make Siberia an attractive and desirable place for the peasantry of European Russia, especially after the government finally permitted the peasants some freedom of movement in 1861. Speransky's awareness of the peculiarities of Siberia led him to try to give these peculiarities greater recognition in the administration of the region. In so doing, he contributed greatly to the development of a "regionalist" approach to local government. This too gave a greater feeling of dignity and self-esteem to the Siberian peoples, while paving the way for greater flexibility in the future administration of Siberia and other border regions of the empire. It was a tragedy that Speransky's successors in St. Petersburg did not follow his precepts wholeheartedly and never fully accepted his regionalistic outlook on local administration. Their failure in this respect had a decisively negative affect on the stability of the imperial regime in times of serious crisis.

It is perhaps a little more difficult to assess fully the meaning and implications of the policy expressed in the statutes in regard to the natives. It must be stated from the outset that, by and large, the Russian government had no clear and consistent attitude on this problem. We should be especially careful not to transpose mechanically the pattern found in one area to another. Except to a very limited degree (and that only after the beginning of the conquest of Central Asia in the 1860's), Siberia was spared the threat of external aggression. The Kazakh and Mongol raiders from across the "line" were nothing more than petty nuisances; China was no more a danger to Russia, even in the Amur region, while Japan had not yet appeared on the scene. Furthermore, the Siberian natives had no cultural, political, and social traditions which might constitute a threat to the foundations of the Russian Empire, as did, for instance, the Polish traditions of independence and aristocratic democracy, the Baltic "feudalism," or the cultural and religious ties which bound the Moslems of the Volga, the Crimea, and the Caucasus to the Turks. For these reasons, the attitude of the imperial administration towards the natives of Siberia was perhaps exceptional, and we should not equate it with governmental policies elsewhere.

Quite clearly, the central government rejected the concept of federation entirely--an attitude which proved a major factor in the collapse of imperial Russia. St. Petersburg considered the whole of Siberia, including the clearly defined areas inhabited by socially well-organized and culturally developed natives, as an integral part of Russia. Siberia could therefore not possess any of the privileges usually accorded to units of a federation. The deviations from the regular Russian administrative pattern which the statutes of 1822 permitted were of local significance only. They reflected practical necessities, imposed by geography and climate, which had to be recognized. In no way could they be construed as paving the way to regional "autonomy."

Logically, the anti-federalistic premise led to the belief that such a unitary empire as the Russian could be preserved only if the social and cultural patterns of its peoples were-- grosso modo --similar. In the absence of such similarity, the aim of the government was to create a Kulturgemeinschaft to support the existing Staatsgemeinschaft. Siberia was to be Russified in two senses: first, its economic and adminis- trative structure was to be linked organically with that of European Russia (this concerned primarily the Russian

population); secondly, the Siberian natives should eventually
enter and merge into the mainstream of the empire's economic, political, social, and cultural life. But to Speransky
and the government of Alexander I Russification did not imply
the forcible imposition of the Russian language, habits,
religion, etc. upon the natives. As we have seen, the government was careful not to destroy the traditional pattern of
native life and left intact its cultural and religious habits
and values. The policy rather was to draw the natives into the
Russian orbit gradually and voluntarily. It was an "organic"
(to use a term then very much in vogue) Russification.
Russification was to be promoted by having the natives realize
the virtues of Russian civilization and the advantages to be
derived from active participation in the social and economic
life of the empire. Such an approach, of course, was directed
more particularly at the native "aristocracy." The process
would also be furthered by the changes in the natives' social
organization that must result from a transformation of their
way of life and economy. It was as much this aim of eventually
bringing about a change in the natives' pattern of life as it
was crude fiscal and political interests which lay behind the
energetic efforts to settle the natives in agricultural pursuits.
As we have seen, the calculation proved quite accurate: to
the extent that the leaders of the more advanced native peoples
took up agriculture, they became interested in landownership
and increasingly tended to identify themselves with the social,
political, and economic values of the Russians, although
they retained many of the spiritual, religious, and cultural
practices of their nomadic ancestors. (Incidentally, a similar
approach was followed by the French colonial administration
in Indo-China, Africa, and the West Indies with varying
success in the late nineteenth and early twentieth centuries.)
     One method by which an organic Russification could be
accomplished was to bring the old customary laws of the
natives into harmony with Russian legal and administrative
norms. Not only would this clarify and improve the administration, but it would also teach the natives Russian concepts
and attitudes without forcing them to abandon their own traditional values abruptly. Codification of native customary law,
then, was undertaken with this aim in mind. This same motive
underlay Speransky's later codification of other regional customary laws, in southwestern Russia and in the Lithuanian-
White Russian provinces. If some of these codifications did not

find legislative implementation, it was the result of political circumstances not foreseen by the government (for example the Polish uprising of 1831 and the revolutions of 1848). In Siberia, as we have noted, the Code of the Steppe was put into practice in fact, though it did not receive full official sanction.

By and large, influential and progressive officials of imperial Russia--at least until the reign of Alexander III-- understood the value of preserving many of the moral and religious, as well as social, traits of the Siberian nation- alities. Not only should the positive elements of the national cultures be preserved, but they also should be incorporated into an imperial, all-Russian, civilization. On the other hand, Speransky and other "liberal" officials after him felt that Russian culture had much to offer the natives; in particular, as devout and sincere Christians, they were convinced that Greek Orthodoxy was the most important value that they could impart to other peoples. It need not be done by force, but neither should other religions be allowed to use "unfair" means to promote their own ends. [2]

To us today, many of the methods and attitudes expressed in the legislation of 1822 seem inadequate or even wrong. But we should not forget the conditions of Siberia and Russia at the beginning of the nineteenth century and should judge the attitudes and work of men like Speransky and the "liberal- conservative" (Prince Viazemskii's characterization of Pushkin) officials of later reigns in the light of these con- ditions. Their merit lay in having understood that a social and economic system founded on individual enterprise and freedom of activity must find support and protection in the administrative structure. And this could be attained only if the old-fashioned, inchoate, arbitrary practices were replaced by a clear, orderly, hierarchical system based on law. But they failed to realize that the full development of such an administration in fact tended to subvert the very essence of Russian autocracy. The emperors and conservatives at the court, however, sensed this implication. They refused to consider any change which would weaken their position and never gave a fair try to the approach and program advocated by enlightened bureaucrats like Speransky. Yet the ideals by which a statesman is guided and the ultimate goals he sets for himself belong to history as much as his actual deeds, for they are often a source of inspiration and a guide to those who come later under more propitious conditions. Thus the ideals upon which the Siberian statutes of 1822 were based are also significant. In spite of the shortcomings in the execution of this legislation, it instilled a new attitude into the people and the bureaucracy; it prepared the ground and indicated the direction for the future evolution of Siberia. Thereby it played a most important role in Siberia's development through-out the nineteenth century and to the very eve of the revolution.

Appendices

Appendices

APPENDIX I
PROMOTION OF AGRICULTURE AMONG THE BURIATS

Excerpts from source materials illustrating the government's promotion of agriculture among the Buriats. Translated from V. P. Girchenko (ed.), Sbornik materialov po istorii Buriatii XVIII i pervoi polovine XIX vv., Tsentral'noe Arkhivnoe Upravlenie Buriat-Mongol'skoi ASSR, vyp. 1 (Verkhneudinsk, 1926), pp. 2-10.

No. 2   Letter from the Chief Shulenga, Khabtagai Butukanov, to the Director of Economy of the Kuda Administration (vedomstvo), dated April 4, 1786:

Ten members of the Abagan Clan have enough land for agriculture, they have households and ploughed fields, "and they do not wish to have arable land lying fallow and wish to extend the area of ploughland, like the best peasants. They have asked to be given any sum of money, under proper security, to buy seed, tools, and as many horses as they need..." Besides these ten, forty-nine more Buriats wish subsidies.

No. 9   Letter of Treskin to the Chief Taisha, Tulaev, of the Buriats of the Kuda Clan, dated May 9, 1807 (under No. 2245):

"Herewith, I am forwarding a copy of my invitation to your fellow clansmen to redouble their efforts in extending

agriculture. I also request you, my dear sir, to make an
appropriate admonition consonant with the expectations of the
authorities. Knowledge of the zeal with which your honorable
predecessors and you yourself, dear sir, have endeavored
to spread among your clansmen all useful institutions, con-
vinces me even now that you will apply all your efforts to
spread agriculture for the benefit of your own clan. This proof
of your concern for the Buriats entrusted to your administration will earn for you the renewed right to expect special favor
from the authorities..." The letter concludes with Treskin's
demand for a list of the best and richest land tillers.

No. 10   Memorandum of Treskin, May, 1807 (No. 24,
          file No. 158):

"Among all the matters which compose the duties of
my office, the first and most important is agriculture; it
attracts all the attention and concern of the higher authorities
[nachal'stvo]; it is the single inexhaustible source of the
contentment, prosperity, and wealth of the inhabitants and
the primary cause of their multiplication. Siberia was unknown, barbarous, and unpopulated to the day agricultural
settlers came into it. They were the first to open the rich
veins of this rich earth. Lavishly rewarded, their labors
proved to the peoples of Siberia that tilling the soil is the
most profitable of all occupations... I address myself to
you, settlers, with the invitation, sweetest to my heart, to
follow their [first peasant settlers'] example at the first sign
of the coming of spring, and to direct all your industry to the
working of your lands, the most useful labor for you and for
society." Treskin continues with a paean to the earth and
then argues that other occupations than agriculture may be
more profitable immediately but less durable and secure in
the long run. "Buriats and other peoples of Siberia! It is to
you, more than to anyone else, that I direct this invitation.
Thanks be rendered to your honorable clansmen who fell in
love with agriculture and have shown to their fellow tribesmen its advantages over all occupations!... Besides your
personal economic profit, you will see the consideration and
benefactions which our most gracious Sovereign, the Emperor,
will shower on those who turn to agriculture.... All necessary
aid will be rendered and appreciable rewards given to those

agriculturists whose industry will be certified by the authorities.

The Civilian Governor of Irkutsk, Treskin "

APPENDIX II
M. M. SPERANSKY ON FREEDOM OF TRADE

Speransky's views on freedom of economic activity are best set forth by himself in the following two documents given in full by Vagin, Istoricheskie svedeniia..., Vol. I, pp. 178 and 350-52.

1

Excerpts from Speransky's instructions to Tseidler (Zeidler), Civilian Governor of Irkutsk, September 4, 1821:

"a. Freedom of Grain Trade: The curbs permitted during the last years, the erroneous rules under which grain supplies were collected, the compulsory and arbitrary prices which were established, and the abuses which accompanied all this, led to complete disorganization in this area. While the grain was not purchased from the peasants but collected on the basis of per capita assessment, while its price was arbitrarily lowered and maintained at a forced low, agriculture naturally declined instead of expanding. And though on paper and according to official reports the amount of ploughed acreage increased year by year, in reality the amount planted was barely sufficient for the minimum needs. Surplus and reserves were insignificant. To this must be added that the last years were years of crop failure; there were also early freezes and big floods. Together, all these causes produced a rise in prices. One could have kept the prices within their previous limits if one had permitted the former arbitrary rules. But I considered it much more useful to bring the building of a grain reserve into a legal framework, and allow a temporary rise in prices rather than continue the previous errors and prepare the way to an unavoidable decline in agriculture for the sake of a temporary alleviation of the situation. I am convinced that if God blesses the present year with even an average harvest, free grain prices will be moderate, and that the agriculturist will find in the free sale [of his crop] the needed incentive if he also is assured that the government will buy the grain from him and will not collect it through arbitrary assessments."

2

Speransky's proposals to the City Duma of Irkutsk, June 19, 1820:

"In considering the ways of supplying the city of Irkutsk with grain, I find, on the basis of the information submitted to me, that already for a long time they differ from the usual method common to all cities. To the burgher of average or small means [the Irkutsk method] provides neither advantageous prices nor the necessary regularity [of supply]. The method practiced now consists in that the wealthy build up a reserve in due time, while the average or poor burgher must buy grain either from peasants coming to the market irregularly and bringing insufficient quantities, or else from the so-called state flour shops [labaz]; consequently, there is no permanent free trade [in grain] at all. The inconveniences of this situation are quite important: (a) the limited quantity of flour coming to the market raises its prices to a level at which it brings hardship to the burghers; (b) state stores, which in other cities exist exclusively to help the poorest and neediest citizens and to lower the prices only in extreme cases, have here [in Irkutsk] become a regular means of meeting the city's supply needs and have arrogated a trade which is oppressive for private individuals and contrary to the rules. It is known that in Irkutsk there had once existed a free trade in grain, that there had existed private reserves and unimpeded private sale [in grain]. [Speransky's italics]

"Without entering here into a consideration of the causes which produced a change in that system, I consider it my duty to submit the following to the City Duma of Irkutsk:

"(1) Article 167 of the Statute on Towns provides that 'among other affairs, it is the concern of the City Duma to supply the inhabitants of the town with the necessary foodstuffs for the nourishment and sustenance of its citizens.' On the basis of this provision the Irkutsk Duma will not fail to begin considering measures to re-establish a permanent private trade in grain in the city and to open private [free] flour shops.

"(2) In the name of the Government, the Duma will assure

all private individuals wishing to open this type of [grain] trade, that there will be absolutely no curbs on their purchases [of grain] in the districts [uezds] or on the sales price [of grain] in that city; on the contrary, the Government will firmly maintain the rule that the trade in domestic products, and particularly in foodstuffs, is to be completely open and free both in the country districts and in the city to all those legally entitled to engage in it.

"(3) It is well known that many regulations which are hampering private traders have occasionally been permitted under the pretext of [preventing] monopoly [perekup]. In its true and legal meaning, there is monopoly when one, two, three, or more traders of merchandise which is brought from the villages to the city and already on its way buy up the goods on the road in secret agreement among themselves for the benefit of one [group or individual], prevent their direct sale to others, and then impose their own arbitrary and excessive prices. That is why the purchase and storage of grain by private individuals in the country districts, which was common practice at one time, and the transporting of this grain to the cities on a contractual basis can never be and should never be called a monopoly. Anyone who has the legal right to engage in trade is free to buy grain in the district and to sell it in the city, without any restrictions, either as to price or as to quantity; and the only curb consists in limiting an excessive rise in prices by the [existence of] state stores.

"(4) As a consequence of the loss of habit for such an [open] trade and because of ingrained distrust, merchants with small capital will certainly be afraid to start such a trade. It is, therefore, the task of well-meaning and enlightened citizens to encourage such a type of enterprise by their example and concern; they must show the way in helping the common good, not so much for the sake of their own private interests, as for the honor of their class. They should not permit that one of the first towns of Siberia be alone, not only in Siberia but perhaps also in the whole of Russia, in depending for its supply of food on state stores, which had been established for the poor, and on a small and irregular market.

"(5) The City Duma shall not fail to report to me [the names of] those who will indicate their willingness to establish flour stores starting next year, i.e., 1821, and the quantity [of flour] they will deal in, so that on the basis of this information I can give orders concerning the quantity of grain to be kept in reserve by state stores."

APPENDIX III
THE SIBERIAN ADMINISTRATION

1. The Administrative Division of Siberia (PSZ, 29,125)

Type of Division	Governor-generalship	Province (gubernia)	Region (oblast')	District (okrug)	Town (gorod)	Township Russian (volost')	Township Native (inorodnaia uprava)	Village Russian (selenie)	Village Native (ulus)
Name of Division	Western Siberia / Eastern Siberia	Tomsk, Tobolsk / Irkutsk, Eniseisk	Omsk / Iakutsk, Maritime*, Troitsko-Savsk*	Tomsk 6, Tobolsk 9, Omsk 4 / Irkutsk 5, Eniseisk 5, Iakutsk 5					
Type of Administration	Main Administration (Governor-general and Council)	Provincial Administration (Civil governor and council)	Regional Administration (Chief combining civil and military functions and council)	District Administration (Chief and council) 3 types: 1) general 2) separate-division 3) under-populated	Mayor (golova) and Council (duma)	Head (golova) and Elder (starosta) and Clerk (pisar')	Head (golova) and 2 Elders (starosta) and Clerk (pisar')	Elder (starosta) and Assistants (desiatniki)	Clan Elder and Assistants

* Special administrative arrangement (see section 2 of this appendix)

2. The Regional Administrations

The regions of Omsk and Iakutsk had identical organizations. The region was headed by a chief of the region (oblastnoi
nachal'nik), who was at the same time the divisional commander of the military forces stationed there. Like the civil
governor of a regular province, the chief of the region was
assisted by a council composed of the president of the general
administration (like the provincial board), the president of the
regional court, the regional procurator, the military ataman
(the chief of the local Cossacks), the regional engineer, and
the military auditor (ober-auditor). The functions of this
administration were similar to those of the provincial administration, except that the chief of the region also exercised
military justice and maintained relations with representatives
of the foreign countries across his region's borders.

The districts included in the regions were administered
as follows: at the head of their administration was the chief
of the district, who was also the commandant of the local
fortress, assisted by a council. The district council was
composed of the commandant of the capital town (plats-
maior), the town police chief (gorodnichii), the district
judge, the treasurer, and the elected town mayor, if any.
The three functions of administration--police, economy, and
justice--were taken care of by a land court, the district
treasury administration, and the district court. The composition of the land court differed somewhat from that of
the land courts of the regular Siberian districts; it consisted
of the eldest Cossack regimental commander (as chairman),
a Cossack official, and one or two civilian deputies.

In the Omsk region, the districts situated along the
Kirghiz steppe line did not have any functional division of
administrative duties. Police, economy, and justice were
taken care of by a district bureau (prikaz) composed of the
eldest Kirghiz sultan, two Russian deputies, and two men
chosen from the Kirghiz nobility. (PSZ 21, 125, pars. 321-398)

The Maritime region (on the shores of the Pacific Ocean)
had no over-all administration. It consisted of two autonomous
subdivisions, each on the same level as a district: Kamchatka
and Okhotsk. The administration of Kamchatka paralleled
that of a general district, except that its chief was the military commander of the area. The administration of Okhotsk
was also like that of a general district, but its chief was the

naval officer commanding the port of Okhotsk. In addition to his regular duties as naval commander and district chief, this officer was to see to it that the Russian-American Trading Company did not use government facilities for its own private advantage and in general did not exceed the rights and privileges granted to it under its charter. (PSZ 29,125; pars. 399-436)

The Troitsko-Savsk Frontier administration had as its main function the guarding of the Siberian-Chinese border. Its head was the border chief (pogranichnyi nachal'nik),who was an official of the Ministry of Foreign Affairs. The border chief was assisted by a council of six representatives elected by Russian and native Cossacks, and one councilor nominated upon the recommendation of the civil governor of Irkutsk. The Troitsko-Savsk frontier was subdivided into three divisions (otdelenie): Tsurukhaisk, Kharatsaisk, and Tunka. In each division the administration--similar to that of a separate district--was taken care of by a frontier commissary (pogranichnyi pristav), who was chosen from among the Russian Cossack officers. (PSZ 29,125, pars. 436-472)

APPENDIX IV
THE NATIVE PEOPLES OF SIBERIA

1. List and classification by the Ministry of the Interior in 1810.

The list and classification of Siberian natives given by the anonymous author of an official publication serves as a good illustration of the Imperial Government's inadequate information and "unscientific" methods. The list is found in the official Statisticheskoe obozrenie Sibiri, sostavlennoe na osnovanii svedenii, pocherpnutykh iz aktov pravitel'stvennykh i drugikh dostovernykh istochnikov (Statistical survey of Siberia based on data taken from government documents and other reliable sources), Ministerstvo Vnutrennikh Del, St. Petersburg, 1810:

I. Of Finnish origin: Permiaks, Zyrians, Votiaks, Cheremisy, Voguls, Ob' Ostiaks

II. Of Tatar origin: Turalintsy, Tatars (from Tobolsk,

Tomsk, Ob' river, Baraba, Chulyma, Kachin),
Teleuts, Kistinsk Tatars, Abintsy, Tatars from
Verkhne-Tomsk and Saian, Biriusy, Bel'shiry,
Bashkirs, Meshchery, Bukhars, Kirghiz (i.e.,
Kazakhs), Iakuts.

III. Of Mongol origin: Buriats, Kalmyks, Mongols proper.

IV. Manchu peoples: Tungus.

V. Of unknown origin: Samoeds, Iukagirs, Kamchadals,
Koriaks, Chukchi, Kurilians, Aleutians.

2. A modern list and classification (1927)

A modern list and classification is found in N.I. Zarubin,
Spisok Narodov SSSR (List of Nationalities of the USSR) (Trudy
Kommissii po izucheniu plemennogo sostava naseleniia SSSR
i sopredel'nykh stran; N. 13, Leningrad, 1927), pp. 24 ff.
Reproduced below is the section of the list which deals with
the population of Siberia within its appropriate 1820 boundaries
(figures in parentheses indicate date of census quoted).

Compare population figures with those of 1796 quoted
in section three of this appendix.

Finno-Ugrians: Northeastern (Perm') Finns:
    93. Zyrians   186,108 (1920) (about 10,000 in Tobolsk
and Tomsk regions)
    94. Permiaks   128,132 (1920)
    95. Votiaks   466,182 (1920)
Ugrians:
    97. Ostiaks   18,591 (1911)
    98. Voguls (Mans, Iugres) 6,814 (1911)
Samoeds
    99. Samoeds   18,021 (1920)
Turkic peoples: Northwestern branch:
    101. Kumandintsy   873 (1917)
    102. Altaians (mountain or white Kalmyks) 26,084 (1897)
    103. Telengets   9,200 (1897)
    104. Teleuts   7,000 (1923)
    113. Bashkirs   320,743 (1897)
    117. Tobolsk Tatars   37,637 (1898)

118. Siberian Bukhars   11,659 (1897)
119. Baraba Tatars   4,433 (1897)
121. Kazakhs ca. 4 million (Kirghiz, Kirghiz-Kaisak)
122. Chulyma Turks   11,123 (1897)
123. Kyrgyz (Kara Kirghiz) 643,099 (1924)
Southeastern branch:
134. Black Tatars   6,342 (1897) (in Altai)
135. Tomsk-Kuznetsk Tatars   8,164 (1897)
Northeastern branch:
136. Shortsy   14,809 (1897) (Kuznetsk)
137. Lebedintsy   907 (1897) (on Bii river)
138. Kyzyl'tsy   7,959 (1897) (Achinsk district)
139. Sagaitsy   3,019 (1897)
140. Kachintsy   11,974 (1897)
141. Bel'tirs   7,959 (1897)
142. Koibals   1,015 (1897)
143. Kamasintsy   137 (1890) (Kansk district)
144. Soiots   ca. 2,500
145. Karagas   389 (1897)
146. Iakuts   220,040 (1917)
147. Dolgans   967 (1897)
Mongols:
148. Buriats   220,442 (1924)
149. Kalmyks   140,000 (1920)
150. Sart Kalmyks   2,405 (1917) (Kirghiz ASSR)
Tungus-Manchus: Tungus
151. Tungus (properly speaking)   53,194 (1897)
152. Lamuts   9,049 (1897)
153. Negidal'tsy   423 (1897)
Manchus:
154. Gol'ds   5,441 (1897)
155. Ol'chians   2,204 (1897)
Paleo-asiatic peoples:
157. Chukchi   12,000 (1900)
158. Koriaks   6,702 (1924)
159. Kamchadals   5,700 (1924)
160. Iukagirs   1,003 (1901)
161. Chuvantsy   452 (1901)
162. Enisei Ostiaks   1,281 (1917)
163. Giliaks   4,298 (1911)
164. Asiatic Eskimos   1,134 (1925)
165. Aleutians   501 (1909)
Another list, less complete and detailed, on the basis of

the 1897 census (as reported and analyzed by S. Patkanov) is
to be found in M. A. Czaplicka, Aboriginal Siberia: a study
in social anthropology (Oxford University, 1914), pp. 18-20.

3. Population figures on the natives (1796)

Figures giving a breakdown by peoples and closest to
the period studied were those of the Fifth Census (1796) as
quoted in the Statisticheskoe obozrenie Sibiri published by
the Ministry of the Interior in 1810. Figures given here indicate only taxable souls and cannot be considered as absolutely
correct. The administrative divisions are those of the pre-
Speransky period: part of Perm' province was incorporated
into the West Siberian Governor-generalship; the province
of Iakutsk was still a subdivision of Irkutsk.

PEOPLES	PERM' Prov.	TOBOLSK and TOMSK	IRKUTSK	TOTAL
Voguls	847	2,017		2,864
Cheremis	639			639
Tetery	1,838			1,838
Ostiaks		18,691		18,691
Tatars	5,629	26,093		31,722
Bashkirs	13,508			13,508
Bukhars		2,895		2,895
Iakuts		258	50,676	50,934
Buriats			58,765	58,765
Kalmyks		1,158		1,158
Mongols			96	96
Tungus-Lamuts		2,306	13,807	16,113

Samoeds	3,398	163	3,561
Iukagirs		505	505
Kamchadals		1,782	1,782
Koriaks, Omotry		1,470	1,470
Kurilians		100	100
TOTAL (souls)	22,461	56,816	127,364	206,641

Notes

ABBREVIATIONS

AGS   Arkhiv Gosudarstvennogo Soveta

The following symbols identify the volumes in the series:

I-2   Otdelenie iuridicheskoe - Protokoly tsarstvovaniia imperatritsy Ekateriny II (1768-1796)

II   Soviet v Tsarstvovanie Imperatora Pavla I (1796-1801)

III   Vols. 1 and 2, Tsarstvovanie Imperatora Aleksandra I (1801-1810)

IV   Tsarstvovanie Imperatora Aleksandra I (1810-1825)
     IV,A   Vols. 1-5, Zhurnal po delam Departamenta Grazhdanskikh i Dukhovnykh Del
     IV,B   Vols. 1-2, Zhurnal po Departamentu Zakonov
     IV,C   Vol. 1 (1818-20), Zhurnal Departamenta Zakonov po grazhdanskomu otdeleniu
     IV,D   Vols. 1-2, Departament Gosudarstvennoi Ekonomii

V   Tsarstvovanie Imperatora Nikolaia I (1825-1826)

Chtenniia...   Chteniia Imperatorskogo Obshchestva Istorii i Drevnostei Rossiiskikh pri Moskovskom Universitete

PSZ   Polnoe Sobranie Zakonov Rossiiskoi Imperii s 1649 goda

Sbornik IRIO   Sbornik Imperatorskogo Rossiiskogo Istoricheskogo Obshchestva

ZhKM   Zhurnaly Komiteta Ministrov - tsarstvovanie imperatora Aleksandra I, 1802-1826

Notes

INTRODUCTION

    1. F. F. Vigel', Zapiski (Moscow, 1892), p. 196.

    2. This circumstance reduces our sources and materials to a few well-defined categories which need no special critical comment at this point. Suffice it to list them: in the first place ranks the Polnoe Sobranie Zakonov, a compendium which includes all official general legislation as well as many orders, decrees, and instructions issued to individuals on specific occasions. Further, we are very fortunate to possess the records and minutes of the Council of State and the Committee of Ministers for the reign of Alexander I, and in them we can follow the story of many local events and problems whose import otherwise would have remained unknown or unclear to us. There are also several source collections (of unequal value) for official material on specific problems (for example, the China border). Next to these official, government sources, we are able to draw on some memoir literature. Unfortunately, it is limited in scope and poor in quality; it has to be used with great caution, the more so since its information cannot always be checked against more reliable sources. Finally, for the history of the natives in particular, the descriptions and reports of travels and explorations by scientists and amateurs are of great help.

PART I

CHAPTER I

    1. For example the nakaz (instruction) to Siberian

voevodas in 1670, 1694, quoted by V. I. Ogorodnikov, "Russkaia gosudarstvennaia vlast' i sibirskie inorodtsy XVI-XVIII vv.," Sbornik trudov professorov i prepodavatelei Gosudarstvennogo Irkutskogo Universiteta, otd. I, vyp. 1 (Irkutsk, 1921), p. 89. See also N. Koz'min, "Istoriia Sibiri," Sibirskaia Sovetskaia Entsiklopediia, II, 394.

2. There is no need for us to describe the Siberian colonial administration in the seventeenth century. This has been done excellently by G. V. Lantzeff, Siberia in the XVIIth century - a study of the colonial administration (Berkeley, 1943).

3. Pogranichnyi dozorshchik or pogranichnyi komissar established to supervise the Russo-Chinese border posts and to administer the border region. See Sychevskii, Istoricheskaia zapiska o kitaiskoi granitse (St. Pbg., 1846), pp. 25-36 passim.

4. Voltaire, Essai sur les moeurs et l'esprit des nations, in Oeuvres complètes (Paris, 1878), XIII, 182.

5. See S. G. Svatikov, Rossiia i Sibir' (Prague, 1929), p. 6.

6. PSZ, 11,989 (Dec. 15, 1763), par. 17, reads: "The Siberian Prikaz is not to be [any more], and the Siberian Province, like the others, has to refer all matters to the relevant Colleges, and, therefore, all affairs heretofore dealt with in the above mentioned Prikaz should be distributed among the Colleges and Chanceries..."

7. PSZ, 15,327 (Jan. 19, 1782), established the Lieutenancy of Tobolsk; 15,675 (Mar. 2, 1783) established the province of Irkutsk; 15,679 (Mar. 6, 1783) established Kolyvansk province.

8. "Because of the large size of the region [Irkutsk province] the zemskie ispravniki [land captains] are to be assisted by 'noblemen's deputies' in the lower land courts, and because there are no noblemen there, the positions are to be filled by nobles from other provinces [i.e., officials]," PSZ, 15,675 (Mar. 2, 1783), par. 3. Similar regulations are given for the courts in equity, PSZ, 15,680 (Mar. 6, 1783).

9. For instance, Peter the Great specifically forbade the election of Siberian merchants to the office of burmistr in the towns. S. Prutchenko, Sibirskie okrainy (St. Pbg., 1899), Vol. I, p. 45, cites PSZ, 1,708 (Oct. 27, 1699).

10. Cf. F. A. Kudriavtsev, Istoriia buriat-mongol'skogo naroda ot XVIII v. do 60 kh godov XIX v. (Moscow-Leningrad, 1940), p. 129.

11. PSZ, 15,680, quoted in note 8 above. This should not lead to the conclusion that the nobility in European Russia had true self-government and autonomy. In practice the Russian government never allowed even the nobility to administer its own affairs freely. The history of local government in Russia from 1775 until the middle of the nineteenth century is one of perennial, though not always effective, bureaucratic interference and control.

12. The statute on the provinces, 1775, is in PSZ, 14, 392.

13. I. Blinov, Gubernatory - istoriko-iuridicheskii ocherk (St. Pbg., 1905), p. 174; A.D. Gradovskii, "Istoricheskii ocherk uchrezhdeniia general-gubernatorov v Rossii," Russkii Vestnik, XI (Nov., 1869), 5-31, and XII (Dec., 1869), 396-413; see especially pp. 16-17. This tendency of the governors-general to assume viceregal power explains the rapid disappearance of the office of governor-general in Russia proper, except in special cases.

14. Obozrenie glavnykh osnovanii mestnogo upravleniia Sibiri (St. Pbg., 1841), pp. 15-17.

15. AGS, III-1, pp. 70-71.

16. AGS, III-1, p. 71.

17. PSZ, 19,910, pp. 693-94. See also Ministerstvo Vnutrennikh Del, Statisticheskoe obozrenie Sibiri (St. Pbg., 1810), pp. 72-73.

18. A mayor (gorodskoi golova) was in those days the spokesman of the merchant class. He was elected by his fellow burghers, usually on the basis of a rather limited franchise. He represented and spoke for the burghers of his city and transmitted those orders and regulations of the government which concerned the townspeople, as for example, distributing the fiscal burden and assigning individuals to public services and works. He also had limited disciplinary powers over the burghers, in case of nonfulfillment of obligations, and often served as mediator in civil and monetary litigation between members of his class.

19. AGS, III-2, pp. 989-99 (minutes for session of Mar. 8, 1809).

20. PSZ, 20,771. See also "Otchet Ministerstva Vnutrennikh Del za 1803 god" in ZhKM, I, 76.

21. A contemporary observer described the function of these commissariats in the following terms: "In the districts with commissariats the executive department of the provincial administration [gubernskoe pravlenie] nominates local land commissars [zemskii komissar] as staff members of the land police [zemskaia politsiia]. [These commissars] see to the good conduct and order in the villages and ulus or the encampments of nomads under the jurisdiction of the commissariats; they conduct all kinds of investigations and in particular enforce the collection of government taxes." There were five such districts with a total of nineteen commissariats. N. Semivskii, Noveishie i dostovernye povestvovaniia o Vostochnoi Sibiri (St. Pbg., 1817), Appendix, p. 73.

22. Obozrenie glavnykh osnovanii..., pp. 18-22.

23. See V.V. Sviatlovskii, Istoriia ekonomicheskikh idei v Rossii (Petrograd, 1923), Chap. VI, in particular pp. 95-100.

24. R.M. Kabo, Goroda Zapadnoi Sibiri (Moscow, 1949), p. 115; Sviatlovskii, op. cit., p. 96.

25. An interesting illustration of this newly discovered awareness is provided by the comments of a Polish observer, a member of the anti-Russian Confederation who came to Siberia as an exile in the 1770's: "We had heard much about Siberia as a deserted and unpopulated country; actually we found everywhere [in Western Siberia] surplus, prosperity, populated villages with a people much more humane than in Russia. [Near Tiumen'] we had to travel through relatively prosperous villages." M. Serno-Solov'evich (ed.), "Zapiski poliaka-konfederata soslannogo v Sibir' 1768-1776," Russkii Arkhiv, 1886, No. 1, p. 289.

26. This did not preclude the illegal and elemental migration of peasants to Siberia, particularly in the seventeenth century. But if we recall the role played in the history of the Rostov, Vladimir, Suzdal', and Moscow areas by a colonization stimulated and sponsored by the appanaged princes, grand dukes, and other noblemen, the lack of interest of the nobility in Siberia becomes noteworthy. No doubt the government's tardy awareness of Siberia's agricultural wealth reflects the nobility's lack of interest in the area.

27. For example, an eighteenth century ukaz reminded the local officials "to see strictly to it that persons from the clergy do not engage in commerce under the pretext of traveling for the needs of the spiritual salvation of mankind."

Quoted in N. M. Iadrintsev, Sibir' kak koloniia (St. Pbg.,
1882.), p. 416. See also A. P. Shchapov, "Sibirskoe obshchestvo
do Speranskogo," Sochineniia A. P. Shchapova, Vol. III (St.
Pbg., 1908), p. 647, and V. K. Andrievich, Istoriia Sibiri
(St. Pbg., 1887), II, 236.

28. The "line" (liniia, in European Russia called cherta)
was the border between the settled area of Siberia, under the
firm control of the administration, and the uncontrolled
expanse of territory occupied by nomadic peoples. The line
consisted of a string of military outposts--small fortresses at
strategic crossroads--inhabited by Cossacks, some peasants,
merchants, or friendly native tribes. It was never completely
fixed and moved with the expansion of Russian settlement
and the establishment of firmer political control over the
neighboring tribes. Not until the end of the nineteenth century
did the "line" coincide with the empire's international borders,
and then it disappeared.

29. See S. S. Shashkov, "Sibirskie inorodtsy v XIXm
stoletii," Istoricheskie etiudy, II (St. Pbg., 1872), p. 175.

30. A. N. Radishchev noted that even peasants combined
into one partnership to trade in Kiakhta. "Pis'mo o kitaiskoi
torgovle," Polnoe Sobranie Sochinenii, ed. V. V. Kallash
(Moscow, 1907), Vol. II, pp. 76-77. See also Radishchev,
"Zapiski puteshestviia v Sibir'," Polnoe Sobranie Sochinenii,
p. 34, and Statisticheskoe obozrenie Sibiri, p. 81.

31. Shchapov, op. cit., pp. 648-49.

32. Shashkov, "Rabstvo v Sibiri," Istoricheskie etiudy
(St. Pbg., 1872), pp. 121-22.

33. Iadrintsev, op. cit., p. 412, for example. On slavery
in Siberia, see article by Shashkov, "Rabstvo v Sibiri."

34. P. A. Slovtsov, Istoricheskoe obozrenie Sibiri, II,
213; Iadrintsev, op. cit., p. 415. Further on this question,
consult Lantzeff, op. cit., and Raymond H. Fisher, The
Russian Fur Trade, 1550-1700 (Berkeley, 1943).

35. Iadrintsev, op. cit., p. 423. For more details on the
demands of Siberian deputies, see Prutchenko, op. cit., I,
76-93.

36. For a contemporary opinion, see "Otryvki o Sibiri,"
in Dukh Zhurnalov for 1815, p. 572.

37. Radishchev, "Pis'mo o kitaiskoi torgovle," Polnoe
Sobranie Sochinenii, pp. 68, 78.

38. Koz'min, op. cit., II, 381.

39. Radishchev, "Zapiski puteshestviia v Sibir'," Polnoe

Sobranie Sochinenii. Also, on peasant trade with western
Mongolia, see Andrievich, op. cit., II, 268.

40. AGS, III-1, p. 401.

41. ZhKM, II, 428 (under May 7, 1812).

42. See Lantzeff, op. cit., pp. 162-71; V.I. Shunkov,
Ocherki po istorii kolonizatsii Sibiri v XVII i nachale XVIII v.
(Moscow, 1946), p. 22, quotes excerpts from an interesting
order of Boris Godunov. Statisticheskoe obozrenie Sibiri,
p. 76; ukaz of Mar. 26, 1752, in G.N. Potanin, "Materialy
dlia istorii Sibiri," Chteniia..., 1866, No. 4, p. 22.

43. On the central government's attitude toward the
nobility and serfdom in general, see the suggestive pages of
P.B. Struve, "Istoricheskii smysl russkoe revoliutsii," in
Sotsial'naia i ekonomicheskaia istoriia Rossii (Paris, 1952).

44. For example, on state subsidies to the Nerchinsk
factories, see ZhKM, I, 12 (under Sept. 23, 1802); Slovtsov,
op. cit., II, 33.

45. Potanin, "Materialy...," Chteniia..., pp. 261-62.
See also the exhaustive study of the factory system in the
Urals by R. Portal, L'Oural au XVIIIième siècle (Paris,
1950), in particular pp. 43-46.

46. Statisticheskoe obozrenie Sibiri, p. 84. Kantseliariia
Komiteta Ministrov, ed. N. Razumov, Zabaikal'e: svod
materialov... (St. Pbg., 1899), p. 22; V. Kliuchevskii,
Kurs Russkoi istorii (Moscow, 1937), V, 121.

47. V. Girchenko, Iz istorii pereseleniia v Pribaikal'e
staroobriadtsev semeiskikh (Verkhneudinsk, 1921?), p. 3.

48. Slovtsov, op. cit., II, 34; Girchenko, op. cit., p.3.

49. For details, see Girchenko, op. cit., pp. 1-8.

50. AGS, II, pp. 571-82 (under Oct. 15, 1799); PSZ,
19, 157.

51. AGS, IV, D-2, pp. 993-1020 (minutes for Oct. 21,
1810, Sept. 21, 1817, Dec. 8, 1822); also Prutchenko, op. cit.,
I, 71-72 (ukaz of Dec. 15, 1801).

52. Razumov, Zabaikal'e..., pp. 57-58; Girchenko,
op. cit., p. 9.

CHAPTER II

1. F. Vigel', Zapiski (Moscow, 1892), p. 166; V.
Shteingel', "Sibirskie satrapy," Istoricheskii Vestnik, vol. 17
(Aug., 1884), p. 376.

2. For example of Pestel's insistence on bureaucratic

help, see AGS, IV, A-1, pp. 33-36 (under June 30, 1810).

3. On Pestel consult: P. Maikov, "I.B. Pestel'," Russkii Biograficheskii slovar', XIII (St. Pbg., 1902), pp. 593-99; N.N. Firsov, Chteniia po istorii Sibiri (Moscow, 1920-21), II, 12; I. Kalashnikov, "Zapiski irkutskogo zhitelia," Russkaia Starina, vol. 123 (July, 1905), p. 193.

4. Descriptions of and comments on Treskin can be found in: E.I. Stogov-Mozhaiskii, "Ocherki, rasskazy, vospominaniia," Russkaia Starina, vol. 23 (1878), pp. 503-7; V.I. Shteingel', op. cit., p. 377; Kalashnikov, op. cit., pp. 222-23; Shchapov, op. cit., pp. 674-77 (who cites Treskin's popularity in spite of his harshness); many statements of contemporaries were gathered forty years later by Vagin who interviewed the survivors. They are reproduced in part in the appendix to Vol. I of V.I. Vagin's book Istoricheskie svedeniia o deiatel'nosti grafa M.M. Speranskogo v Sibiri s 1819 po 1822 g. (St. Pbg., 1872). They should be used with caution.

5. Hereafter, we shall use the names of Treskin and Pestel interchangeably, as synonymous. For indeed, during Pestel's ten years' stay in St. Petersburg, Treskin governed Siberia in his name; and all the opinions, information, and recommendations presented by Pestel to the Council of State, Senate, and Ministries were in fact conceived and written by Treskin.

6. Kalashnikov, op. cit., pp. 202, 236-37; Shteingel', op. cit., pp. 382-83; Vagin, op. cit., I, 87. Cf. the representation made by the governor-general of Siberia to the Committee of Ministers for a greater police force in Irkutsk, ZhKM, I, 323 (July 20, 1809).

7. In addition to the references in note 4, note the comment of Shteingel', usually highly inimical to Treskin, "I confess it: I like, even respect Treskin...." Op. cit., p. 385.

8. Iadrintsev, Sibir' kak koloniia, p. 552; Vagin, op. cit., II, 129-31.

9. AGS, IV, A-5, pp. 133-36 (July 20, Nov. 16, Nov. 20, 1811). Approved by the emperor Dec. 18, 1811. It is true that in this Treskin followed up an idea of Governor-general Jacobi under Catherine II.

10. ZhKM, I, 278 (April, 14, 1809). These measures also show to what extent business transactions were hamstrung by bureaucratic red tape and the excessive centralization of Russia's administration.

11. ZhKM, II, 174 (May 3, 1811). Strictly speaking, only nobles could own estates, i.e., land inhabited and worked by serfs.

12. AGS, IV, D-1, p. 504.

13. Quoted in Girchenko, op. cit., p. 14.

14. ZhKM, II, 657 (Dec. 24, 1812).

15. ZhKM, II, 7 (Jan. 19, 1810).

16. "Inasmuch as these people have become inhabitants of Siberia, they should, of course, have the opportunity of seeking their well-being and the conveniences offered by local conditions. Otherwise, they cannot attain the good circumstances which are desired by the government itself, while the good of the community demands it and even stimulates them [ex-convicts] to it...." ZhKM, II, 339 (Feb. 14, 1812).

17. AGS, III-2, pp. 1118-22.

18. The Decembrist N.A. Bestuzhev exaggerated somewhat when he described the origin of the new Buriat economy: "The former governor of Irkutsk, Treskin, was the first to establish agriculture among the Buriats. A Buriat told me how he had ploughed the land first given by the government with a plough or more correctly a hoe...." N.A. Bestuzhev, "Buriatskoe khoziaistvo," Dekabristy v Buriatii (Verkhneudinsk, 1927), p. 12.

19. AGS, IV, D-2, pp. 681-84 (Feb. 15, 1818). See the sources given in Appendix I.

20. In the terminology of the period studied here, the Kirghiz properly speaking were not differentiated from the Kazakh tribes. As a matter of fact, in all instances of concern to us, where the contemporary Russian sources speak of the Kirghiz (or Kirghiz-Kaissaks), they refer to the Kazakhs of present-day Kazakhstan (approximately the Kazakh SSR).

21. ZhKM, II, 429-30 (May 7, 1812).

22. 1 chetvert = 2 hectoliters.

23. AGS, IV, D-2, p. 1819.

24. On village and state granaries, see Entsiklopedicheskii Slovar', Vol. XXV (book 49), pp. 354-61 passim. After 1817, only Siberia and some outlying border provinces preserved state stores; cf. S.M. Seredonin, Istoricheskii obzor deiatel'nosti Komiteta Ministrov (St. Pbg., 1902), I, 159; ZhKM, II, 173 (May 3, 1811).

25. ZhKM, II, 320 (Jan. 24, 1812).

26. As illustrated by the order of the Ispravnik Geden-shtrom to the elder of the Pesterovskoe village, Oct. , 1814: "I prescribe to you to assemble immediately all the peasants under your jurisdiction and to inform them that they have to present themselves, all without fault, next morning before dawn, for the sale of grain, in the town of Tarbagataisk." Quoted by Girchenko, op. cit. , p. 16; also cf. AGS, IV, D-2, p. 1808.

27. ZhKM, II, 627 (Nov. 28, 1812).

28. PSZ, 21,273.

29. ZhKM, I, 212 (Oct. 16, 1808).

30. AGS, IV, D-1, pp. 459-61 (Dec. 1, 1811).

31. ZhKM, I, 301 (June 16, 1809) and II, 143-44 (Feb. 8, 1811).

32. Shchapov, op. cit. , pp. 656, 657, 673; Iadrintsev, op. cit. , p. 421.

33. Iadrintsev, op. cit. , pp. 398-401; also Andrievich, Sibir' v XIX st. (St. Pbg. , 1889), I, 219-20.

34. ZhKM, II, 700.

35. ZhKM, II, 627 (Nov. 28, 1812).

36. Shchapov, op. cit. , pp. 669-70; also Lantzeff, Struve, and standard works on Russian economic life in the seven-teenth century. In some ways this situation is reminiscent of the conditions in Flanders at the time of the outbreak of the Hundred Years' War.

37. ZhKM, II, 562-66 (Sept. 24, 1812).

38. ZhKM, II, 180, 272 (May 17, 1811 and Nov. 22, 1811).

39. ZhKM, II, 627-29 (Nov. 28, 1812); AGS, IV, D-2, pp. 1814 ff. (Jan. 4 and 18, 1818).

40. "But in Russia, perhaps, one should add some restric-tions [to full freedom of enterprise]. When industry has reached, so to say, its full age, then one can and should let it proceed alone and follow its path from afar. But in its first steps, when its weakness prevents it from being secure in its enterprises, when its experience has not yet clarified its aims, when many fields of economy are still unknown to it: then the Government must direct it, indicate to it possible benefits, promote it by encouraging it, and even complement the inadequacy of capital from its [treasury's] pocket." "Otchet Ministerstva Vnutrennikh del za 1803 god," ZhKM, I, 61.

41. AGS, V, pp. 577-620 (No. 93) passim, in particular pp. 579-80. See also references in notes 24, 26, 27 of this chapter.

42. In addition to the official sources cited in the previous note, see Girchenko, op.cit., p. 17; I.P. Basnin, "Iz proshlogo Sibiri," Istoricheskii Vestnik, vol. 90 (Nov., 1902), pp. 534-35.

43. Vagin, op. cit., I, 582-83. Gedenshtrom, at one time an energetic official and assistant to Treskin, offered the following judgment on Loskutov's administrative methods: "Pitiless and unrelenting severity transformed even the most depraved convicts into peaceful peasants. The clearing of fields and pastures... was done at the price of unthinkable efforts, but it was finally accomplished by means of unrelenting compulsion and supervision." M. Gedenshtrom (Hedenström), Otryvki o Sibiri (St. Pbg., 1830), pp. 72-73.

44. Treskin was compared to Caliph Harun al-Rashid for his constant personal inspections of Irkutsk (Vagin, op.cit., I, 572--the testimony of N.P. Bulatov).

45. Girchenko, op.cit., p. 13.

46. AGS, IV, C, pp. 277-82 (Oct. 30, 1818). The matter was serious enough to come to the attention of the Council of State eventually--hence our information. But how many abuses never came up for redress?

47. These details are told by Shchapov, Vagin, Iadrintsev, Firsov and in the literature referred to in notes 3 and 4 of this chapter.

48. Shteingel', op.cit., p. 374.

49. ZhKM, II, 171 (April 26, 1811).

50. The plight of Sibiriakov and Myl'nikov and the persecution of other merchants has been related by all the memoir writers we have read. Details are also to be found in Iadrintsev, Vagin (most complete), Shchapov, Firsov, and others. For Derzhavin's participation in this affair see Sochineniia Derzhavina, ed. Grot (St. Pbg., 1871), vol. 6.

51. See Basnin, op.cit., p. 541.

52. Potanin, "Goroda Sibiri," Sibir' i ee sovremennoe sostoianie i ee nuzhdy (St. Pbg., 1908), p. 240; Basnin, op.cit., pp. 561-62.

53. An anecdote of the time had it that at some dinner Alexander I complained about his poor eyesight. Thereupon Prince Naryshkin remarked that His Majesty should talk about it to Pestel. "Why?" asked Alexander I. "Well, Sire, Pestel has the best eyeglasses in Russia; he lives in St. Petersburg and sees exactly what is going on in Siberia." Kalashnikov, op.cit., p. 193; Stogov-Mozhaiskii, op.cit., p. 504.

CHAPTER III

1. On Speransky during this period, see M. A. Korff, Zhizn' grafa Speranskogo (St. Pbg., 1861), Vol. II; I. Bychkov, "M.M. Speranskii general gubernator Sibiri i vozvrashchenie ego v Sankt Peterburg," Russkaia Starina, vol. 112 (Oct., 1902), pp. 35-56 A. Fateev, "Speranskii - general gubernator Sibiri: Part 2, Upravlenie Sibir'iu," Zapiski Russkogo Nauchnoissledovatel'skogo Ob'edineniia v Prage, Vol. XI, No. 88 (1942), pp. 323-62; N. Iadrintsev, "Speranskii i ego reformy v Sibiri," Vestnik Evropy (1876, No. 5), pp. 93-116; N. Iadrintsev, "Chuvstva Speranskogo k Sibiri," Sbornik gazety "Sibir", Vol. I (St. Pbg., 1876), pp. 397-408; E. Popov, M.M. Speranskii v Permi i Sibiri (Perm', 1879); A. Shchapov, op. cit., Vol. III, pp. 643-717; Vagin, op. cit.

2. See Iadrintsev, "Chuvstva Speranskogo k Sibiri," Sbornik gazety "Sibir".

3. Alexander I to Speransky, letter dated March 22, 1819, quoted in N. K. Shil'der, Imperator Aleksandr Pervyi - ego zhizn' i tsarstvovanie (St. Pbg., 1904), IV, 149.

4. Speransky to Count V. Kochubei, May 20, 1820, in V Pamiat' grafa M. M. Speranskogo (St. Pbg., 1872), p. 313.

5. These details are most fully reported by Vagin, op. cit., II, 154-201, 227-45, 659-63, 682-706 passim. See also, John Dundas Cochrane, Narrative of a Pedestrian Journey through Russia and Siberian Tartary, from the Frontiers of China to the Frozen Sea and Kamchatka (London, 1824), and F. P. Vrangel', Puteshestvie po severnym beregam Sibiri i po Ledovitomu moriu (St. Pbg., 1841), Part I.

6. Letter of Speransky to Count Gur'ev, May, 1820 (?), in V Pamiat'..., pp. 321-23.

7. See Speransky's letters: to Count Kochubei, Sept. 29, 1820, from Tobolsk, in V Pamiat'..., p. 501, and to Count Gur'ev, Oct. 2, 1820, ibid., p. 485.

8. Speransky's letter to his daughter, Tobolsk, June 14, 1819, Russkii Arkhiv, 1868, No. 11, p. 1684.

9. Letter to his daughter, Sept. 5-6, 1819, from Irkutsk, Russkii Arkhiv, 1868, No. 11, p. 1697.

10. I take the liberty of referring the reader to my articles on this subject: "The Philosophical views of M. Speransky," Slavonic and East European Review, Vol. XXXI, No. 77 (June, 1953), pp. 437-51; "The Political Philosophy of Speranskij," The American Slavic and East European Review,

Vol. XII (Feb., 1953), pp. 1-21.

11. Dominique Dufour de Pradt, Des colonies (et de la
révolution actuelle de l'Amérique), 2 vols. (Paris, Warsaw,
1817).

12. O. Kozodavlev, "Mnenie ministra vnutrennikh del po
delam sibirskim," Chteniia..., 1859, No. 3, p. 62.

13. Ibid., p. 63.

14. The original composition of this Siberian Committee,
which lasted from 1821 to 1838 (to supervise the implementa-
tion of the statutes of 1822), was as follows: Count V.
Kochubei (chairman), Count A. Arakcheev, Count Gur'ev, Prince
Golitsyn, Comptroller General Kampenhausen, Speransky.
Obozrenie glavnykh osnovanii..., pp. iv-v.

15. Vigel', Zapiski, p. 165.

16. Ibid., p. 187.

17. In addition to the literature dealing with Speransky in
Siberia and his own letters and diary, see the Memoirs of
Basnin, Kalashnikov, Stogov-Mozhaiskii; also N. Shchukin,
Poezdka v Iakutsk (2nd ed.; St. Pbg., 1844), p. 227.

18. Cf. P.A. Slovtsov, Pis'ma iz Sibiri 1826 (Moscow,
1828). Slovtsov gives the following list of secondary schools
in Siberia in 1826 (ibid., pp. 111-12): The Irkutsk School
District (direktsiia) comprised a total of 13 schools with 620
pupils: (a) the Irkutsk gymnasium--39 pupils; (b) the district
schools (uezdnaia shkola)--113 pupils, Kirensk--16, Iakutsk--
51, Nizhneudinsk--15, Troitskosavsk--71, Verkhneudinsk--42,
Nerchinsk--57; (c.) the parish schools (prikhodskaia shkola) of
Irkutsk--160, Tunka--20, Kiren'--13, Oninsk--13, Seleng-
insk--10. The Tomsk-Eniseisk School District comprised
the following 5 district schools: Tomsk--87, Krasnoiarsk--70,
Eniseisk--69, Kuznetsk--44, Kainsk--48, with a total of 318
pupils. The Tobolsk School District included: (a) the Tobolsk
gymnasium--42 pupils; (b) district schools in: Tobolsk--120,
Berezovo--35, Turino--21, Tiumen'--84, Ialutorovo--50,
Kurgan--67, Tara--52, Ishim--32; and (c) the parish schools
in: Tobolsk (2 schools with a total of 92 pupils), Tura--21,
Tiumen'--42; or a total of 13 schools with 650 students. The
grand total for Siberia was 31 schools with 1,588 pupils.
The total operating capital of these schools amounted to
231,047 rubles.

19. Iadrintsev, "Nachalo pechati v Sibiri," Literaturnyi
sbornik (St. Pbg., 1885), pp. 375-76. Iadrintsev, Sibir'
kak koloniia, pp. 555-59; I.D. Zavalishin, Opisanie Zapadnoi

Sibiri (Moscow, 1862), pp. 75-77; Potanin, "Goroda Sibiri," Sibir' i ee sovremennoe sostoianie..., p. 249.

20. Stogov-Mozhaiskii, op.cit., p. 526.

21. M. Azadovskii, M. Zolotarev, B. Kubalov (eds.), Sibir' i dekabristy, has an extensive bibliography on this subject. Further references can be found in the Bibliografiia Dekabristov published in 1925 and the sources and books published in Soviet Russia in 1950. See Bibliography.

22. A. Erman, Reise um die Erde durch Nord Asien und die beiden Oceane, Historischer Theil (Berlin, 1833-48), II, 80-81.

23. PSZ, Vol. XXXVIII (1822-23), pp. 342-565, a total of 3,027 paragraphs. The complete list of the laws is as follows: 29,124: General Introduction; 29,125: General Administrative Statute; 29,126: Statute on the Natives; 29,127: Statute on the Kirghiz; 29,128: Statute on the Exiles; 29,129: Convoys and Transportation of Exiles; 29,130: Statute on Land Transportation; 29,131: Statute on the Siberian Cossacks; 29,132: Zemskie povinnosti (local dues); 29,133: State Grain Stores; 29,134: Statute on Loans and Debts.

24. The task of the government in Siberia is "to leave freedom to private enterprise, have all possible correct information about its successes; in particular remove from it all fetters; in this consists the general principle of government in this domain...." "Otchet Ministerstva Vnutrennikh Del za 1803 god," ZhKM, I, 63. The economic theories current in the early 1820's were those of maximum freedom in economic life, based on the work of Adam Smith which had been translated a decade earlier. All prominent Russian statesmen of the time subscribed to these theories, sometimes with minor qualifications to take care of Russian conditions.

25. For example, Loskutov traded with the Karagass peoples, Shchapov, op.cit., p. 663.

26. Vagin, op.cit., I, 178, 352. See Appendix II for some source materials on this.

27. "The Main Administration [glavnoe upravlenie] protects, with all its power and through its ordinances, the freedom of enterprise and trade, the freest exchange of the necessities of life throughout all of Siberia without any distinction between districts and provinces," PSZ, 29,125, par. 523; see also pars. 561, 397, 95.

28. "It is forbidden to all officials serving in the provinces

to enter into debt relations with peasants and natives, in their own name or under the cover of the name of a third person. All debt obligations contracted in this manner, with written proof or without it, private or communal, are invalid; there can be no judiciary action on them and their collection cannot be enforced." PSZ, 29,134, par. 53. The same injunction is repeated in the statute on the natives.

29. PSZ, 29,127, par. 188.

30. "The first and principal means for supplying the people with bread [i.e., grain] is private enterprise and trade. The second means, serving as aid and complement to the first in years of crop failure, is the network of village stores in the countryside and communal stores in the towns. But because in Siberia, due to the character of its population, communal supplies cannot be established in every town, there must be added a third means to the former two--state supplies." PSZ, 29,133, par. 26.

31. Zavalishin, Opisanie Zapadnoi Sibiri, p. 68; Seredonin, Istoricheskii obzor..., II-2, p. 228-29.

32. PSZ, 29,127, par. 191.

33. PSZ, 29,127, pars. 202, 193, 194. In European Russia only members of the first guild could engage in foreign trade.

34. PSZ, 29,130, pars. 375, 376.

35. PSZ, 29,134, par. 44. In the preliminary considerations on Siberia, Speransky had written: "The condition of the peasants and nomads has changed considerably since the issuance of the original rules on debt relations. The development of enterprise, the change in the ways of life, and the movement of trade have introduced among them such needs and means which were not in existence before and with which present rules and laws have to be brought into harmony." Obozrenie glavnykh osnovanii..., pp. 133-34.

36. PSZ, 29,134, par. 95.

37. PSZ, 29,134, par. 66. This regulation could also become a source of abuses by the local officials. Probably Speransky felt that this contingency would be taken care of by the general rules governing the duties of local officials.

38. PSZ, 29,134, par. 79.

39. PSZ, 29,125, par. 49.

40. Erman, op.cit., I, 602. See also Shchukin, Poezdka v Iakutsk, pp. 243-26, who reports a similarly successful attempt on the initiative of an official near Iakutsk.

41. Girchenko, op.cit., p. 15.

42. Obozrenie glavnykh osnovanii..., pp. 126-27.

43. "...(2) not to prevent, but by all means foster private grain trade; (3) that state grain stores serve only as aid in case of necessity, but not as a means of introducing exclusive grain trade by the Treasury." PSZ, 29,133, par. 7.

44. PSZ, 29,133, par. 7.

45. PSZ, 29,133, pars. 9, 10.

46. The need of enlightening examples to stimulate agriculture in Siberia was also felt by Speransky's old school friend and Siberian expert, P. A. Slovtsov. See Slovtsov, Pis'ma iz Sibiri, p. 92.

47. PSZ, 29,127, pars. 163, 164.

48. PSZ, 29,133, pars. 56-59.

49. Iadrintsev, Sibir' kak koloniia, p. 419.

50. The need of greater agricultural settlement was a recurring theme in all contemporary writings and articles devoted to Siberia. Cf. Gedenshtrom, op. cit., pp. 13 and 147-48; Shchukin, op.cit., pp. 14-15 (Siberia "should give space to be used by other parts of the world which are over-populated"); Semivskii, op.cit., Foreword (no pagination); "Otryvki iz zamechanii o Sibiri" in Dukh Zhurnalov, No. IX, 1812, pp. 507-8; A.M. Kornilov, Pribavleniia k zamechaniiam o Sibiri (St. Pbg., 1829), pp. 109-10.

51. N.M. Druzhinin, Gosudarstvennye krest'iane i reforma P. D. Kiseleva, Vol. I (Moscow-Leningrad, 1946), p. 172; for summaries of various projects of the period, see ibid., pp. 121-95 passim. Fuller material on this question is to be found in the classical works of V. Semevskii.

52. PSZ, 28,997 (April 10, 1822); this decree was not part of the reorganization of Siberia but was very closely connected with it.

53. Speransky's protégé and eventual successor in Western Siberia, S.B. Bronevskii, continued this policy and promoted the settlement of the southwestern (Altai) border region. Zavalishin, Opisanic Zapadnoi Sibiri, I, 158. For another approach to the promotion of agricultural settlement by extending serfdom into Siberia, see Primechaniia o Sibiri, an anonymous manuscript of the late 1820's by a local official (in Hoover Library, manuscript division).

54. Lantzeff, op.cit., p. 165.

55. Cf. Statisticheskoe obozrenie..., p. 88; Obozrenie glavnykh osnovanii..., pp. 79-102; Iadrintsev, Sibir' kak koloniia, p. 246; Firsov, op.cit., II, 44.

56. PSZ, 29, 128, par. 1.

57. PSZ, 29, 128, par. 226.

58. PSZ, 29, 128, par. 262.

59. PSZ, 29, 128, pars. 203, 206.

60. PSZ, 29, 128, pars. 260, 261.

61. PSZ, 29, 128, par. 401.

62. PSZ, 29, 130, pars. 190, 193, 618.

63. PSZ, 29, 128, pars. 345, 346, 347, 350-93.

64. PSZ, 29, 128, par. 255.

65. PSZ, 29, 128, pars. 314, 315.

66. Iadrintsev, Sibir' kak koloniia, p. 246.

67. The exiles were unfree only temporarily. And in an economic sense many, as we have seen, always remained free labor in agriculture.

68. Andrievich, Istoriia Sibiri, II, 404; see also article by Shashkov, "Rabstvo v Sibiri," Istoricheskie etiudy.

69. AGS, IV, B-2, pp. 362-64.

70. PSZ, 29, 134, par. 9.

71. PSZ, 29, 134, par. 40.

72. AGS, IV, B-2, pp. 367-68.

73. In fact, their position was much more comparable to that of the Streltsy in seventeenth-century Muscovy than to that of their "free" namesakes, the Cossacks of the Dnieper Zaporozh'e and the Don. A brief, though pedestrian, description of the Streltsy in English can be found in C. Bickford O'Brien, Russia under Two Tsars 1682-1689 (The Regency of Sophia Alekseevna) (Berkeley, 1952), Part I. See also P. Struve, op. cit., pp. 212-16.

74. Quoted in V. Vatin, Minusinskii krai v XVIII v. (Minusinsk, 1913), p. 46.

75. Vatin, op. cit., pp. 50-53.

76. Ibid., p. 86.

77. N. Koz'min, Ocherki proshlogo i nastoiashchego Sibiri (St. Pbg., 1910), p. 48, note 2.

78. Obozrenie glavnykh osnovanii..., pp. 114-25.

79. There were organized seven regiments of City Cossacks: (1) the Tobolsk Regiment (with six "hundreds"), (2) the Siberian Tatar Regiment (composed of Moslems from Tobolsk province), (3) the Tomsk Regiment, (4) the Eniseisk Regiment, (5) the Irkutsk Regiment, (6) the Transbaikal (Zabaikal'skii) Regiment, (7) the Iakut Regiment. A. Gagemeister (Hagemeister), Statisticheskoe obozrenie Sibiri (St. Pbg., 1854), II, 82.

80. PSZ, 29,131, par. 143.

81. A similar principle for determining possession and ownership of land had prevailed in medieval Russia. See V.B. El'iashevich, Istoriia prava pozemel'noi sobstvennosti v Rossii, 2 vols. (Paris, 1948-1951).

82. PSZ, 29,131, pars. 114-17.

83. PSZ, 29,131, pars. 149-53.

84. PSZ, 29,131, par. 123.

85. PSZ, 29,131, par. 176.

86. PSZ, 29,131, par. 161.

87. PSZ, 29,131, pars. 165,172.

88. PSZ, 29,131, par. 182.

89. PSZ, 29,131, par. 169. They could trade only in authorized merchandise; alcoholic beverages, for instance, were excluded.

90. PSZ, 29,131, pars. 188, 190, 195.

91. Slovtsov, Istoricheskoe obozrenie Sibiri, II, iv; V.V. Kir'iakov, Ocherki pereselencheskogo dvizheniia v Sibiri (Moscow, 1902), pp. 57,58.

92. PSZ, 29,124, par. 3.

93. PSZ, 29,125, par. 385.

94. PSZ, 29,127, pars. 172, 174, 178, 179.

95. AGS, IV, D-2, pp. 1000-18.

96. PSZ, 29,134, par. 108.

97. "The method for fulfilling these obligations is established on a special basis for the Siberian provinces. The maintenance of roads and the convoying of exiles are replaced in part by the organization of special road and convoy units [kommanda] and in part by money dues. The maintenance of [postal] relays is transformed into a money tax." PSZ, 29,132, par. 3. See also Girchenko, op.cit., pp. 10, 12.

98. PSZ, 29,130, pars. 1, 399.

99. PSZ, 29,132, pars. 20, 25.

100. Kalashnikov, op.cit., p. 248.

101. Obozrenie glavnykh osnovanii..., pp. 13-14.

102. "To transform personal power into [the power of] an institution; and having reconciled the unity of its action with its public character, preserve this power by legal means against arbitrariness and abuses.... To establish the action of this power in such a manner that it be neither personal nor 'domestic,' but public and official." Obozrenie glavnykh osnovanii..., pp. 50-52 and PSZ, 29,125, par. 474.

103. Obozrenie glavnykh osnovanii..., p. 8.

104 . PSZ, 29, 125, par. 63 (note). See also Appendix III.

105. PSZ,. 29, 124, par. 1.

106. PSZ, 29, 125, par. 105.

107. PSZ, 29, 127, par. 316.

108. PSZ, 29, 125, pars. 57, 62. Hereafter, unless indicated otherwise, all paragraph references will be to PSZ, 29, 125 -- the principal administrative statute of 1822.

109. Pars. 573, 574.

110. Quoted in A.D. Gradovskii, op. cit., p. 20.

111. Par. 511.

112. Speransky wrote to Kozodavlev: "In theory I am in agreement with your ideas, but in practice I don't know." Quoted in Iadrintsev, Sibir' kak koloniia, p. 519. One may doubt Speransky's sincerity on this.

113. Quoted in Iadrintsev, Sibir' kak koloniia, pp. 519-20; Prutchenko, op.cit., I, 215-17.

114. Pars. 18, 19.

115. Pars. 14, 15, 16, 20.

116. Par. 522.

117. Par. 158.

118. Pars. 582, 583.

119. Pars. 543, 544.

120. Pars. 545, 546.

121. V.V. Ivanovskii, "Administrativnoe ustroistvo nashikh okrain," Uchenye Zapiski Kazanskogo Universiteta, vol. 58, No. 6 (Nov. -Dec., 1891), p. 38.

122. Par. 590.

123. Pars. 591, 594.

124. Pars. 597, 607.

125. Pars. 572, 575.

126. Pars. 537, 538.

127. Pars. 501, 502, 503.

128. Par. 480.

129. Pars. 500, 486.

130. Pars. 321-472. See Appendix II for details.

131. Pars. 21-35

132. Already in his earlier state papers Speransky had put forth very strongly and clearly the idea that the provincial administration was to take care of these three functions of police, economy, and justice. He had copied this division, which made for better control and for more participation by people well acquainted with local circumstances, from the

ideas on local government expressed by Turgot in France
and later developed in a bureaucratic direction by Napoleon
and along looser and more autonomous lines by vom Stein in
Prussia.

133. Pars. 39-44.
134. Pars. 45-53.
135. Pars. 54-56.
136. Pars. 64-69.
137. Pars. 75-79.
138. Pars. 80-85 and 70-74.
139. PSZ, 15,680; PSZ, 29,125, pars. 86-98.
140. Pars. 99-102.
141. Pars. 107-133.
142. Pars. 135-141.
143. Par. 142.
144. Par. 134.
145. See; Plan gosudarstvennogo preobrazovaniia grafa
M. M. Speranskogo (1809), izd. Russkaia Mysl' (Moscow,
1905), pp. 1-120; "Proekt uchrezhdeniia dlia upravleniia
gubernii" in Sbornik IRIO, vol. 90 (St. Pbg., 1894), pp. 274-
358.
146. Division of functions was the rage of the period.
But it should not be confused with the classical doctrine of
separation of powers, of checks and balances, as embodied
in the American Constitution, or "discovered" by Montesquieu
in the English. In contrast to the latter, division of functions
was mainly a bureaucratic device for more efficient administration and clearer legal relations.
147. Zavalishin, Opisanie Zapadnoi Sibiri, p. 54.
148. As one contemporary put it, the bureaucracy could
bring forth a man of Speransky's caliber, whereas the merchant class produced only Baranov, "a vicious and drunken
muzhik."
149. Letter to his daughter, Irkutsk, Feb. 1, 1820, No. 37,
in Russkii Arkhiv, 1868, No. 11, p. 1735.
150. Prutchenko, op. cit., I, 279.

PART II

CHAPTER IV

1. See Appendix IV for a list of the native peoples of
Siberia.

2. Recently a summary account of this process as it occurred among the Buriats was given by Professor N.N. Poppe
in an article (in manuscript) prepared for the Russia in Asia
Project of the Far Eastern and Russian Institute of the University of Washington.

3. For example, the treaty of Jan. 15, 1689, summarized
by M.N. Bogdanov, Ocherk istorii buriat-mongol'skogo
naroda (Verkhneudinsk, 1926), pp. 68-69.

4. See K.V. Bazilevich, Vneshniaia politika russkogo
tsentralizovannogo gosudarstva, vtoraia polovina XV v.
(Moscow, 1952), pp. 58-59; B. Nolde, La formation de
l'Empire russe, Vol. I (Paris, 1952), pp. 63-128 passim
(especially pp. 97-107).

5. See, for example, N. Koz'min, K voprosu o tiurko-
mongol'skom feodalizme (Moscow-Irkutsk, 1934), pp. 100-101.

6. "The Russian central authorities tried to pursue a
mild policy towards the natives, to attract--not to repel them.
The practice of the local authorities had usually a different
character. Complaints by the natives about injuries and acts
of violence, exactions and abuses of the local authorities were
never ceasing." V. Riasanovsky (Riazanovskii), Mongol'skoe
pravo - preimushchestvenno obychnoe (Harbin, 1931), p. 147.

7. Sychevskii, Istoricheskaia zapiska o kitaiskoi granitse..., pp. 34-46.

8. V.I. Ogorodnikov, "Russkaia gosudarstvennaia vlast'
i sibirskie inorodtsy XVI-XVIII vv.," Sbornik trudov professorov i prepodavatelei Gosudarstvennogo Irkutskogo
Universiteta, otd. I, vyp. 1, p. 79.

9. Ibid., p. 77. Cf. also ukaz of July 8, 1710, to the
Voevoda of Irkutsk, Larion Siniavin, to collect the iasak from
the Ashabagat clan in money, N.N. Stepanov reviewing,
Istoriia Buriat-Mongol'skoi ASSR, t. I (Ulan-Ude, 1951)
in Voprosy Istorii, April, 1952, p. 112.

10. Ogorodnikov, op.cit., p. 78.

11. "Materialy dlia severovostochnoi Sibiri v XVIIIm v.
(1751-1752)," ed. S. Shashkov, Chteniia..., 1864 (No. 3),
pp. 82-89.

12. V. P. Girchenko, Iz istorii pereseleniia v Pribaikal'e....

13. In the words of a contemporary well placed to know,
"everybody traveled and made use of the [transportation]
service--a distance of 500 versts was of no consequence...."
S. Cherepanov, "Otryvki iz vospominanii Sibirskogo kazaka

1810-1848," Drevniaia i novaia Rossiia, 1876, Nos. 6-10.

14. "Dzakiia - nakaz 1793" (quoted in Riasanovsky, Mongol'skoe pravo..., Appendix 4), p. 5.

15. Ogorodnikov, op.cit., p. 84.

16. Ibid., p. 80.

17. Eventually (in 1851), the land granted to these Cossacks became a part of the territory of the Transbaikal Cossack Army. The above description is based on: Sychevskii, op.cit., pp. 20, 25 (texts of Burinsk treaty and instructions of Count Raguzinskii), 221; D. Samokvasov (ed.), Sbornik obychnogo prava sibirskikh inorodtsev (Warsaw, 1876), p. 150; N. Razumov (ed.), Zabaikal'e: svod materialov... (St. Pbg., 1899), p. 63-68; R. Okun', "Sibirskii komitet: obzor arkhivnykh fondov," Arkhivnoe Delo, vol. 38 (1936), p. 98; S. Patkanov, "Opyt geografii i statistiki tunguskikh plemen Sibiri," Zapiski Gosudarstvennogo Geograficheskogo Obshchestva po otdelu etnografii, No. 31 (St. Pbg., 1906), vyp. 2, pp. 202-3; F. Kudriavtsev, Istoriia buriat-mongol'skogo naroda ot XVIII do 60kh godov XIX v., pp. 88-89.

18. The evacuation of the Ingoda Valley took place in 1802 at the behest of Councilor Laba, author of the settlement regulations of 1806. See V. Girchenko, K istorii buriat-mongolov, khorintsev pervoi poloviny XIX v. (Verkhneudinsk, 1928), pp. 9-10.

19. Koz'min, K Voprosu o tiurko-mongol'skom feodalizme, p. 122; Kudriavtsev, op.cit., p. 101.

20. For example, "these tribute-paying natives are to come with their furs [remaining after payment of the iasak] to the Tsar's traders and entrepreneurs, and only through them are they to sell or exchange their pelts." Quoted in Bogdanov, op.cit., p. 91.

21. See Shashkov, "Sibirskie inorodtsy v XIXm stoletii," Istoricheskie etiudy, II.

22. V.G. Kartsov, Ocherk istorii narodov severo-zapadnoi Sibiri (Moscow, 1937), pp. 88-89.

23. Iadrintsev, Sibir' kak koloniia, p. 414.

24. See the decree of July 20, 1748, in Riasanovsky, Mongol'skoe pravo..., p. 173.

25. Quoted in Riasanovsky, op.cit., p. 174, and "Stepnoe ulozhenie khorintsev 1808," par. 97, ibid., Appendix, p. 23.

26. The fullest picture is in the article of Shashkov, "Rabstvo v Sibiri," Istoricheskie etiudy.

27. "The subjects of the Eleven Clans take merchandise

on credit and at high interest to the value of big sums without our [elders'] approval and knowledge. Unable to repay the merchant for the merchandise bought on credit, they borrow money from one another at high interest. But often, not finding the money to repay the debt, they give promissory notes to the merchants without our knowledge and permission and convert their old debt into a new one at new interests. Then, unable to repay this debt, they ruin themselves and as a result are forced to go into indentured service, so that they are unable to contribute to the state's iasak and the various expenses and collections of the Eleven Clans. These people become incapable of supporting their children, their father and mother. Moreover, it turns out that...for many such debts made by the father, his son has to go into indentured service. While the son cannot manage this debt, the father makes new ones, and as a result sons are forced to remain in debt to the end of their days; they stop contributing to the iasak and cease to be useful members of the community." Quoted in Riasanovsky, op. cit., p. 174. See also Ogorodnikov, op. cit., pp. 95-96; Shashkov, "Rabstvo v Sibiri," Istoricheskie etiudy, pp. 158 ff.

28. Iadrintsev, Sibirskie inorodtsy, ikh byt i sovremennoe polozhenie (St. Pbg., 1891), p. 103.

29. To prevent mass starvation the government had organized state granaries to accumulate reserves of grain, but this institution too became a source of exploitation of the natives. Government rules required the state granaries to be replenished every year. This was done by collecting part of the peasants' crops. Natives who lived by hunting and fishing were required to pay a sum of money in lieu of their grain assessment. Thus the state granaries, instead of serving the humanitarian function of alleviating hardships, were an added burden on the native economy.

30. Iadrintsev, Sibir' kak koloniia, p. 152; N.N. Firsov, Chteniia po istorii Sibiri, II, 14.

31. Shashkov, "Sibirskie inorodtsy...," Istoricheskie etiudy, p. 286. M. Czaplicka, Aboriginal Siberia: a study in social anthropology (Oxford, 1914), p. 21, summarizes the problem in the following words: "If we consider the question of the increase of Siberian natives from the geographic or territorial point of view, we can draw the following conclusion, The natives who live in regions almost wholly

barren, and those in the northern part of the southern provinces, where agriculture is possible indeed but is at best an
uncertain means of livelihood, are not increasing." However,
the writer says that the natives who lived where agriculture
was possible were increasing in numbers in spite of epidemics
and famines.

32. Patkanov, op.cit., vyp. 2, pp. 95-96.

33. Razumov, Zabaikal'e..., pp. 31-36; Patkanov, op.
cit., p. 99.

34. Patkanov, op.cit., vyp. 2, pp. 204-5; S. Tokarev,
Ocherk istorii iakutskogo naroda (Moscow, 1940), p. 112.

35. Kudriavtsev, op.cit., p. 120.

36. Kudriavtsev, quoting translation of the chronicle by
N.N. Poppe, ibid., pp. 170-71.

37. S.V. Bakhrushin, "Istoricheskie sud'by Iakutii,"
Iakutiia: sbornik statei (Leningrad, 1927), p. 307; also see
Sychevskii, op.cit., p. 95; "Obychai Selengiiskikh Bratskikh,"
in Samokvasov, op.cit., p. 193 (No. 167).

38. Razumov, Zabaikal'e..., p. 36; Riasanovsky, op.cit.,
pp. 147, 167; Bogdanov, op.cit., p. 101. For a recent Soviet
view see N.N. Stepanov, "Istoricheskoe znachenie prisoedineniia narodnostei krainego severa k Rossii," Voprosy Istorii,
July, 1952, p. 83.

39. Girchenko, K istorii buriat-mongolov, khorintsev...,
p. 9; Tokarev, op.cit., p. 114.

40. Tokarev, op.cit., p. 123.

41. Girchenko, K istorii buriat-mongolov, khorintsev...,
p. 3; full details on the Galsanov affair are found in Vagin,
Istoricheskie svedeniia o deiatel'nosti grafa M.M. Speranskogo
v Sibiri s 1819 po 1822 g., I, 263-80.

42. After 1809 the clan chief received the ninth rank (chin);
see Riasanovsky, op.cit., p. 165.

43. Resistance against baptism was also due to the unwillingness of the natives to lose their nationality along with
their religion and traditional customs. I. Pestov, Zapiski ob
Eniseiskoi gubernii i Vostochnoi Sibiri (Moscow, 1833),
pp. 181-82; Shashkov, "Sibirskie inorodtsy...," Istoricheskie
etiudy, p. 229.

44. Bogdanov, op.cit., pp. 156-57; Bakhrushin, op.cit.,
p. 308; G. Sarychev, Puteshestvie po severovostochnoi
chasti Sibiri, Ledovitomu moriu i Vostochnomu okeanu (St.
Pbg., 1802), pp. 35-36.

45. Sychevskii, op.cit., pp. 35-36.

46. In an effort to limit the number of lamas, the administration established the category of officially recognized
(shtatnyi) lamas who enjoyed various privileges, foremost
of which was tax exemption. But there were many lamas
outside of this officially recognized category and these supernumerary (zashtatnyi) lamas eventually made up the majority
of the Buddhist clergy. See Archbishop Nil (of Iaroslav),
Buddizm rassmatrivaemyi v otnoshenii k posledovateliam ego
obitaiushchikh v Sibiri (St. Pbg., 1858); Kudriavtsev, op. cit.,
pp. 138-43.

47. Bogdanov, op. cit., pp. 108, 124, 153, 155; Razumov,
Zabaikal'e..., p. 45; B.I. Vladimirtsev, Obshchestvennyi
stroi mongolov (Leningrad, 1934), pp. 191, 192.

48. For instance, the inspections of 1733, 1748, 1763. See
Ogorodnikov, op. cit., p. 96.

CHAPTER V

1. Iadrintsev, Sibir' kak koloniia, p. 167; Iadrintsev,
Sibirskie inorodtsy..., p. 203.

2. Instructions dated Feb. 6, 1763, in PSZ, 11,749
(Vol. XVI, pp. 153-54).

3. The basis of the Russian system of direct taxation
was the capitation tax imposed on all males of working age.
Only these taxable individuals (who were classified as "souls")
were the object of the statistical census.

4. Iadrintsev, Sibir' kak koloniia, p. 168; Ogorodnikov,
op. cit., p. 77.

5. Obozrenie glavnykh osnovanii..., p. 57.

6. I.I. Mainov, "Russkie krestiane i osedlye inorodtsy
Iakutskoi oblasti," Zapiski Imperatorskogo Russkogo Geograficheskogo Obshchestva po otdelu statistiki, Vol. XII (St. Pbg.,
1912), pp. 50-51.

7. "Khyn-tok-togol," in Riasanovsky, Mongol'skoe
pravo, Appendix 5, pp. 6-7.

8. AGS, I-2, p. 257.

9. Mainov, op. cit., p. 14; Tokarev, op. cit., pp. 126-27.

10. Iadrintsev, Sibirskie inorodtsy..., p. 204; Stepanov,
"Istoricheskoe znachenie...," Voprosy Istorii, July, 1952,
p. 83.

11. AGS, IV, A-1, p. 466.

12. A. de Levchine, Description des hordes et steppes
des Kirghiz-Kazaks, trans. Ferry de Pigny (Paris, 1840).

13. Ibid., pp. 314, 315 (note), 413; S. Bronevskii, "Zapiska o Kirgiz-Kaisakakh," Otechestvennye Zapiski, vol. 42 (1830), pp. 192-93.

14. AGS, I-2, p. 261. See also Appendix I.

15. PSZ, 27,501; AGS, IV, D-2, pp. 681-84; Razumov, Zabaikal'e..., p. 74. The change in the government's views on the natives' possession of land is illustrated by the following two decrees concerning the Voguls: in 1795 (PSZ, 17,347, pars. 714 ff.) their land was taken away by the Treasury under the pretext that they were a nomadic people; in 1815 (PSZ, 25,763, par. 3) land was set aside to the Voguls so that they could till it, establish pastures, and learn a sedentary way of life. P. Keppen, Khronologicheskii ukazatel' materialov dlia istorii inorodtsev Evropeiskoi Rossii (St. Pbg., 1861), pp. 74-75.

16. Kudriavtsev, op. cit., p. 112. In 1802, the Khori Buriats brought 15,000 poods of flour to Irkutsk for sale.

17. P. Liubomirov, "Pervye 10 let sushchestvovaniia irkutskoi kazennoi sukonnoi fabriki 1793-1802," Ocherki po istorii russkoi promyshlennosti (Moscow, 1947), pp. 674-75; Kudriavtsev, op. cit., p. 97.

18. Riasanovsky, Fundamental Principles of Mongol Law (Tientsin, 1937), pp. 79-80.

19. Riasanovsky, Mongol'skoe pravo..., p. 161 (Prigovor Selenginskikh Bratskikh, June 5, 1823) and p. 205 (Prigovor khorintsev o poriadke upravleniia ot maia 1818).

20. PSZ, 15,680 and 20,771.

21. "The Northern Buriats are governed by their clan chiefs. In each ulus [encampment] there is an ulus elder or headman. At the head of each clan there is a clan chief [zaisan or shulenga]. Separate clans are united into administrations; for example, the Verkholensk vedomstvo united the seven clans of the Verkholensk Buriats.... At the head of each vedomstvo was a chief taisha; usually he also had an assistant [zaisan-noyon]. Several vedomstvos usually combined into another administrative unit, a common office [kontora]. The Northern Buriats had three offices, the Balagansk, Idinsk, and Alar; the Kitoi Buriats had only one common office; the Kuda, Kapsal, Verkholensk, and Lena Buriats had another; the Tunka Buriats formed a third office. The chief taisha was president of the office and there were also special deputies." Riasanovsky, Mongol'skoe pravo..., pp. 212-13.

22. Obozrenie glavnykh osnovanii..., p. 59.

23. "The first efforts of the government to find out the peculiarities of the native way of life through bureaucratic means, with the help of local administrative institutions, arose under Catherine II when the Lieutenancy of Irkutsk demanded the following information from the ispravniks: the origins of the various tribes, and also the important events in their history, the traditions that have been preserved among them, etc. (Archives of the Olekma District Administration, order of the Lieutenant in Irkutsk of Nov. 23, 1784)." Mainov, op. cit., p. 91, note 2.

24. Ogorodnikov, op. cit., p. 88. Or as Levchine described the Kazakh administration set up in 1787 by Governor Igelstrom with the assistance of Batyr-Syrym: "La plus importante est l'établissement de tribunaux sous le nom de rasprava. On ouvrit deux raspravas dans les races d'Alimoul et de Baiouline, à cause du nombre de ceux qui les composent; la race de Semirodsk n'en eut qu'une. Chaque rasprava était composée d'un président et de deux membres qui étaient obligés de se réunir tous les jours, d'examiner, tous présents, les suppliques qu'on leur adressait, d'y donner leurs décisions, de faire satisfaction aux offensés et aux opprimés et de laisser aux mécontents la faculté de demander appel au tribunal de la frontière, siégeant à Orenbourg; mais comme les membres de ces tribunaux ne savaient pas lire, toute la partie des écritures fut confiée à un mollah, ou sécrétaire qui se trouvait attaché à chaque tribunal avec un aide; son devoir était de marquer les papiers qui entraient, de les inscrire au journal, de composer les notes, les protocoles, de faire les interrogatoires, de tenir les régistres, d'établir, d'inscrire les heures d'audience, de composer les rapports, les communications, les ordres: le tout selon les formes données par le gouvernement à Orenbourg. En outre, dans chacune des trois races de la Petite Horde on choisit un ancien principal et quelques uns de seconde classe pour veiller à la conduite du peuple." Levchine, op. cit., pp. 278-79. In 1798 there was established a court at Petropavlovsk to try cases arising from disputes between Kazakhs and Siberians. Ibid., pp. 295, 403.

25. AGS, I-2, p. 249.

26. Riasanovsky, Mongol'skoe pravo..., p. 206.

27. Koz'min, K voprosu o tiurko-mongol'skom feodalizme, p. 91.

28. See S. V. Pakhman, Istoriia kodifikatsii grazhdanskogo

prava (St. Pbg. , 1876), II, 479-81; A. Nol'de, "K istorii
sostavleniia proekta 'Svoda stepnykh zakonov kochevykh
inorodtsev Vostochnoi Sibiri,'" Sbornik S. F. Platonovu,
ucheniki, druz'ia i pochitateli (St. Pbg. , 1911), p. 506. For
Speransky's instructions to the Peking Mission and a description of the measures he took concerning the text of the Mongol
code brought back by the mission's convoy officer, see Vagin,
op. cit. , II. To his daughter, Speransky wrote from Irkutsk
(April 7, 1820) after a visit to Kiakhta: "How much interesting
information about the history and language of this wonderful
people [the Chinese] I shall bring back to you. Two hundred
million heads, i. e. , more than the population of all Europe,
under one hat! This is the first marvel, a marvel of politics,
education heretofore unheard of and nonexistent in the history
of the world. Then follow other marvels no less remarkable
which no less lower the pride of European enlightenment.
One has to confess that our teachers, the Greeks and Romans,
were not greater experts on national education, and apparently
it is fated that the East will always prevail over the West."
Russkii Arkhiv, 1868, No. 11, p. 1747.

   29. Riasanovsky cites the following from the Regulations
of 1789 which are reminiscent of the rules for the Kazakhs:
"The judiciary was not separated from the administration but
closely connected with it. The first tribunal was the Djassak-
prince or Taidji (administrator of a Hoshun or division).
Appeals against the decisions of these could be lodged with
the President of the Seim and appeals against the latter with
the Chinese Board of Foreign Relations.... Appeals to the
Board, before cases were heard by the Djassak and President
of the Seim, were strictly forbidden under threat of punishment. (VII, 5)." Fundamental Principles of Mongol Law,
p. 131.

   30. Strongly influenced by the contemporary Romantic
interests of Western Europe, Russian intellectuals (and
Speransky among them) were also very excited by things
Oriental. For instance, the Sibirskii Vestnik for 1823 had
several articles on Orientology, some of them translations
of Abel Rémusat's writings.

   31. Tokarev, op. cit. , p. 117; Mainov, op. cit. , p. 49
(note).

   32. Riasanovsky, Mongol'skoe pravo... , p. 209 (note).

   33. Full lists of the codes and decisions collected in
preparation for the general Code of the Steppe are given in

Samokvasov and Riasanovsky (Mongol'skoe pravo...). Both
authors reprinted most of the texts (in Russian) of these
decisions. See also E. Iakushkin, "Obychnoe pravo russkikh
inorodtsev: materialy dlia bibliografii obychnogo prava,"
Chteniia..., 1899, No. 3, pp. 1-370.
    34. See pp. 125-26.

CHAPTER   VI

    1. Letter to his daughter, July 10, 1819, in V Pamiat'...,
p. 198.
    2. See Speransky's diary: "Puteshestvie v Sibir' s 31. III.
1819 po 18. II. 1821 - Dnevnik," in V Pamiat'..., pp. 103-
330 passim.
    3. In his interest in Buddhism Speransky also followed
a current intellectual romantic fad which saw in the religious
life of the Far East a potential source for the renovation of
Western spirituality and religion. See the illuminating pages
of Raymond Schwab, La Renaissance orientale (Paris, 1950).
    4. In addition to Speransky's diary and letters from
Siberia to his daughter and friends, see Vagin, op.cit., I,
280-84, 721-26; Bogdanov, op.cit., pp. 162 ff.; B. Laufer,
Ocherk mongol'skoi literatury (Leningrad, 1927), pp. 78,
90-91; for a contemporary description and judgment, see
A. Martos, Pis'mo o Vostochnoi Sibiri 1823-1824 (Moscow,
1827), pp. 67-71.
    5. Iadrintsev, Sibirskie inorodtsy..., pp. 230-40 passim;
Bogdanov, op.cit., p. 164; Kudriavtsev, op.cit., p. 219.
    6. In Riasanovsky's words: "The provisions of the statute
of 1822 defined the relations towards the natives for the
duration of the entire nineteenth century, although in themselves they did not introduce novelties of principle but were
adapted to what had existed until then and to the clan way of
life which retained its significance in the nineteenth century."
Riasanovsky, Mongol'skoe pravo..., p. 150.
    7. Samokvasov, op.cit., pp. 87-89, 102; see also
Riasanovsky, Mongol'skoe pravo..., pp. 212-13 for Northern
Buriats.
    8. Riasanovsky, Mongol'skoe pravo..., p. 231.
    9. Obozrenie glavnykh osnovanii..., pp. 60-61.
    10. It may be noted that the statute of 1822 introduced the
term inorodets (native; literally, "from another clan") into
the regular administrative and legal vocabulary of the Russian
Empire.

11. PSZ, 29,126, pars. 12, 13, 17-23, 88-92. Unless indicated differently, paragraphs hereafter will refer to PSZ, 29,126, the statute on the natives.

12. Shashkov, "Sibirskie inorodtsy...," Istoricheskie etiudy, pp. 186-87.

13. Par. 170.

14. Par. 170, section 1.

15. Imperial Russia recognized only three classes, each having its special legal status: the nobility, the peasantry, and the others. The determining characteristic of the peasantry was that its members were subject to a capitation tax and were strictly circumscribed in their right to move about the country; also, they did not have juridical status (on matters of civil suits, giving testimony in courts, making wills, etc.). This legal status had but an indirect relation to the occupation of the persons or groups concerned. Thus, a person could live and work in the city, be a craftsman or trader (with some limitations), and still be legally a peasant. In other words, this provision merely stated that the native nomad was neither a nobleman nor a member of the.third estate.

16. Pars. 25, 68, 70, 72.

17. Pars. 61-62. A partial list of vagrants was given in the statute: natives from Okhotsk, Gizhiga, Kamchatka (the Koriaks and Iukagirs), Turukhansk, Obdorsk; the Aleutians, the Karagas, the Samoeds.

18. Pars. 111-13.

19. Pars. 172-86.

20. Pars. 187-201.

21. Par. 124.

22. Pars. 214-22.

23. Kudriavtsev, op.cit., p. 123.

24. Pars. 114-21, 202-22.

25. Pars. 122-32, 223-35.

26. Pars. 142-46.

27. Pars. 147-56.

28. Pars. 157-62.

29. Pars. 14-16, 81-87.

30. Pars. 246-51, 254.

31. Suglan (or, to use the Russian equivalent given in the statute, mir) was the assembly of all members of a given tribe for purposes of paying their taxes, delivering the iasak in furs, trading, settling minor disputes, having their census taken, etc. For tribes of vagrant or nomadic peoples this

was the nearest equivalent to a yearly village assembly.

32. Pars. 133-41, 296-339.

33. Obozrenie glavnykh osnovanii..., p. 57.

34. For example, pars. 29, 46.

35. Pars. 45, 52.

36. Pars. 28, 30, 31, 300.

37. Pars. 270-85.

38. Pars. 53, 55, 56, 57, 58, 59, 63-67, 286-92.

39. Shashkov, "Sibirskie inorodtsy...," Istoricheskie etiudy, p. 246.

40. One traveler, A. Martos, recorded on Dec. 16, 1823, that he met a group of Buriat elders going to Irkutsk to help make a collection of the laws of the steppes at the invitation of the government. Martos, op. cit., pp. 43-44.

41. The materials for this code and information on the native assemblies where they were collected are given by Riasanovsky and Samokvasov.

42. The degree of neglect shown by the government in this question can be gauged from the fact that the original source material used by the Commission was lost; only by accident did Professor Samokvasov discover it a few decades later in the private archives of a member of the Commission on Codification. See A. Nol'de, "K istorii sostavleniia proekta...," Sbornik S. F. Platonovu.... For the historical circumstances which contributed to the failure of all the codifications of regional customary law, see A. Nol'de, Ocherki po istorii kodifikatsii mestnykh grazhdanskikh zakonov pri gr. Speranskom (St. Pbg., 1906), I, 243-47.

43. Riasanovsky, Mongol'skoe pravo..., p. 153; Fundamental Principles of Mongol Law, p. 76.

44. Riasanovsky, Mongol'skoe pravo..., p. 232.

45. Kartsov, op. cit., pp. 78-79; Mainov, op. cit., pp. 93-94; Bogdanov, op. cit., p. 101. Already in 1782 a diploma (attestat) had been issued to the Khori taisha, Damba Dugar Irincheiev, which stated "that he has tried to bring his subjects to [adopt] customs similar to Russian ones in all fields of economic life, the building of houses, in agriculture." Speransky's statute only continued and more effectively implemented this policy.

46. Pars. 31, 32.

47. R. Okun', "Sibirskii Komitet...," Arkhivnoe Delo, p. 96.

48. Shashkov, "Sibirskie inorodtsy...," Istoricheskie

etiudy, pp. 190-91, 195. Okun', op. cit., p. 97.

49. The article by Shashkov often referred to gives the fullest and most balanced discussion of this aspect of Speransky's
reform and illustrates it by numerous figures comparing the
old and new tax burdens and costs of administration. See in
particular pp. 201-5. For an emotionally laden analysis see
Iadrintsev, Sibirskie inorodtsy... and Sibir' kak koloniia.

CHAPTER VII

1. For an application of the American concept of "frontier"
to the study of Russian--and in particular Siberian--history,
see Donald W. Treadgold, "Russian Expansion in the Light
of Turner's Study of the American Frontier," Agricultural
History, Vol. XXVI, No. 4 (Oct., 1952), pp. 147-52.
2. It may be noted that this was also the basic attitude
of the influential younger Slavophile, Iurii Samarin, in regard
to the Baltic Provinces and Poland in the 1850's and 1860's.

Bibliography

Bibliography

The following bibliography includes the most important
and useful source collections, special studies, and contemporary accounts consulted in the preparation of the present
volume. I have omitted those works to which only casual
reference has been made in the text. Neither have I included
the standard general histories of Russia.

For purposes of convenience the spelling of titles has
been modernized before transliteration.

The bibliographical references have been arranged under
the following headings:

I. Sources:
   1. Administration
   2. Siberia
   3. Speransky
   4. Siberian Natives

II. Contemporary Descriptions, Reports, Memoirs, etc.

III. Contemporary Periodicals

IV. Selective List of Monographic Literature on Russian
    Administration

V. Secondary Works on Russian Siberia:
   1. Bibliographies, Encyclopedias
   2. Secondary studies

VI. Siberian Natives:
   1. Contemporary Descriptions and Reports
   2. Studies on Native History
   3. Native Law and Its Codification

I SOURCES

1. Administration

Arkhiv Gosudarstvennogo Soveta (Archives of the State Coun-
    cil). Vols. I-V. St. Petersburg, 1869-1901.
"Instruktsii maioru Shcherbachevu" (Instructions to Major
    Shcherbachev), in I. Bulychev, Puteshestvie po Vostochnoi
    Sibiri (Journey through Eastern Siberia). St. Petersburg,
    1856, pp. 251-68.
Kozodavlev, O. "Mnenie ministra vnutrennikh del po delam
    sibirskim" (Opinion of the Minister of the Interior on
    Siberian affairs), October 24, 1818, Chteniia..., 1859
    (No. 3), pp. 59-64.
Polnoe Sobranie Zakonov Rossiiskoi Imperii s 1649 g. (Com-
    plete collection of the laws of the Russian Empire since
    1649). 48 vols. St. Petersburg, 1830.
Seredonin, S.M. Istoricheskii obzor deiatel'nosti Komiteta
    Ministrov (Historical survey of the activities of the
    Committee of Ministers). Vols. I-IV. St. Petersburg,
    1902.
Zhurnaly Komiteta Ministrov - tsarstvovanie Imperatora
    Aleksandra I, 1802-1826 (Minutes of the Committee of
    Ministers - reign of Emperor Alexander I, 1802-1826).
    2 vols. (1802-1812). St. Petersburg, 1888-1891.

2. Siberia

"Materialy dlia istorii severovostochnoi Sibiri v XVIIIm v.
    (1751-1752)" (Materials for the history of northeastern
    Siberia in the eighteenth century, 1751-1752), ed. S.
    Shashkov. Chteniia..., 1864 (No. 3), pp. 62-93.
"Materialy dlia istorii Sibiri" (Materials for the history of
    Siberia), Sbornik gazety "Sibir'", Vol. I, St. Petersburg,
    1876, pp. 435-60.
Ministerstvo Vnutrennikh Del (Ministry of Internal Affairs).
    Statisticheskoe obozrenie Sibiri (sostavlennoe na osnovanii
    svedenii, pocherpnutykh iz aktov pravitel'stvennykh i
    drugikh dostovernykh istochnikov) (Statistical survey of
    Siberia based on data taken from government documents
    and other reliable sources). St. Petersburg, 1810.
Pamiatniki Sibirskoi istorii XVIII v. (Monuments of Siberian
    history of the eighteenth century). 2 vols. St. Petersburg,

1882-1885.

Potanin, G.N. "Materialy dlia istorii Sibiri" (Materials for the history of Siberia), Chteniia..., 1866 (No. 4), pp. 1-128; 1867 (No. 1), pp. 129-230; 1867 (No. 2), pp. 231-324.

Sychevskii. Istoricheskaia zapiska o kitaiskoi granitse, sostavlennaia sovetnikom Troitsko--Savskogo pogranichnogo pravleniia Sychevskim v 1846 g. (Historical note on the Chinese border, prepared by the Councilor of the Troitsko-Sava border administration, Sychevskii, in 1846). Communicated by V. N. Basnin. St. Petersburg, 1846.

"Zhurnal druzheskogo svidaniia Irkutskogo grazhdanskogo gubernatora Treskina s kitaiskim pogranichnympravitelem 19.II - 13.III.1810" (Diary of the friendly meeting between the civilian governor of Irkutsk, Treskin, and the Chinese border governor, February 19 to March 13, 1810). Moscow, 1860, and also Chteniia..., 1860 (No. 1), pp. 167-250.

3. Speransky

Bychkov, A.F. (ed.). V Pamiat' grafa M. M. Speranskogo (In memory of Count M. M. Speransky). St. Petersburg, 1872.

Kochubei, V. "Pis'ma k Speranskomu" (Letters to Speransky), Russkaia Starina, vol. 112 (November, 1902), pp. 301-322.

Obozrenie glavnykh osnovanii mestnogo upravleniia Sibiri (po bumagam Speranskogo i Sibirskogo Komiteta 1821-1822) (Survey of the principal foundations of Siberia's local government, based on the papers of Speransky and of the Siberian Committee 1821-1822). St. Petersburg, 1841.

"Raport Speranskogo Gosudariu Imperatoru, 1-go iunia 1820" (Report of Speransky to H.M. the Emperor, June 1, 1820), Russkii Arkhiv, 1870, pp. 598-99.

Speranskii, M. "Pis'ma k A.A. Stolypinu s 23.II.1813 do 18.IX.1819" (Letters to A. A. Stolypin from February 23, 1813, to September 18, 1819), Russkii Arkhiv, 1869 (Nos. 10 and 11), pp. 1682-1708 and 1966-84.

————. "Pis'ma k V. P. Kochubeiu" (Letters to V. P. Kochubei), Russkaia Starina, vol. 111 (July, 1902), pp. 51-54.

————— . "Pis'ma M. M. Speranskogo k ego docheri iz Penzy i s dorogi v Sibir'; 22 oktiabria 1816 - 18 maia 1819" (Letters of M. M. Speransky to his daughter from Penza and from the road to Siberia), Russkii Arkhiv, 1868 (Nos. 7 and 8), pp. 1103-1212.

————— . "Pis'ma Speranskogo k ego docheri iz Sibiri; 30 maia 1819 - 17 marta 1821" (Letters of Speransky to his daughter from Siberia), Russkii Arkhiv, 1868 (No. 11), pp. 1682-1811.

————— . "Proekt dlia upravleniia gubernii" (Project for the administration of the provinces), Sbornik IRIO, vol. 90 (St. Petersburg, 1894), pp. 274-358.

4. Siberian Natives

Akademiia Nauk Kazakhskoi SSR (Academy of Sciences of the Kazakh SSR). Materialy po kazakhskomu obychnomu pravu (Materials on Kazakh customary law). Sbornik 1. Alma Ata, 1948.

"Dzakiia - nakaz 1793," in Riasanovsky, Mongol'skoe pravo, Appendix 4.

"Dokladnaia zapiska i khyn-tok-togol khorintsev" (Petition and the khyn-tok-togol of the Khori Buriats), in Riasanovsky, Mongol'skoe pravo, Appendix 5.

Girchenko, V. P. (ed.). Sbornik materialov po istorii Buriatii XVIII i pervoi poloviny XIX v. (Collection of materials on the history of the Buriat country in the eighteenth and first half of the nineteenth centuries). Vyp. 1. Verkhneudinsk, 1926.

Leontovich, F. I. K istorii prava russkikh inorodtsev. Drevnii mongolo-kalmytskii ili oiratskii ustav vzyskanii (On history of the law of Russian natives - The ancient Mongol-Kalmyk or Oirat code). Odessa, 1879.

"Prigovor khorintsev o poriadke upravleniia 18. XII. 1817" (Decision of the Khori Buriats on administration, December 18, 1817), in Riasanovsky, Mongol'skoe pravo, Appendix 7.

"Prigovor khorintsev o poriadke upravleniia maia 1818" (Decision of the Khori Buriats on administration of May, 1818), in Riasanovsky, Mongol'skoe pravo, Appendix 8.

Samokvasov, D. I. (ed.). Sbornik obychnogo prava sibirskikh

inorodtsev (Collection of the customary law of the Siberian
    natives). Warsaw, 1876.
"Stepnoe ulozhenie khorintsev 1808" (Steppe Code of the Khori
    Buriats of 1808), in Riasanovsky, Mongol'skoe pravo,
    Appendix 6.
Svod stepnykh zakonov kochevykh inorodtsev Vostochnoi
    Sibiri (Code of the steppe laws of the nomadic natives
    of Eastern Siberia). St. Petersburg, 1841.

II   CONTEMPORARY DESCRIPTIONS,
      REPORTS, MEMOIRS, ETC.

Basnin, I. P. "Iz proshlogo Sibiri" (From the Siberian
    past), Istoricheskii Vestnik, vol. 90 (November, 1902),
    pp. 532-74.
Borisovskii, N. F. "Iz doreformennoi Sibiri - iz dnevnika
    starozhila" (From pre-reform Siberia - from the diary
    of an old settler), Istoricheskii Vestnik, vol. 75 (1899),
    pp. 538-63.
Bronevskii, S. B. "Ob otkrytii Omskoi oblasti Sibiri, 10. XI.
    1823" (On the formal opening of the Omsk region of
    Siberia, November 10, 1823), Sibirskii Vestnik, 1823
    (No. 4), pp. 191-95.
Cherepanov, S. "Otryvki iz vospominanii Sibirskogo Kazaka
    1810-1848" (Excerpts from the memoirs of a Siberian
    Cossack, 1810-1848), Drevniaia i Novaia Rossiia, 1876
    (Nos. 6-10), pp. 187-92, 258-72, 376-85, 79-84, 180-87.
Cochrane, John Dundas. Narrative of a Pedestrian Journey
    through Russia and Siberian Tartary, from the Frontiers
    of China to the Frozen Sea and Kamchatka. London,
    1824.
Erman, A. Reise um die Erde durch Nord Asien und die
    beiden Oceane (Historischer Theil). 3 vols. Berlin,
    1833-1848.
Gedenshtrom, M. M. (Hedenström). Otryvki o Sibiri (Excerpts
    on Siberia). St. Petersburg, 1830.
Georgi, I. G. Russia: or a Compleat Historical Account of
    All the Nations which Compose that Empire. London,
    1780.
I. R. (Full name unknown). "Primechaniia o Sibiri" (Notes
    on Siberia). Unpublished manuscript, no pagination,
    182?, in Hoover Library, Stanford University.
Kalashnikov, I. "Zapiski irkutskogo zhitelia" (Notes of an

Irkutsk inhabitant), Russkaia Starina, vol. 123 (July, 1905), pp. 187-251; (August, 1905), pp. 384-409; (September, 1905), pp. 609-46.

Kornilov, A. M. Zamechaniia o Sibiri (Remarks on Siberia). St. Petersburg, 1828.

————— . Pribavleniia k Zamechaniiam o Sibiri (Additions to the remarks on Siberia). St. Petersburg, 1829.

Khvostov, V. S. "Zapiska Khvostova o Sibiri" (Notes of Khvostov on Siberia), Russkii Arkhiv, 1870, pp. 601-10.

Kotsebu, O. Puteshestvie v iuzhnyi okean i v Beringov proliv dlia otyskaniia severo-vostochnogo morskogo prokhoda, predpriniatoe v 1815, 1816, 1817, i 1818 gg. na korable "Riurike" (Journey to the Southern Ocean and the Bering Straits in search of a northeastern sea passage, undertaken in 1815, 1816, 1817, and 1818 on the vessel "Riurik"). 3 vols. St. Petersburg, 1821-23.

Krashennikov, S. Opisanie zemli Kamchatki (Description of the land Kamchatka). 2nd ed. St. Petersburg, 1786.

Martos, A. Pis'mo o Vostochnoi Sibiri 1823-1824 (Letter about Eastern Siberia). Moscow, 1827.

Martynov, A. Zhivopisnoe puteshestvie ot Moskvy do kitaiskoi granitsy (A picturesque journey from Moscow to the Chinese border). St. Petersburg, 1819.

"Otryvki iz zamechanii o Sibiri odnogo iz byvshikh v onoi prezhde Irkutskim a potom Tobol'skim gubernatorom" (Excerpts from notes on Siberia of a former governor first in Irkutsk and then Tobolsk), Dukh Zhurnalov, No. IX (1812), pp. 505-20, 567-74, 607-16, 627-50.

Pallas, P. S. Reise durch verschiedene Provinzen des russischen Reichs. St. Petersburg, 1773-1778.

Parshin, V. Poezdka v Zabaikal'skii krai (Journey to the Transbaikal Region). Moscow, 1844.

"Pereezd s Gumboldtom po Sibiri, 1829"(Travel with Humboldt through Siberia, 1829), Russkii Arkhiv, 1865, pp. 1125-41.

Pestov, I. Zapiski ob Eniseiskoi gubernii i Vostochnoi Sibiri 1831 g. (Notes on the provinces of Eniseisk and Eastern Siberia 1831). Moscow, 1833.

"Puteshestvie po Sibiri g-na Trunina" (Travel in Siberia of Mr. Trunin), Novosti Russkoi Literatury na 1802 god, Part III, pp. 81-115.

Radishchev, A. N. Polnoe Sobranie Sochinenii (Complete works), ed. V. V. Kallash. Moscow, 1907. Vol. II

(Includes his articles "Zapiski Puteshestviia v Sibir'," 1790; "Pis'mo o kitaiskom torge," 1792; "Dnevnik puteshestviia iz Sibiri," 1797).

Sarychev, G. Puteshestvie po severovostochnoi chasti Sibiri, Ledovitomu moriu i Vostochnomu okeanu (v prodolzhenii os'mi let, pri geograficheskoi i astronomichesko-morskoi ekspeditsii, byvshei pod nachal'stvom flota kapitana Billingsa 1785 po 1793 g.) (Journey in the northeastern part of Siberia, the Arctic Ocean, and the Eastern Ocean...). 2 vols. St. Petersburg, 1802. Re-edited, Moscow, 1952.

Semivskii, N. Noveishie i dostovernye povestvovaniia o Vostochnoi Sibiri (iz chego mnogoe donyne ne bylo vsem izvestno) (Most recent and most reliable accounts about Eastern Siberia, much of which has not, until now, been known to everybody). St. Petersburg, 1817.

Serno-Solov'evich, M. (ed.). "Zapiski poliaka-konfederata soslannogo v Sibir' 1768-1776" (Memoirs of a Polish Confederate exiled to Siberia 1768-1776), Russkii Arkhiv, 1886 (No. 1), pp. 278-304.

Shchukin, N. Poezdka v Iakutsk (Journey to Iakutsk). St. Petersburg, 1833. 2nd ed., 1844.

Slovtsov, P. Pis'ma iz Sibiri (Letters from Siberia). Moscow, 1828.

—————. Progulki vokrug Tobol'ska v 1830 g. (Walks near Tobolsk in 1830). Moscow, 1834.

Stogov-Mozhaiskii, E. I. "Ocherki, rasskazy i vospominaniia; Speranskii i Treskin v Irkutske, 1819 g." (Sketches, tales, and reminiscences; Speransky and Treskin in Irkutsk, 1819), Russkaia Starina, vol. 23 (1878), pp. 499-530.

Vagin, V. I. "Sorokovye gody v Irkutske" (The 1840's in Irkutsk), in Literaturnyi Sbornik, ed. Iadrintsev, St. Petersburg, 1885, pp. 249-80.

Vigel', F. F. Zapiski (Memoirs). Moscow, 1892; also in 2 vols., Moscow-Leningrad, 1928.

"Vozrazhenie na stat'iu 'Statisticheskie svedeniia o lovle zverei i ptits v Rossii i Sibiri'" (Objection to the article "Statistical data on the hunting of animals and birds in Russia and Siberia"), Anonymous, Syn Otechestva, vol. 48 (1821), pp. 49-68.

Vrangel', F. Puteshestvie po severnym beregam Sibiri i po Ledovitomu moriu (Expedition to the northern shores of

Siberia and the Arctic Ocean). St. Petersburg, 1841.
Part I.
"Zametki o Sibiri" (Remarks about Siberia), Anonymous,
Chteniia..., 1861 (No. 3), pp. 78-91.
Zavalishin, I. D. Opisanie Zapadnoi Sibiri (Description of
Western Siberia). Moscow, 1862.

III CONTEMPORARY PERIODICALS

Muza. Ed. I. I. Martynov. St. Petersburg, 1796.
Novosti Russkoi Literatury na 1802, 1803, 1804, 1805 god.
Moscow, 1802-05.
Severnyi Vestnik. St. Petersburg, 1804.
Litsei. Ed. I. Martynov. St. Petersburg, 1806.
Syn Otechestva. St. Petersburg, 1812-52.
Dukh Zhurnalov. St. Petersburg, 1815. (Published until 1820,
but later issues inaccessible to me.)
Sibirskii Vestnik. Ed. G. Spasskii. St. Petersburg, 1818-24.
Severnyi Arkhiv. St. Petersburg, 1822-1826.

IV SELECTIVE LIST OF MONOGRAPHIC LITERATURE
ON RUSSIAN ADMINISTRATIVE AND POLITICAL
PROBLEMS OF THE PERIOD

Blinov, I. Gubernatory - istoriko-iuridicheskii ocherk (Governors, an historico-juridical study). St. Petersburg,
1905.
Bliumin, I. G. Ocherki ekonomicheskoi mysli v Rossii v
pervoi polovine XIX v. (Studies on the economic thought
in Russia in the first half of the nineteenth century).
Moscow-Leningrad, 1940.
Bogdanovich, M. Istoriia tsarstvovaniia imperatora Aleksandra I i Rossiia v ego vremia (History of the reign
of Alexander I and the Russia of his time). 6 vols.
St. Petersburg, 1869.
Danevskii, P. Ob istochnikakh mestnykh zakonov nekotorykh
gubernii i oblastei Rossii (On the sources of local laws of
some provinces and regions of Russia). St. Petersburg,
1857.
Ditiatin, I. I. Ustroistvo i upravlenie gorodov Rossii (Organization and administration of Russian towns). St. Petersburg, 1875.
Dovnar-Zapol'skii, M. V. Obzor noveishei russkoi istorii

(Survey of most recent Russian history). Vol. I. Kiev, 1914 (2nd ed.).

Gradovskii, A. D. "Istoricheskii ocherk uchrezhdeniia general-gubernatorov v Rossii" (Historical study of the institution of governors-general in Russia), Russkii Vestnik, November-December, 1869, pp. 5-31 and 396-413.

Ivanovskii, V. V. "Administrativnoe ustroistvo nashikh okrain" (The administrative organization of our border-lands), Uchenye Zapiski Kazanskogo Universiteta, vol. 58, No. 6 (November-December, 1891), pp. 27-70.

Khodnev, A. I. Istoriia Imperatorskogo Vol'nogo Ekonomi-cheskogo Obshchestva s 1765 do 1865 (History of the Imperial Free Economic Society from 1765 to 1865). St. Petersburg, 1865.

Korkunov, N. M. Russkoe gosudarstvennoe pravo (Russian public law). 2 vols. St. Petersburg, 1909.

Latkin, V. N. Uchebnik istorii russkogo prava perioda imperii XVIII i XIX st. (Manual of the history of Russian law in the period of the Empire, eighteenth and nineteenth centuries). 2nd ed. St. Petersburg, 1909.

Lazarevskii, N. I. Lektsii po russkomu gosudarstvennomu pravu (Lectures on Russian public law). 2nd ed. St. Petersburg, 1910.

Okun', S. Istoriia SSSR 1796-1825 (History of the USSR 1796-1825). Leningrad, 1948.

Pakhman, S. V. Istoriia kodifikatsii grazhdanskogo prava (History of the codification of civil law). St. Petersburg, 1876.

Romanovich-Slavatinskii, A. Posobie dlia izucheniia russkogo gosudarstvennogo prava po metodu istoriko-dogmati-cheskomu (Manual for the study of Russian public law from an historico-dogmatic viewpoint). Kiev, 1872.

Semevskii, V. I. Krestianskii vopros v Rossii v XVIIIm i pervoi polovine XIX veka (The peasant question in Russia in the eighteenth and first half of the nineteenth centuries). St. Petersburg, 1888.

Shil'der, N. K. Imperator Aleksandr Pervyi - ego zhizn' i tsarstvovanie (Emperor Alexander I - his life and reign). 4 vols. 2nd ed. St. Petersburg, 1904.

Sviatlovskii, V. V. Istoriia ekonomicheskikh idei v Rossii (History of economic ideas in Russia). Petrograd, 1923.

Vernadskii, G. V. Ocherk istorii prava russkogo gosudar-
    stva XVIII-XIX vv. (Period imperii) (Essay on the history
    of the law of the Russian state, eighteenth to nineteenth
    centuries, period of the Empire). Prague, 1924.

V   SECONDARY WORKS ON RUSSIAN SIBERIA

1. Bibliographies, Encyclopedias

Brokgauz i Efron. Entsiklopedicheskii slovar'. 86 vols.
    St. Petersburg, 1890-1907.
Kerner, R. J. Northeastern Asia: a selected bibliography.
    Berkeley, 1939.
Mezhov, V. Bibliografia Sibiri. 4 vols. St. Petersburg, 1905.
Mintslov, S. R. Obzor zapisok, dnevnikov, vospominanii,
    pisem i puteshestvii otnosiashchikhsia k istorii Rossii i
    napechatannykh na russkom iazyke (Survey of memoirs,
    diaries, reminiscences, letters, and travelogues re-
    lating to the history of Russia and printed in the Russian
    language), Novgorod, 1912.
Russkii Biograficheskii Slovar'. Ed. A. Polovtsov. 25 vols.
    (Incompleted series). St. Petersburg, 1897-1917.
Sibirskaia Sovetskaia Entsiklopediia. 3 vols. (Of the four
    volumes announced, only three were published.) Novo-
    sibirsk, 1929-33.
Sistematicheskii ukazatel' statei kasaiushchikhsia materika
    Azii pomeshchennykh v izdaniiakh Russkogo Geografi-
    cheskogo Obshchestva s 1846 do 1897 g. (Systematic
    index of articles pertaining to the continent of Asia and
    published in the publications of the Russian Geographic
    Society from 1846 to 1897). Irkutsk, 1898.

2. Secondary works

Andrievich, V. K. Istoriia Sibiri (History of Siberia). 5 vols.
    St. Petersburg, Irkutsk, Tomsk, Odessa, 1887-1889.
    ————. Sibir' v XIX st. (Siberia in the nineteenth century).
    2 vols. St. Petersburg, 1889.
Azadovskii, M. "Stranichki kraevedcheskoi deiatel'nosti
    dekabristov v Sibiri" (Pages on the regionalistic activities
    of the Decembrists in Siberia), in Sibir' i Dekabristy,
    Irkutsk, 1925, pp. 77-112.
Azadovskii, M., Zolotarev, M. and Kubalov, B. (eds.).

Sibir' i Dekabristy (Siberia and the Decembrists). Irkutsk,
    1925.
Bakhrushin, S. V. "Istoricheskie sud'by Iakutii" (Historical
    destiny of Iakutiia), in Iakutiia: sbornik statei, Leningrad,
    1927, pp. 275-322.
Bazanov, A. G. Ocherki po istorii missionerskikh shkol na
    krainom severe (Studies in the history of missionary
    schools in the extreme north). Leningrad, 1936.
Bogolepov, M. "Torgovlia v Sibiri" (Trade in Siberia), in
    Sibir' i ee sovremennoe sostoianie i ee nuzhdy, St.
    Petersburg, 1908, pp. 169-200.
Bychkov, I. A. "M. M. Speranskii general gubernator Sibiri i
    vozvrashchenie ego v Sankt Peterburg" (M. M. Speransky,
    governor-general of Siberia, and his return to St. Peters-
    burg), Russkaia Starina, vol. 112 (October, 1902),
    pp. 35-56.
Chukovskaia, L. K. Dekabristy, issledovateli Sibiri (The
    Decembrists, explorers of Siberia). Moscow, 1951.
Dekabristy v Buriatii (The Decembrists in Buriatiia). Verkh-
    neudinsk, 1927.
Fateev, A. N. "Speranskii - general gubernator Sibiri"
    (Speransky - governor-general of Siberia), Zapiski
    Russkogo Nauchno-Issledovatel'nogo ob'edineniia v
    Prage, Vol. XI, Nos. 82 and 88 (Prague, 1942), pp. 111-
    51 and 323-62.
Firsov, N. N. Chteniia po istorii Sibiri (Readings on the
    history of Siberia). 2nd ed. 2nd fascicle. Moscow, 1920-
    21.
Fisher, E. I. Sibirskaia istoriia s samogo otkrytiia Sibiri
    do zavoevaniia vsei zemli rossiiskim oruzhiem (History
    of Siberia from the very discovery of Siberia to its com-
    plete conquest by Russian arms). St. Petersburg, 1774.
Gagemeister (Hagemeister), A. G. Statisticheskoe obozrenie
    Sibiri (Statistical survey of Siberia). 3 vols. St. Peters-
    burg, 1854.
Girchenko, V. Iz istorii pereseleniia v Pribaikal'e staro-
    obriadtsev semeiskikh (From the history of the resettle-
    ment in the Baikal region of the "Family Old Believers").
    Verkhneudinsk, ca. 1921.
Golodnikov, K. "K biografii P. A. Slovtsova" (Concerning
    the biography of P. A. Slovtsov), in Sbornik gazety
    "Sibir'", I (St. Petersburg, 1876), pp. 423-31.
Guliaev, S. N. "Istoriko-statisticheskoe opisanie goroda

Barnaula v Tomskoi gubernii, sostavlennoe S. N.
Guliaevym v 1864 g." (Historical-statistical description
of the city of Barnaul in the Tomsk province, prepared
by S. N. Guliaev in 1864). Manuscript in the Hoover
Library, Stanford University.

Iadrintsev, N. M. "Chuvstva Speranskogo k Sibiri" (Feelings
of Speransky towards Siberia), Sbornik gazety "Sibir'",
I (St. Petersburg, 1876), pp. 397-408.

———— (ed.). Literaturnyi sbornik (Literary collection).
St. Petersburg, 1885. (Includes his article, "Nachalo
pechati v Sibiri" (Beginnings of the press in Siberia),
pp. 352-406.)

————. Sibir' kak koloniia (Siberia as a colony). St. Petersburg, 1882.

————. "Speranskii i ego reformy v Sibiri" (Speransky and
his reforms in Siberia), Vestnik Evropy (1876), No. 5,
pp. 93-116.

Kabo, R. M. Goroda Zapadnoi Sibiri (Towns of Western
Siberia). Moscow, 1949.

Kantseliariia Komiteta Ministrov. Zabaikal'e: svod materialov
Vysochaishe uchrezhdennoi Kommissii dlia issledovaniia
mestnogo zemlevladeniia i zemlepol' zovaniia pod pred-
sedatel'stvom stats-sekretaria Kulomzina (Transbaikalia:
collection of materials of the commission appointed by
imperial order for the investigation of local landownership
and land tenure under the chairmanship of State-secretary
Kulomzin), ed. N. I. Razumov. St. Petersburg, 1899.

Kir'iakov, V. V. Ocherki istorii pereselencheskogo dvizheniia
v Sibir' (Studies of the history of the colonization movement into Siberia). Moscow, 1902.

Koz'min, N. "Istoriia Sibiri" (History of Siberia), Sibirskaia
Sovetskaia Entsiklopediia, Vol. II (1931), pp. 380-402.

————. Ocherki proshlogo i nastoiashchego Sibiri (Studies
of the past and the present of Siberia). St. Petersburg,
1910.

Krypton, C. The Northern Sea Route: its place in Russian
economic history before 1917. New York, 1953.

Kubalov, B. "Dekabristy v Iakutskoi oblasti" (The Decembrists
in the Iakutsk region), Sbornik trudov professorov i
prepodavatelei Gosudarstvennogo Irkutskogo Universiteta,
otdel I, vyp. 2 (Irkutsk, 1921), pp. 108-38.

————. Dekabristy v Vostochnoi Sibiri (The Decembrists
in Eastern Siberia). Irkutsk, 1925.

————. "Sibirskoe obshchestvo i dekabristy" (Siberian society and the Decembrists), Katorga i Ssylka, vol. 8 (21) (1925), pp. 139-71.

Lantzeff, G. V. Siberia in the XVIIth Century (a study of the colonial administration). Berkeley, 1943.

Maak, R. Viliuskii okrug iakutskoi oblasti (The Viliusk district of the Iakutsk region). 2 vols. St. Petersburg, 1883-1886.

Maikov, P. "I. B. Pestel'," Russkii Biograficheskii Slovar', Vol. XIII (St. Petersburg, 1902), pp. 593-99.

Ogorodnikov, V. I. Ocherki istorii Sibiri do nachala XIX v. (Studies in the history of Siberia before the nineteenth century). Irkutsk, 1920. Only Part II, sect. 3 accessible to me: "Russkaia gosudarstvennaia vlast' i sibirskie inorodtsy XVI-XVIII vv." in Sbornik trudov professorov i prepodavatelei Gosudarstvennogo Irkutskogo Universiteta, otd. I, vyp. 1 (Irkutsk, 1921), pp. 69-113.

Okun', S. The American-Russian Company. Translated by Carl Ginsburg. Cambridge, Mass., 1951.

————. "Sibirskii komitet: obzor arkhivnykh fondov" (The Siberian Committee: survey of archival deposits), Arkhivnoe Delo, vol. 38 (1936), pp. 92-103.

Patkanov, S. Glavneishie dannyia po statistike naseleniia krainego vostoka Sibiri (Main data for the statistics of the population of the extreme east of Siberia). 3 fascicles. St. Petersburg, 1903.

Popov, G. A. Iakutskii krai (The Iakut region). Vyp. 2. Iakutsk, 1926.

Potanin, G. N. "Goroda Sibiri" (The towns of Siberia), in Sibir' i ee sovremennoe sostoianie i ee nuzhdy (St. Petersburg, 1908), pp. 235-60.

Prutchenko, S. Sibirskie okrainy: oblastnye ustanovleniia, sviazannye s Sibirskim Uchrezhdeniem 1822 g. v stroe upravleniia russkogo gosudarstva (Siberian borderlands: regional institutions connected with the Siberian Statute of 1822 in the system of administration of the Russian state). 2 vols. St. Petersburg, 1899.

Razumov, I. (ed.). Zabaikal'e: svod materialov.... See Kantseliariia Komiteta Ministrov.

Selishchev. Zabaikal'skie staroobriadtsy-semeiskie (Trans-baikal "Family Old Believers"). Irkutsk, 1920.

Serebrennikov, I. I. Sibirovedenie ("Sibiriology"). Harbin, 1920.

Shashkov, S. S. Istoricheskie etiudy (Historical studies).
St. Petersburg, 1872. Includes "Rabstvo v Sibiri" (Slavery
in Siberia), pp. 97-166.

Shchapov, A. P. "Sibirskoe obshchestvo do Speranskogo"
(Siberian society before Speransky), in Sochineniia
A. P. Shchapova, Vol. III (St. Petersburg, 1908),
pp. 643-717.

Shcheglov, I. V. Khronologicheskii perechen' vazhneishikh
dannykh iz istorii Sibiri 1032-1882 (Chronological list
of the most important data of Siberian history 1032-1882).
Irkutsk, 1883.

Sherstoboev, V. N. "Zemledelie severnogo Predbaikal'ia v
XVII-XVIII vv." (Agriculture of the northern pre-Baikal
region in the seventeenth to eighteenth centuries), in
Materialy po istorii sel'skogo khoziaistva SSSR, Vol. I
(Moscow, 1952), pp. 279-302.

Shteingel', V. I. "Sibirskie satrapy 1765-1819" (Siberian
satraps 1765-1819), Istoricheskii Vestnik, Vol. 17
(August, 1884), pp. 366-86.

Shunkov, V. I. "K istorii razvitiia zemledeliia v Zapadnoi
Sibiri - konets XVII - nachalo XVIII vv." (On the history
of the development of agriculture in Western Siberia -
end of the seventeenth and beginning of the eighteenth
centuries), Istoricheskie Zapiski, Vol. XI (1941),
pp. 201-35.

————. Ocherki po istorii kolonizatsii Sibiri v XVII i nachale
XVIII v. (Studies in the history of Siberia's colonization
in the seventeenth and beginning eighteenth centuries).
Moscow-Leningrad, 1946.

Slovtsov, P. A. Istoricheskoe obozrenie Sibiri (Historical
survey of Siberia). Part I, St. Petersburg, 1838; Part II,
St. Petersburg, 1844. Both parts reprinted without
changes, St. Petersburg, 1886.

Svatikov, S. G. Rossiia i Sibir' (Russia and Siberia), Prague,
1929.

Treti'iakov, P. I. Turukhanskii krai, ego priroda i zhiteli
(The Turukhansk region, its nature and inhabitants).
St. Petersburg, 1871.

Vagin, V. I. Istoricheskie svedeniia o deiatel'nosti grafa
M. M. Speranskogo v Sibiri s 1819 po 1822 g. (Historical
data on the activities of Count M. M. Speransky in Siberia
from 1819 to 1822). 2 vols. St. Petersburg, 1872.

Vatin, V. A. Minusinskii krai v XVIII v. (The Minusinsk

region in the eighteenth century). Minusinsk, 1913.

Viatkin, M. Ocherki po istorii kazakhskoi SSR (Studies in
the history of the Kazakh SSR). Vol. I. Moscow, 1941.

Vittenburg, P. V. (ed.). Iakutiia. Leningrad, 1927.

Zavalishin, D. I. Zapiski Dekabrista (Memoirs of a Decembrist). Munich, 1904.

VI SIBERIAN NATIVES

1. Contemporary descriptions and reports

Bestuzhev, N. A. "Buriatskoe khoziaistvo" (Buriat economy),
in Dekabristy v Buriatii (Verkhneudinsk, 1927), pp. 11-
18.

Bronevskii, V. B. "Zapiski o kirkiz kaisakakh Srednei Ordy"
(Notes on the Kirghiz-Kaisaks of the Middle Horde),
Otechestvennye Zapiski, vols. 41, 42, 43 (1830).

Hyakinth (Mönch) (Iakinf Bichurin). Denkwuerdigkeiten ueber
die Mongolei. Berlin, 1832. Recent Russian edition:
Sobranie svedenii o narodakh obitavshikh v Srednei Azii
v drevnie vremena. 2 vols. Moscow-Leningrad, 1950.

Levchine (Levshin), A. de. Description des hordes et steppes
des Kirghiz-Kazaks. Translated by Ferry de Pigny.
Paris, 1840.

Zuev, V. F. Materialy po etnografii Sibiri XVIII v. (1771-
1772) (Materials on the ethnography of Siberia in the
eighteenth century). Re-edited, Moscow-Leningrad,
1947.

2. Studies on native history

Bogdanov, M. N. Ocherk istorii buriat-mongol'skogo naroda
(Essay on the history of the Buriat-Mongolian people).
Verkhneudinsk, 1926.

Bogoras, W. The Chukchee ("Memoirs of the American
Museum of Natural History," Vol. VII), New York, 1904-
1909.

Czaplicka, M. A. Aboriginal Siberia, a study in social
anthropology. Oxford, 1914.

Girchenko, V. P. K istorii buriat-mongolov, khorintsev
pervoi poloviny XIX v. (On the history of the Buriat-
Mongols, the Khori Buriats of the first half of the nineteenth century). Verkhneudinsk, 1928.

Iadrintsev, N. M. "Inorodtsy Sibiri i ikh vymiranie" (The
    natives of Siberia and their dying out), Russkaia Mysl'
    (1883), No. 3, pp. 81-128.

————— . Sibirskie inorodtsy, ikh byt i sovremennoe polozhenie
    (Siberian natives, their customs and contemporary con-
    ditions). St. Petersburg, 1891.

Kartsov, V. G. Ocherk istorii narodov severo-zapadnoi
    Sibiri (Essay on the history of the peoples of northwestern
    Siberia). Moscow, 1937.

Keppen, P. Khronologicheskii ukazatel' materialov dlia
    istorii inorodtsev Evropeiskoi Rossii (Chronological index
    of materials for the history of the natives of European
    Russia). St. Petersburg, 1861.

Koz'min, N. P. K voprosu o tiurko-mongol'skom feodalizme
    (On the problem of Turko-Mongolian feudalism). Moscow-
    Irkutsk, 1934.

Kudriavtsev, F. A. Istoriia buriat-mongol'skogo naroda ot
    XVIII v. do 60kh godov XIX v. (History of the Buriat-
    Mongol people from the eighteenth century to the 1860's).
    Moscow-Leningrad, 1940.

Laufer, B. Ocherk mongol'skoi literatury (Survey of Mongolian
    literature). Leningrad, 1927.

Mainov, I. I. "Russkie krestiane i osedlye inorodtsy Iakutskoi
    oblasti" (Russian peasants and settled natives of the
    Iakut region), Zapiski Imperatorskogo Russkogo Geografi-
    cheskogo Obshchestva po otdelu statistiki, Vol. XII,
    St. Petersburg, 1912.

Miropiev, M. A. O polozhenii russkikh inorodtsev (On the
    situation of Russia's natives). St. Petersburg, 1901.

Nil (Archbishop of Iaroslav). Buddizm rassmatrivaemyi v
    otnoshenii k posledovateliam ego obitaiushikh v Sibiri
    (Buddhism considered in relation to its followers who
    live in Siberia). St. Petersburg, 1858.

Ogorodnikov, V. I. "Russkaia gosudarstvennaia vlast' i
    sibirskie inorodtsy XVI-XVIII vv." (Russian state power
    and Siberian natives in the sixteenth to eighteenth cen-
    turies), Sbornik trudov professorov i prepodavatelei
    Gosudarstvennogo Irkutskogo Universiteta, otd. I, vyp. 1
    (Irkutsk, 1921), pp. 69-113.

Okladnikov, A. P. Ocherki iz istorii zapadnykh Buriat-
    Mongolov XVII-XVIII vv. (From the history of the Western
    Buriat Mongols in the seventeenth to eighteenth cen-
    turies). Leningrad, 1937.

Patkanov, S. Statisticheskie dannyia pokazivaiushchie ple-
mennoi sostav naseleniia Sibiri - na osnovanii dannykh
perepisi 1897 g. (Statistical data showing the tribal
make-up of the population of Siberia - on the basis of
the census of 1897). 3 vols. St. Petersburg, 1912.

————— ."Opyt geografii i statistiki tunguskikh plemen Sibiri"
(Essay on the geography and statistics of the Tungus
tribes of Siberia), Zapiski Gosudarstvennogo Geografi-
icheskogo Obshchestva po otdelu etnografii, No. 31,
St. Petersburg, 1906.

Shashkov, S. S. "Sibirskie inorodtsy v XIXm stoletii" (Siberian
natives in the nineteenth century), Istoricheskie etiudy,
II (St. Petersburg, 1872), pp. 165-292.

Stepanov, N. N. "Istoricheskoe znachenie prisoedineniia
narodnostei krainego severa k Rossii" (Historical significance of the accession of the peoples of the extreme north
to Russia), Voprosy Istorii, July, 1952, pp. 74-88.

————— . "Istoriia Buriat-Mongol'skoi ASSR, tom I" (History
of the Buriat-Mongol ASSR, vol. I [a review article]),
Voprosy Istorii, April, 1952, pp. 108-13.

Tokarev, S. A. Obshchestvennyi stroi iakutov XVII-XVIII vv.
(The social system of the Iakuts in the seventeenth to
eighteenth centuries). Iakutsk, 1945.

————— . Ocherk istorii iakutskogo naroda (Survey of the
history of the Iakut people). Moscow, 1940.

————— . "Proishozhdenie sel'skoi obshchiny u Iakutov" (Origin
of the village commune among the Iakuts), Istoricheskie
Zapiski, Vol. XIV (1945), pp. 170-99.

Vladimirtsev, B. Ia. Obshchestvennyi stroi mongolov (Social
system of the Mongols). Leningrad, 1934.

Zarubin, N. I. Spisok narodnostei SSSR (List of nationalities
of the USSR). Leningrad (Akademiia Nauk SSSR - Trudy
Komissii po izucheniu plemennogo sostava naseleniia
SSSR i sopredel'nykh stran, No. 13), 1927.

3. Native law and its codification

A.R. "O zakonakh nekotorykh vostochno-sibirskikh inorodtsev"
(On the laws of some Eastern Siberian natives), Sibirskii
Vestnik, 1823 (No. 1), pp. 1-12.

Iakushkin, E. I. "Obychnoe pravo russkikh inorodtsev -
materialy dlia bibliografii obychnogo prava" (Customary
law of Russian natives - materials for a bibliography

of customary law), Chteniia..., 1899 (No. 3), pp. 1-370.
(Pp. 49-95, item's 220-360, deal directly with Siberian
native customary law).

Khangalov, M. "Iuridicheskie obychai Buriat" (Legal customs
of the Buriats), Etnograficheskoe obozrenie, 1894 (No. 2),
pp. 100-42.

Leontovich, F. I. K istorii prava russkikh inorodtsev (On
the history of the law of Russian natives). 2 vols. Odessa,
1879-1880.

Nol'de, A. "K istorii sostavleniia proekta 'Svoda stepnykh
zakonov kochevykh inorodtsev Vostochnoi Sibiri'" (On
the history of the project of a code of the steppe laws
of the nomadic natives of Eastern Siberia), in Sbornik
S. F. Platonovu, ucheniki, druz'ia i pochitateli (St.
Petersburg, 1911), pp. 502-21.

Riasanovsky (Riazanovskii), V. A. Fundamental Principles
of Mongol Law. Tientsin, 1937.

————. "Dva pamiatnika obychnogo prava mongol'skikh
plemen: 2. Svod stepnykh zakonov kochevykh inorodtsev
Vostochnoi Sibiri" (Two monuments of the customary
law of Mongol tribes: 2. Code of the steppe laws of the
nomads of Eastern Siberia), Vestnik Manzhurii (Harbin,
1930), No. 1, pp. 1-13.

————. Mongol'skoe pravo - preimushchestvenno obychnoe
(Mongol law - principally customary law). Harbin, 1931.

————. Obychnoe pravo mongol'skikh plemen (Customary
law of Mongol tribes). Harbin, 1924.

Index

Index